The Ethics
of Management

The Ethics
of Management

Sixth Edition

LaRue Tone Hosmer

Professor Emeritus of Corporate
Strategy and Managerial Ethics
Ross School of Business
University of Michigan

McGraw-Hill
Irwin

Boston   Burr Ridge, IL   Dubuque, IA   New York
San Francisco   St. Louis   Bangkok   Bogotá   Caracas   Kuala Lumpur
Lisbon   London   Madrid   Mexico City   Milan   Montreal   New Delhi
Santiago   Seoul   Singapore   Sydney   Taipei   Toronto

McGraw-Hill Irwin

THE ETHICS OF MANAGEMENT

Published by McGraw-Hill/Irwin, a business unit of The McGraw-Hill Companies, Inc., 1221 Avenue of the Americas, New York, NY, 10020. Copyright © 2008, 2006, 2003, 1996, 1990, 1987 by The McGraw-Hill Companies, Inc. All rights reserved. No part of this publication may be reproduced or distributed in any form or by any means, or stored in a database or retrieval system, without the prior written consent of The McGraw-Hill Companies, Inc., including, but not limited to, in any network or other electronic storage or transmission, or broadcast for distance learning.

Some ancillaries, including electronic and print components, may not be available to customers outside the United States.

This book is printed on acid-free paper.

3 4 5 6 7 8 9 0 DOC/DOC 0 9

ISBN 978-0-07-340503-2
MHID 0-07-340503-5

Managing developmental editor: *Laura Hurst Spell*
Editorial assistant: *Sara Knox Hunter*
Associate marketing manager: *Kelly Odom*
Project manager: *Kathryn D. Mikulic*
Senior production supervisor: *Debra R. Sylvester*
Lead designer: *Matthew Baldwin*
Lead media project manager: *Cathy L. Tepper*
Cover image: © *Getty Images*
Typeface: *10/12 Times New Roman*
Compositor: *Laserwords Private Limited*
Printer: *R. R. Donnelley*

Library of Congress Cataloging-in-Publication Data

Hosmer, LaRue T.
    The ethics of management/LaRue Tone Hosmer.—6th ed.
      p. cm.
    Includes index.
    ISBN-13: 978-0-07-340503-2 (alk. paper)
    ISBN-10: 0-07-340503-5 (alk. paper)
    1. Business ethics. 2. Industrial management—Moral and ethical aspects. I. Title.
HF5387.H67 2008
174'.4—dc22   2007032963

www.mhhe.com

Contents

Chapter 6
How Can a Business Organization Be Made Moral?   145

About the Author

LaRue Hosmer is a mechanical engineer who, in 1955, founded a company to build waste-reduction equipment for sawmills and paper mills. The company was sold in 1968, and Professor Hosmer returned to the academic community and received a PhD in Corporate Strategy and the Economics of Competition in 1971. He has taught at the University of Michigan ever since, with visiting appointments at Stanford, Yale, Virginia, the Naval Post Graduate School, and Alabama. His interest in ethics dates from experiences while running the machinery company, and he offered the first course in ethics of management at the Michigan Business School in 1984. He currently is emeritus.

Preface

The Growing Importance of Ethics in Management

Over the period 1998 to 2002, when the fifth edition of this text was being written, the ethical problems at business firms that dominated the headlines tended to have a financial orientation. Enron, Tyco, and WorldCom were probably the most famous examples; those companies deliberately falsified their income statements and balance sheets. Martha Stewart was doubtless the most infamous example, though perhaps undeservedly so; she cannot have been the only person in America who traded stocks based upon insider information. Bank of America and approximately 100 other retail bankers and brokers were—in my view—the most egregious; they were found to have permitted the exploitive trading of the mutual funds they had sold to smaller investors. Citygroup and many of the other investment banks may—again in my view—have been the most bogus; they were shown to have deliberately encouraged their stock analysts to mislead the public to gain favor and business from their large clients. But—and once more this is my personal view—I do not believe that all this past evidence of widespread wrongdoing within the financial services industry was due to some inherent moral failure on the part of the men and women who worked within that industry. I believe that the wave of wrongdoing was due, instead, to the extreme pressures, risks, and rewards that characterized that industry.

My concern is that the extreme pressures, risks, and rewards that previously characterized the financial services industry are now spreading to other sectors of the economy. In 2006, while this sixth edition is being prepared, the ethical problems at business firms that are being reported in our daily newspapers and on our evening newscasts, and that consequently ought to be discussed in our management classes, are found in the pharmaceutical industry, the electronics industry, the insurance industry, and the accounting profession, among many others. Merck and Guidant, two very reputable firms in health care, are accused of having failed to inform physicians and patients when their products were found to be defective. Hewlett Packard, without doubt the most respected name in electronic goods and service, has been shown to have engaged in a tawdry investigation of telephone records. Aetna, UnitedHealth, and WellPoint, three well known companies in employee benefit insurance, are claimed to have made undisclosed payments to private consulting firms that recommended their policies. And 11 partners from KPMG, once the oldest and proudest of the public accounting firms, are now on trial for having assisting clients in the manipulative preparation of their income taxes.

I believe that companies in almost all industries and employees at almost all levels have now become subject to the huge pressures, risks, and rewards that previously characterized just the financial-service firms. This, I assume, is the result of the increased level of global competition. More and more companies are offering more and more products in more and more markets, and some of those companies have inherent advantages in lower wage costs, greater governmental supports, and fewer productive restrictions. The result can be that employees at all levels in many firms will feel forced to take morally inappropriate actions that hurt or harm other people or organizations in order to hide problems or improve profits within their own firms. I say this result "can be," not "will be," because some companies have already taken actions to reduce the pressures upon their employees and improve the societies of which they form a part. Those companies are clearly to be congratulated.

There are not many of these companies that should be congratulated for having already taken remedial action, however, and most of the students in our classes are going to have to deal with the pressures, risks, and rewards of the exceedingly competitive global economy on their own, soon after graduation. They will certainly experience the temptation to "get along by going along." Yet, at the same time, they should recognize the opportunity to "stand out by standing up." My most basic argument is that all members of our courses are going to have to learn how to *convincingly* present their moral point of view to others in order to jointly serve their companies, protect their careers, and improve their societies. There are, in my view, five steps in making such convincing presentations:

1. Recognize that moral problems in business are complex and difficult to resolve. Moral problems in business inherently involve some individuals, groups, or organizations associated with the firm who are going to be hurt or harmed in ways outside their own control, while others will be benefited or helped. Further, some of those individuals, groups, or organizations associated with the firm will have their rights ignored or denied, while others will have their rights recognized and extended. There is a mixture of benefits and harms, of right exercised and rights denied, in the moral problems of management, and this mixture makes it very difficult for business managers to decide upon a course of action that they can confidently say is "right" and "just" and "fair" when faced with a moral problem.

2. Understand that business managers cannot rely upon their moral standards of behavior or the intuitive ways they just automatically feel about what actions are "right" and "just" and "fair"—and which are not—to make their decisions when faced with a moral problem. Moral standards of behavior differ between people, depending upon their personal goals, norms, beliefs, and values, which in turn depend upon their cultural and religious traditions and their economic and social situations. The individuals and groups in a global economy come from very different cultural and religious traditions and live in very different economic and social situations, and, consequently, their moral standards of behavior, being subjective, are bound to differ substantially. Business managers have to understand, and deal with, those differences.

3. Accept that it is not enough for a manager to simply reach a decision on what he or she believes to be a proper balance of benefits for some and harms for others, of rights recognized for some and rights denied for others, in any given situation. Managers have to go further and *be able to explain convincingly why that balance should be viewed as "right" and "just" and "fair."* A convincing explanation requires objective methods of analysis rather than subjective standards of behavior. These objective methods of analysis include (1) economic outcomes based upon impersonal market forces, (2) legal requirements based upon impartial social and political processes, and (3) ethical duties based upon universal human goals. This logical decision process starts with a listing of the benefits and harms, together with an accounting of the rights exercised and the rights denied, for each of the involved individuals, groups,

and organizations to make certain that everyone understands the magnitude of the problem, despite their differences in their personal standards of behavior, and then moves on to the tripartite economic, legal, and ethical analysis. This logical process is shown graphically in the following figure:

The Application of Objective Methods of Moral Analysis in Management

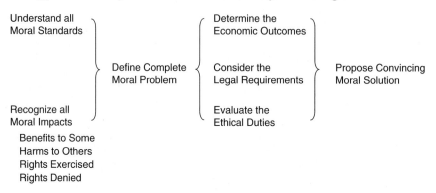

4. Anticipate that if this proposed decision process is followed on a consistent basis, with moral solutions that are logically convincing to the individuals, groups, and organizations associated with the firm, the result will be an increase in the trust, commitment, and effort evidenced by those same individuals, groups, and organizations. Everyone wants to be treated justly in the workplace and in the market, but the only way most people can ensure that just treatment will occur in the future is to be associated with the managers of firms they trust because of the managers' actions in the past. They tend to trust those managers who have logically and convincingly explained the economic, legal, and ethical foundations of their decisions and actions. The argument here is that trust leads to commitment, that commitment leads to effort, and that committed effort is essential for continuing success in a competitively intense, technologically complex, and culturally diverse global economy.

5. Believe that it is not enough for the senior executives in a firm to consistently recognize moral problems and convincingly present moral solutions in order to bring all of the individuals, groups, and organizations associated with the firm into a committed, integral whole. Instead, this sense of corporate integrity has to be spread throughout the firm, and that requires a mission statement based upon accepted organizational values and defined corporate goals, and sustained by financial supports, performance measures, incentive payments, prohibited procedures, and leadership actions. Given the increasing intensity, complexity, and diversity of global competition, companies cannot continue to operate successfully without the resulting cooperation, innovation, and unification that come from trust, commitment, and effort.

It has often been said that ethics is essential for leadership. My argument is that leadership is also essential for ethics. Somebody has to be willing to stand up and say, "This is what we should do, this is why we should do it, and this is how we are going to do it." That is the combined character, skill, and ability that I think we should be teaching in our ethics classes.

Health Care Insurance Companies
and Payments to Customer Consultants

Almost all of the large and medium-sized companies within the United States feel obligated to offer health care insurance to their employees, either as a result of the terms of earlier labor contracts or as a consequence of their current needs to attract and keep highly qualified workers. Many of the smaller, family-owned firms also offer this insurance; here the motivation is more often their personal relationships with employees, whom they see every day and want to help or reward, rather than the terms or conditions of union contracts and labor markets.

The problem is that health care insurance has become exceedingly complex. It is hard to select the right policies. Firstly, there is the issue of the medical conditions and diseases that are covered and the extent of that coverage. Health care insurers differ substantially in the conditions and diseases that are included within their policies and in the nature and extent of the treatments that are provided. Secondly, there is the matter of the co-payments that are required. Health care insurers originally proposed co-payments as incentives to encourage patients to improve their life styles—to lose weight or stop smoking, for example—and thus reduce their demands on the health care system. But now it is alleged that co-payments have become more a means of blocking access to that system and thus reducing the obligations of the insurers. Thirdly, there is the question of the overall cost. Health care insurers do not provide either diagnostic or treatment services; instead, they pay others—hospitals, clinics, physicians, nursing homes, and pharmaceutical companies—for the needed services, and they negotiate the cost and quality of those services on a competitive, or "preferred provider," basis, and then propose a level of annual charges that are hard to compare.

Most business firms, particularly those that are medium-sized or small and family owned, and almost all public organizations—the school systems, police and fire departments, and city and state governments—don't understand this confusing mixture of coverages, co-payments, and costs. They worry about the continually rising level of annual charges, and they frequently turn to health plan consultants for help. Some of these consultants are local 2- to 10-person organizations; others are much bigger regional or national corporations. All of them encourage a presumption that they act solely in the best interests of their clients. However, that presumption was called into question just recently through a series of revelations, many similar to the following account:

> When Kevin Grady took over as an employee-benefits consultant for the Columbus [Ohio] Public Schools District in 2001, he signed a contract promising to act "in the best interests" of the schools. The Ohio district agreed to pay him $35,000 a year to help it choose a health insurer. Officials thought that was all Mr. Grady was getting out of the deal.
>
> It wasn't. After the district switched its health insurance to UnitedHealth Group Inc. on what it says was Mr. Grady's recommendation, he started getting payments and other compensation from the big Minnetonka, Minn., insurer. "Thank you and United for the steaks," Mr. Grady wrote in a Dec. 20, 2001, e-mail to a UnitedHealth employee. "We'll have those on Christmas Eve." (*The Wall Street Journal,* September 18, 2006, p. A1)

Steaks and an occasional bottle of wine might be understandable, but they were not the only extra benefits Mr. Grady got from UnitedHealth. He also received $517,138 in monetary compensation from that company over a two-year period, from 2001, when he recommended the switch in health insurance coverage, to 2003, when the school district learned of these payments, apparently from a dissatisfied employee at UnitedHealth. It quickly became apparent, as a result of the lawsuit filed by the Columbus public schools in an attempt to recover the funds which it claimed were inappropriately paid, that this was not at all an isolated occurrence:

> The episode spotlights a widespread and largely invisible practice that critics say boosts the costs of health care. Many consultants and brokers who are hired to help employers get the best deal on health insurance or prescription-drug coverage have significant financial ties with the health vendors they are supposed to be scrutinizing. The ties may take the form of bonuses for bringing in business, or commissions and consulting fees. Often they are disclosed only partly or not at all. (*The Wall Street Journal,* September 18, 2006, p. A1)[1]

Few of the consulting firms or insurance companies appeared to think of these bonuses, commissions, and fees as inappropriate or improper. Instead—when contacted, and found willing to respond—their spokespersons tended to explain that the practice of making these payments was widespread and accepted, and they generally went on to emphasize that the payments were intended to foster cooperation between consulting firms and insurance companies, and help to control the spiraling costs of health care within the United States:

> "All [insurance] companies offer bonuses," says Joe Grady [president of the local consulting firm that hired his father]. "It's a way to sell the product and saves them [the insurance companies] from hiring 20,000 agents." He denies that his father pushed the district to choose UnitedHealth and contends the district knew all along about the payments. (*The Wall Street Journal,* September 18, 2006, p. A1)

> "Health care finance and delivery are not the core mission of most employers," says Robert O'Brien, the head of health and benefits consulting at Mercer [a large general insurance consultant, with annual revenues from their health care division of $526 million]. "We help employers manage the expense and complexity of their health and benefits programs in a way that maximizes their value for employees." (*The Wall Street Journal,* September 18, 2006, p. A1)

In court documents filed in conjunction with other payment cases, it was found that UnitedHealth typically offered a commission of 1 percent of the premium dollars paid by the client. Aetna Inc., another of the very large health care insurance companies, located in Hartford, Connecticut, computed payments to consulting firms based upon a different formula. If a consultant kept 90 percent of his or her clients loyal to Aetna when their contacts came up for rebidding, generally every three years, the consulting firm received a "retention bonus" of 0.75 percent of the client's premium payments over the life of the contract; if the consultant was able to keep 100 percent of his or

---

[1] *The Wall Street Journal.* Central Edition [only staff-produced materials may be used] by *The Wall Street Journal.* Copyright 2008 by Dow Jones & Company, Inc. Reproduced with permission of Dow Jones & Company, Inc. in the format Textbook via Copyright Clearance Center.

her clients loyal to the firm, the bonus rose to 1.25 percent. WellPoint, of Indianapolis, Inc., the third of the three largest health care insurance companies within the United States, declined to offer details on the formula by which their payments were computed, but did admit that "they continued to offer contingent commissions" (*The Wall Street Journal,* September 18, 2006, p. A1).

Class Assignment

Firstly, think of yourself as a senior executive within one of those three large health care insurance companies: UnitedHealth, Aetna, or WellPoint. Let us say that you are the chief financial officer. You clearly know about these payments. Would you just accept them as a normal and accepted cost of doing business, or would you object to them? Let us further say that an outside member of the board of directors has just heard of the payments, and does object. You know that when he or she raises the issue at the next board meeting, others at that meeting will turn to you. You are known as an intelligent and articulate executive, next in line for promotion to chief executive officer. A major argument of this text is that managers at all levels of an organization should decide for themselves, through analysis, the moral stand they believe to be most appropriate, *but they must be able to logically convince others.* How would you logically convince the others at that board meeting?

Secondly, put yourself in what probably will be a more realistic situation. Assume that you have worked in whatever functional field you are now pursuing—accounting, finance, marketing, human relations—at one of those large insurance companies for two years, ever since you graduated from your college or MBA program. Assume that not only have you just heard of these payments, but that you have also been asked to participate, perhaps as the person authorizing a series of payments to a new consulting firm. Does this involvement disturb you? Assume that the president of your company has what is termed an "open door" policy—employees at any level can make an appointment and come to see him or her about any issue that they believe to be important. Now, what are the risks to your career if you take advantage of that policy, and do go to see the president? What are the risks to your career if you do not? Assume in this case that you truly like your job and your life outside of work. Also recognize that it is always easy to say, "Oh, I wouldn't worry about the risks; I could always just leave and find another job," but understand that it may not be easy to find another job. Potential employers will generally contact past employers, and the indifferent response from a past employer that "It is our policy not to comment on the reasons an employee left, or on the performance of that employee while at our firm" is considered a black mark.

Chapter 1

Moral Problems in Business Management

The preface to the current (sixth) edition expressed the belief that the moral problems in business management appear to be changing in form, frequency, and cause. During the period 1998 to 2002, while the text for the previous (fifth) edition was being prepared, the moral problems that dominated the headlines tended to have a financial orientation. Enron, Tyco, and WorldCom deliberately falsified their income statements and balances sheets. Bank of America, Putnam Investments, and Janus Capital casually permitted the exploitive trading of the mutual funds they had sold to small investors. Citigroup and almost all of the other major investment banks intentionally encouraged their stock analysts to mislead the public to gain favor and business from their large clients. The first conclusion of the preface, however, was that this was not due to some inherent moral failure on the part of the men and women who worked within that industry; instead, the wave of wrongdoing was caused far more by the extreme pressures, risks, and rewards that characterized that industry.

The second conclusion of the preface was that the extreme pressures, risks, and rewards that previously characterized just the financial-services industry are now spreading to other sectors of the economy. The moral problems at business firms that are currently being reported in our daily newspapers and on our evening newscasts are now found in the pharmaceutical industry, the electronics industry, the insurance industry, and the accounting profession, among others. Merck and Guidant, two very reputable firms in health care, are accused of having failed to inform physicians and patients alike when their products were found to be defective. Hewlett Packard, without doubt the most respected name in electronic goods and services, has been shown to have engaged in a tawdry investigation of private telephone records. Aetna, UnitedHealth, and WellPoint, three well-known companies in employee benefit insurance, are said to have made undisclosed payments to the private consulting firms that recommended their policies. And 11 partners from KPMG, once the oldest and proudest of the "Big Four" accounting firms, are now on trial for having assisting clients in the manipulative preparation of their income taxes.

The third conclusion of the preface was that companies in almost all industries and employees at almost all levels have now become subject to the continual pressures, risks, and rewards that were previously concentrated within the financial-service firms. This, it was said, appeared to be the result of the greatly heightened level of global competition. More and more companies are offering more and more products in more and more markets, and some of those companies have inherent advantages in lower wage costs, greater governmental supports, and fewer productive constraints. Now even new hires at many firms will feel either forced or encouraged to take morally inappropriate actions that hurt or harm other people and organizations in order to hide problems or improve profits within their own firms. This is not inevitable. A few companies have already taken actions to reduce the pressures upon their employees, and to focus instead on bringing their workers, customers, suppliers, distributors, and communities into a unified and cooperative whole, as a means of generating profits on a sustainable basis.

This sustainable, or long-term, model of corporate competition is not common, however. Consequently, the fourth conclusion of the preface was that most of the future graduates of our management programs are going to have to be prepared to deal with the pressures, risks, and rewards of the exceedingly competitive global economy on their own, either almost immediately after graduation or somewhat later as functional or technical managers. They will certainly experience the temptation to "get along by going along." Yet, at the same time, they should recognize the opportunity to "stand out by standing up." My most basic argument is that all members of our courses are going to have to learn how to *convincingly* present their moral point of view of what is "right" and "just" and "fair" to other people in order to jointly serve their companies, protect their careers, and improve their societies.

The problem comes in the need to *convincingly* present a given moral point of view. People differ in what they believe to be "right" or "wrong," "just" or "unjust," "fair" or "unfair." Senior executives and mid-level managers alike at the health care insurance companies described in the first case in this book—UnitedHealth, Aetna, and WellPoint—appeared surprised when accused of wrongdoing for having made private payments to the consultants and advisors who were selecting health care policies for their clients at many smaller companies and public organizations. "We've done nothing wrong" was the nearly universal response of managers at almost all levels at both the health care insurers and the health care consultants. It was only the clients, and the employees of those clients who were to benefit from the selected health care policies, who were shocked, discouraged, and angry.

The purpose of this book, then, is to examine the factors that enter into enabling each member of an ethics class to make a convincing presentation of the actions, decisions, and policies that *they* consider to be "right" and "just" and "fair" in any given moral situation. Those factors, and the analytical structure based upon them (also shown in the figure included in the preface), are illustrated in Figure 1.1.

Before going on to describe each of the factors, or steps in the analytical structure, in greater detail, we need to consider an example of a very large and exceedingly complex moral problem. It is one that for many people is much more a managerial dilemma than a moral problem in that there are substantial benefits for some individuals and groups, and at the same time great harms for others, together with a clear recognition of rights for some of those individuals and groups, and an obvious denial of rights for others. We will use this example later in the chapter to illustrate the seven steps in the analytical process.

FIGURE 1.1   **Analytical Process for the Resolution of Moral Problems**

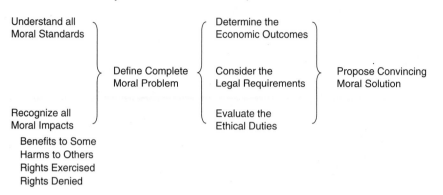

Example of a Large and Complex Moral Problem

Hydro-Quebec is a public utility owned by the province of Quebec that provides electric service to the people of Quebec. To improve that service the company has proposed building a huge hydroelectric generating station in the remote wilderness of northern Canada. The term "huge" has been used advisedly. Hydro-Quebec plans to construct a dam 17 miles long across the valley of the Great Whale River, close to the mouth of that river where it empties into James Bay. The dam will create a lake covering 9,100 square miles, leaving only isolated peaks and upland areas as islands in a partially forested but primarily open tundra region. That region stretches 300 miles to the east, almost to the border with Newfoundland, and 200 miles to the north, nearly to the Arctic Circle. It is an area with heavy snowfall in the winter and plenty of rainfall in the summer. The soil is rocky, and the water does not penetrate the ground; instead, it collects in rivulets and streams. The land has a constant slope towards the west, and the rivulets and streams are channeled into larger rivers which coalesce into the Great Whale River near the James Bay coast. The one long dam will be able to store massive amounts of water covering this very extensive area.

Those massive amounts of water would then serve a single hydroelectric generating station that could produce 14,000 megawatts of electric power, equivalent to the total output of 14 modern coal-fired or nuclear-based generating plants, but of course without the acid emissions or radioactive residues that are associated with those energy sources. Approximately half of the power would be used in southern Quebec, where it would aid in the industrialization of that region. The balance of the power would be sold to the six New England states and New York City; where it would eliminate any need for the utilities in that area to build additional generating capacity for the next 10 years. Profits from the sale of the power—given that Hydro-Quebec is owned by the province of Quebec, not by private stockholders—would then be used to fund improvements in education and health care throughout that province, in both the south and the north.

The electric power to be sold to New England and New York is needed in a region of the United States that for years has been dependent upon the importation of foreign oil for both home heating and industrial expansion. The sale profits are needed in an area of

Canada that for years has suffered from insufficient funding for primary and secondary education, and for health care expansion. Improved health care in the north will bring lower infant mortality and longer life spans. Improved education in the south will bring greater graduation rates and higher personal incomes. The only possible problem with the project is the opposition of a majority of the Cree and Inuit Indians who live in the area to be flooded, a total of 2,000 families. The chief of the Cree has refused to sell the land (which had never been formally deeded to his people by treaty) saying, "It is hard to explain to white people what we mean when we say our land is part of our life. We are like rocks and tree, beaver and caribou. We belong here. We will not leave." A minority of both tribes, about 800 families, however, are perfectly willing to sell the land, and want to adopt what they consider to be more modern and more comfortable ways of living in a cold, harsh, and unforgiving climate.

How do you decide when faced with this issue? Millions of people will benefit. Only 2,000 families, about 8,000 individuals, will be harmed. Certainly you could pay all of the Indian families, majority and minority alike, a fair price for their land. But how do you establish a "fair" price for scrub forests and frozen tundra that has no commercial value but evidently a high emotional worth to many of the families? There is no equivalent land in Canada that is not currently occupied either by native peoples or recent emigrants, so that you cannot simply ask the objecting majority of the Cree and Inuit to either move further east into Newfoundland or further west into Ontario. Both moves would disrupt the lives of other people already there. And, the majority of the Cree and the Inuit say that they do not want your money. They want to stay right where they are, living their lives exactly as they have for hundreds if not thousands of years, on land they consider to belong solely if not legally to them, without interference from the provincial government that wants to build hydroelectric dams and generating plants in what they consider to be their wilderness.

How do you decide, and particularly how do you reach a decision that most can accept as being "right" and "just" and "fair"? It is suggested that you work through the decision process outlined in Figure 1.1 step by step. Understand the moral standards, or the intuitive judgments on "right" and "wrong," and the reasons they differ between different peoples. Look at the benefits and the harms, the rights exercised and the wrongs imposed, for all of those peoples. Then, propose, as clearly as possible, the moral question—is it "right" and "just" and "fair" that we generate these benefits and exercise these rights for some of us, given that others among us will be harmed and have their rights ignored? Finally, answer that moral question by considering the economic outcomes, the legal requirements, and the ethical duties. See if you can reach a solution that you not only believe personally to be "right" and "just" and "fair" but that you believe you could explain understandably and then convincingly to others. The theme of this book is that it is not enough to make up your own mind. You have to be able to justify your decision to others.

Understand the Moral Standards

Most people turn first to their moral standards of behavior when they first encounter a situation in which the well-being of some individuals or groups is going to be hurt or harmed in some way, or in which the rights of those individuals or groups are going to be ignored or compromised in some other way. Moral standards of behavior are our intuitive gauges of individual and organizational actions. They are the means we all use first to decide whether our actions, and those of the other people and other groups with whom we live and work, are "right" or "wrong," "fair" or "unfair," "just" or "unjust."

The problem is that our moral standards of behavior are subjective. They are personal. They are the way we all intuitively feel about our actions and those of our neighbors, friends, and associates, but we can't really justify those feelings. You may feel that lying is wrong under any and all circumstances. I may feel that lying to avoid causing embarrassment or anguish to a close friend is perfectly all right. We can't or at least we generally don't resolve those differences, and so we usually just agree to disagree on the question. Such an understanding is perfectly acceptable when we are dealing with a minor moral problem such as lying to avoid causing discomfort to a friend. However, such an understanding—to agree to disagree—is not acceptable when we are concerned with a substantial moral problem such as building a huge hydroelectric dam that will benefit millions of people who live far away, yet harm the thousands of individuals who live right there.

We have to decide the issue, not ignore the conflict, and the first step is to understand that moral standards are not an adequate framework for decision because they are variable as well as personal. They vary by individual, by group, by region, by country, by culture, and by time. We all have evidence of that variation. Business managers in South and Central America and large parts of Africa and Asia think that it is perfectly acceptable to make small payments to government officials to facilitate needed documents and permits. That is termed *bribery* in the United States. Government officials in the United States feel that it is perfectly acceptable, after they retire, to work for foreign firms that have business relationships with the government. That is termed *treason* in South and Central America and large parts of Africa and Asia.

Moral standards of behavior differ between peoples because the goals, norms, beliefs, and values upon which they depend also differ, and those goals, norms, beliefs, and values in turn differ because of variations in the religious and cultural traditions and the economic and social situations in which the individuals are immersed. These relationships are shown in Figure 1.2.

FIGURE 1.2 **Individual Determinants of Moral Standards**

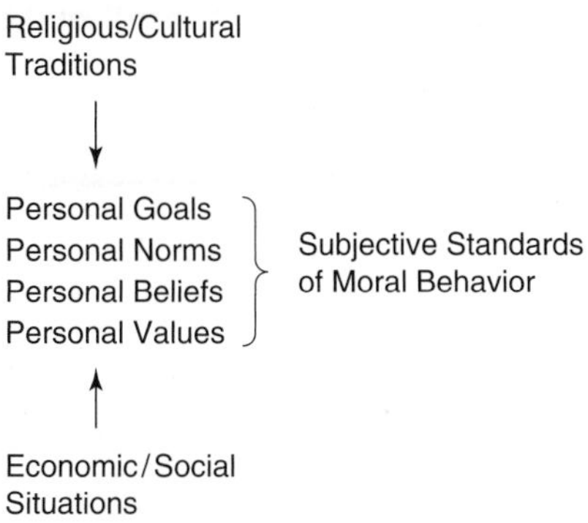

Religious/Cultural
Traditions

↓

Personal Goals ⎫
Personal Norms ⎪   Subjective Standards
Personal Beliefs ⎬   of Moral Behavior
Personal Values ⎭

↑

Economic/Social
Situations

Now we will take up each of the elements in Figure 1.2 in sequence, starting with the personal goals, norms, beliefs, and values, and showing their derivation from the religious and cultural traditions and the economic and social situations of each individual:

- *Personal goals.* Goals are our expectations of outcomes. They are the things we want out of life and the things we expect others probably want out of life as well. They include material possessions (cars, homes, boats, and vacations), lifestyle preferences (money, position, workload, and power), personal goods (family, friends, health, and respect) and social aims (justice, equality, a clean environment, and a world at peace). If I want more money and power and you want greater justice and equality, then probably we are going to differ on what we think is "right" and "wrong."

- *Personal norms.* Norms are our expectations of behavior. They are the ways we expect to act and the ways in which we expect others to act in given situations. Norms differ from moral standards in that they have no close association with judgments about "right" or "wrong." Norms are expectations of behavior; morals are gauges of behavior. I expect you to drive on the right-hand side of the road; that is a norm. If you persist on driving on the left-hand (in the United States), I will say that you are "wrong"; that is a moral standard.

- *Personal beliefs.* Beliefs are our expectations of thought. They are the ways we expect to think, and the ways in which we expect others to think, about given situations. Our beliefs generally support our norms, and our norms usually lead toward our goals. For example, I believe that cigarette smoke causes cancer, and consequently I expect you not to smoke in my presence because one of my goals is good health. If you persist in smoking, despite my repeated (and heated) objections, I am going to say that you are "wrong" for you have acted against my moral standard derived from those goals, norms, and beliefs.

- *Personal values.* Values are our priorities between goals, norms, and beliefs. They are the ways we judge the relative importance of what we want to have, how we want to act, and why we believe as we do. Most people do not consider that all of their goals, norms, and beliefs are of equal importance. Generally there are some that seem more important, more "valued," than others. Let us say that you and I value democracy (a belief) very highly; if someone offers both of us money (a goal) to vote a given way (a norm), we are going to say that they are "wrong."

The goals, norms, beliefs, and values of a person will vary depending upon the cultural and religious tradition of that person, and those variations will in turn affect the person's moral standards. Clearly the cultural and religious traditions of the Cree and Inuit who have long been established in northern Quebec are going to differ markedly from the cultural and religious traditions of the European immigrants who have been comparatively recent (within the past 300 years) settlers in southern Quebec. Assume that both sides hold their religious beliefs and cultural norms in equally high esteem; their differing goals, norms, beliefs, and values are going to affect the ways in which each group views the proposed hydroelectric generating project.

The goals, norms, beliefs, and values of a person will also vary depending upon the economic and social situation of that person. The economic situation includes the relative income and financial security of the individual. The social situation does not mean the social status or standing of the person; instead, it refers to his or her membership in different organizations whose members can influence his or her goals, normal, beliefs, values, and—ultimately—his or her moral standards. Clearly once again, the relative incomes and the organizational memberships of the Cree and Inuit in northern Quebec are going to differ markedly from the relative incomes and organizational memberships of the European immigrants in southern Quebec. Once again, their differing goals, norms, beliefs, and values are also going to affect the ways in which each group views the desirability of the big hydroelectric generating project.

How should you attempt to bridge those different moral standards and project views, and arrive at an ethical solution that you believe to be "right" and "just" and "fair," *and* that you think you could logically explain to all of the other groups involved in the project in order to reach a morally acceptable compromise? The argument of this book is that you work through each of the next six stages in the moral analysis, starting with an explicit recognition of the moral impacts.

Recognize the Moral Impacts

Moral problems were described earlier as being complex because they result in benefits for some and harms for others, and because they exercise the rights of some and deny the rights of others. Those benefits and harms, that exercise and denial of rights, together compose the impacts of the problem. Those "impacts"—the benefits and harms, the rights and wrongs—are what people think about when they consider a morally controversial project such as the construction of the large hydroelectric project in northern Quebec. Consequently, it is suggested that you start your analysis of the problem, and your determination of the solution, by firstly identifying exactly who is going to be benefited and who is going to be harmed. Then identify exactly who is going to be able to freely exercise their rights and who is going to be prevented from an equally free exercise of their rights. People feel strongly about being harmed. People feel even more strongly about being denied their rights. Your first step is to make certain that everyone involved in the moral problem understands what is happening to everyone else:

- *Benefits.* Whose well-being will be substantially improved by the present or proposed action (what is being done, or what is planned to be done) either by yourself or by the organization to which you belong? Focus on material or financial or personal benefits to identifiable groups of people, not to inanimate companies or communities or countries. Moral problems involve a mixture of outcomes. List the positive outcomes of that mixture. Specifically, identify the major groups of people whose well-being you believe will be improved, and give a short description of the nature of that improvement for each group.

- *Harms.* Whose well-being will be substantially harmed by the present or proposed action (what is being done, or what is planned to be done) either by yourself or by the organization to which you belong? Focus on material or financial or personal harms to identifiable groups of people, not to inanimate companies or communities or countries. Moral problems, once again, constitute a mixture of outcomes. List the negative outcomes of that mixture. Identify the major groups of people whose well-being you believe will be damaged, and give once again a short description of the nature of that damage for each group.

- *Rights.* Whose rights will be exercised and made more certain by the present or proposed action either by yourself or by the organization to which you belong? Focus on the rights of identifiable groups of people, not of inanimate companies or communities or countries. Be selective. Make certain that what is being exercised is a clear right or claim of a privilege to do something important, not just a general desire to do something beneficial. Identify the major groups of people whose rights you believe will be sustained or expanded in some way, and give some indication of the nature of those rights.

- *Wrongs.* Whose rights will be denied and made less certain by the present or proposed action either by yourself or by the organization to which you belong? Focus on the wrongs to identifiable groups of people, not to inanimate companies or communities or countries. Again, be selective. Make certain that what is being denied is a clear right or claim of someone to do something important, not just a general desire to do something beneficial. Identify the major groups of these people whose rights you believe will be denied or reduced in some way, and give an indication of the nature of those rights.

The benefits and the harms, the rights and the wrongs, for the different groups involved in the proposed construction of the Great Whale hydroelectric generating project, are summarized in Figure 1.3.

There is a major harm, and an important wrong, that are both shown in Figure 1.3 but were not included in the earlier description of the project. This is the technical issue of the possibility of methyl mercury poisoning. Mercury, which is a highly toxic heavy

FIGURE 1.3 Comparison of the Benefits and Harms, the Rights Exercised and Denied, Associated with the Construction by Hydro-Quebec of the Great Whale Generating Project

Benefits and Harms	Benefits Received	Harms Allocated
Residents of northern Quebec	Improved housing	Loss of flooded land
	Improved health care	Loss of native culture
	Lower infant mortality	Poisoning of local fish
	Longer life spans	Harm to human health
	Better education	
Residents of southern Quebec	Lower priced power	None
	Greater industrial growth	
	More jobs	
	Higher income	
	Better education	
Residents of northeastern U.S.	Available electric power	None
	No new generating plants	
	No acid rain	
	No global warming	

metal, occurs naturally in the soil and consequently in the low scrub vegetation of the tundra area of northern Quebec. When that tundra vegetation is flooded, and submerged under water, the plant matter decays and the mercury combines with the organic hydro-carbons to form methyl mercury, a water-soluble form of the toxic metal. Being water-soluble, it will quickly enter into the aquatic life of the massive lake or reservoir that has been created. It will probably affect the fish and, if humans eat the fish, it will probably affect the humans as well. No one knows the extent of that affect upon either the fish or the people because there has never been a reservoir of this size (9,100 square miles) built this far north (in the tundra area) before. The only proposed solution has been a legal prohibition on eating the fish. Methyl mercury poisoning thus is a probable harm (loss of the local fish as a food product) and possible wrong (denial of the right to health) for the Cree and Inuit peoples that must be included, though, as stated earlier, the exact impact is not known with certainty.

The rights exercised and rights denied perhaps need greater explanation than can be compressed into the short descriptions in the table of Figure 1.3. The residents of southern Quebec would doubtless feel that, if an election were held on building the hydroelectric project, the percentage voting "yes" would easily win because the benefits of lower priced power, greater industrial growth, more jobs, and higher incomes would go to a vast majority of the population. Those residents of southern Quebec would prob-ably also feel that, if a trial were held on the issue, the verdict would be "go ahead" because the right of eminent domain (right of the government to expropriate private land for a public use, such as a highway or airport) is solidly established in the law. Even further, the legal ownership of the land by the Cree and Inuit has never been formally established; their concept of ownership does not extend to land. Land in their culture is owned communally by the tribe, not individually by the person. It is possible in their culture for a person to own a house; it is not possible for that person to own the land upon which that house rests. This is another example of the way in which misunder-standings between Indian and Western cultures are so easily possible. The next step, then, in the analytical process is to clearly state the moral problem so that everyone fully comprehends the issues, regardless of their religious and cultural traditions, and of their economic and social situations.

State the Moral Problem

If your listed balance of benefits received and harms imposed, and your described contrast of rights exercised and rights denied, conflict with your personal moral stan-dards, then clearly you have what you believe to be a moral problem. But, remember that—due to the differences in moral standards that come from variations in goals, norms, beliefs, and values, and from the contrasts in religious and cultural traditions and economic and social situations—not everyone will agree with you.

To reach a solution, you want to get everyone to fully comprehend your side of the issue. Doubtless other groups will want to get everyone—including you—to fully comprehend their sides of the issue as well. If all groups fully comprehend all sides, clearly and accurately, then a compromise that meets the tests of economic benefits, legal requirements, and ethical duties is at least possible. That is why you want to first define and then state the moral problem as clearly as you can. Get agreement here, and the rest of the decision process will be far easier.

It is strongly suggested that you state the moral problem in the form of an extended question. A question is much less threatening and far more considerate than a statement. And the question format explicitly recognizes the concerns of others and makes it possible to include those concerns in the subsequent analysis, discussion, and conclusion:

> Is it "right" that Hydro-Quebec build a large hydroelectric generating plant in northern Quebec, on land that has been inhabited by the Cree and Inuit Indians for centuries? The project will result in substantial benefits (lower-priced power, greater industrialization, more jobs, higher incomes, reduced pollution, improved education, and better health care) for large groups of people in southern Quebec. It will even result in substantial benefits (better housing, education, and health care, and longer life spans and reduced infant mortality) for the native peoples of northern Quebec. But it will also result in a loss of their land and culture, and possible harms to their health. A strong majority of the Indian peoples in the North do not want the project built. A strong majority of the European immigrants in the South do want the project built. The residents of southern Quebec have a right to democratic rule and legal process regarding that project, but the inhabitants of northern Quebec have an equal right to decide their own future and a critical right to ensure their own health.

Determine the Economic Outcomes

In moral analysis the phrase *economic outcomes* refers to the net balance of benefits over costs for the full society, given that the values of those benefits and costs are determined by all of the people within that full society, acting through open and free markets. This is the concept known as Pareto Optimality. The underlying belief is that people, through output product markets, express their preferences for the goods and services they most want, and through input factor markets, express their preferences for the capital (money), labor (time), and land (raw materials) they least desire. Capital, labor, and land are the resources owned by members of society. Producing firms purchase or rent that capital, labor, and material at the lowest possible costs, convert those factors into products with the greatest possible efficiencies, and then sell the output goods and services at the highest possible prices. Competition in the output product markets keeps the prices from becoming improperly high, and competition in the input factor markets keeps the costs from becoming unfairly low. The full society, then, gets as many as possible of the products they most want while having to give up as little as possible of the factors they least want.

The analytical method of "economic outcomes" can also be expressed as three easily understood dictums: (1) More is better than less. (2) Specifically, more is better than less when that "more" consists of what people really want, as expressed through their preferences in the product markets. (3) And even more specifically, that "more" of what people really want is better than less when that "more" is produced as efficiently as possible by using as little as possible of what people least want, as expressed by their preferences in the factor markets.

In the example of the huge hydroelectric generating plant proposed by Hydro-Quebec, the analytical method of "economic outcomes" would firstly conclude—following the first two dictums—that more electricity, as long as it was wanted in the output product markets and would not be surplus, would be better than less. The problem would come in the third dictum. People would have to give up what they least wanted in the input factor markets. But there are no input factor markets for tundra land and native culture, and, consequently, the members of the full society are unable to express their preferences in an economically understandable way. Also, there is the troubling issue of the methyl mercury poisoning. This is termed an "external cost" in economic theory; it is outside the production process, but the potential consequences will be imposed upon the native peoples without their consent.

The concept of the greatest possible economic benefits at the least possible economic costs, which is called the "more is better than less" doctrine or the Pareto Optimality theory, is considered to be a valid means of morally evaluating the benefits and harms of a moral problem as long as three conditions are met:

- *All markets must be free.* Open and competitive product markets must exist for all goods and services, and open and competitive factor markets must exist for all input capital, labor, and material, to generate a true net benefit for society. Without open and free markets the preferences of the members of that society cannot be expressed.

- *All laws must be obeyed.* The analytical method of economic benefits does not consider the balance of rights exercised and rights denied. It focuses on the outcomes, not on the rights. It is assumed that all legitimate rights are expressed by democratically enacted laws, and therefore the spirit, as well as the letter, of those laws must be followed.

- *All costs must be included.* External costs are those outside the productive process; they are frequently ignored because no one in the producing firm has to write out a check as they must to purchase capital, labor, and material. It is assumed that they will be recognized, computed, and then included in the purchase price of the output goods and services.

Consider the Legal Requirements

Legal requirements in moral analysis refer to the laws adopted by members of society to regulate the behavior of members of that society. Clearly some regulation is needed. If everyone pursued their own self-interests, without regard to the self-interests of others, there would be disruption and chaos, and no economic benefits would be possible for anyone. The problem is that every regulation limits, to some extent, the rights of some individuals and groups within society, even though it protects the rights of other individuals and groups within that same society. Legal requirements, in one sense, are very similar to economic outcomes. Economic outcomes in moral analysis focus upon a balance between benefits and harms. Legal requirements in moral analysis also focus upon a balance, though in this instance it is a balance between rights and wrongs, or between rights exercised and rights denied.

The balance between rights exercised and rights denied clearly has to be "fair," which would mean equitable to the full society. The idea of economic outcomes attempts to determine what would be beneficial to the full society. The idea of legal requirements attempts to determine what would be equitable, or evenhanded, to that society. I own a considerable amount of land in a pleasant residential community. You are my next door neighbor. I own the land outright and, consequently, I think that I have a right to do what

I please with that land and make as large a profit as possible. A real estate developer offers me a very high price to build a very large shopping center. My right to sell what I own without interference will be exercised. Your right to live quietly, in your own home, will be denied.

How do we determine what would be equitable under those circumstances? We could take a vote, and because there will be many more residents who don't want a new shopping center in our community than there will be those that do, you will win. But would that be "right"? A majority can override the rights of a minority. The method proposed in the legal requirements method of moral analysis to determine fairness is to consider what would be the balance of rights vs. wrongs if everyone within society considered what regulations should be adopted *while ignorant of his or her own self-interest*. This is the concept known as the "Social Contract". It is usually expressed as a question: What regulations would people agree should be the basic laws of our society *if they did know the position they held within society?*

This is obviously an impossible condition. People do know the positions they hold within society. I know that I own the land and want to build the shopping center. You know that you are my next-door neighbor, and don't want the shopping center built. You particularly don't want it built because I plan to keep it open until 12:30 every night to maximize revenues, with bright lights in the parking lot that will shine directly into your bedroom windows, and loud music on the speaker system that will prevent you from sleeping. But let us say that we move back in time, before there were shopping centers and residential communities. What agreement would we make then as to regulations that would limit the rights of ownership of land? I would be as worried as you about the possibility that my neighbors might use their land in ways that would detract from my use of my land. If we could reach an agreement and pass a law under those conditions, termed the "Veil of Ignorance," then it would be possible to say that that agreement and that law would be "right" and "fair" and "just." It would reflect the social interests of all of us rather than the self-interests of a portion of us.

In the example of the huge hydroelectric generating plant proposed by Hydro-Quebec, the analytical method of legal requirements, following the concept of the Veil of Ignorance, would help each side to understand the rationale of the other side. The native peoples of northern Quebec would be forced to recognize the many benefits and rights of the residents of the south. The residents of southern Quebec would be forced to recognize the many harms and wrongs of the peoples of the north. The concept of a law that focuses on the social interests of all of society rather than on the self-interests of a portion of society can be considered to be a valid means of evaluating the balance of rights and wrongs of a moral problem as long as one condition exists:

- All parties must be willing to evaluate the balance of benefits and harms, and of rights and wrongs, as if they were ignorant of their positions within society. Everyone must be willing to adopt the method of the Veil of Ignorance to examine the issue, and look at social interest rather than self-interest. This is a difficult condition, but it is not an impossible one.

Evaluate the Ethical Duties

The doctrine of Ethical Duties in moral analysis refers to the obligations owed by members of society to other members of that society. Clearly, some obligations do exist.

We ought not to lie to each other, or agreements will not be possible. We ought not to cheat each other, or contracts will not be possible. And we ought not to steal from each other, or communities will not be possible. A society without agreements, without contracts, and without communities, would be impossible to sustain. The problem is that if I could lie just a little bit, cheat just a little bit, and steal just a little bit, the society could still be maintained, weakened but still in existence, and I would be advantaged though you would be harmed. Once again, the focus in moral analysis is between self-interest and social interest.

Ethical duties are a method of moral analysis that attempts to provide a set of rules as to what would be in the interest of society under all conditions and/or situations. There is no moral balance between social interest and self-interest as there is in the analytical methods of economic outcomes and legal requirements. The doctrine of economic outcomes attempts to find a balance, between benefits for some people within society and harms for others, that will result in an overall improvement for the full society. The doctrine of legal requirements attempts to find a similar balance, between rights for some people and wrongs for others, that will also result in an overall improvement for our society. The doctrine of ethical duties does not look for a balance between duties. It does not say that a little more lying, cheating, or stealing by one group can be balanced by a little less lying, cheating, and stealing by another, and society will be better off. Instead, it attempts to set the rules or conditions under which *some* very specific instances of lying, cheating, and stealing would be permissible.

I feel, as I explained in an example given earlier in this chapter in the section on moral standards of behavior, that lying to avoid causing discomfort to a friend is permissible. You may disagree. But how about stealing to save the life of a child, particularly if the theft is from persons or groups who have more than enough for their own sustenance? Is that morally correct in your judgment? Ethical duties get down to the absolute essence of what is "right" and "just" and "fair" for everyone. Remember this "for everyone" condition; an ethical principle is meaningless unless it can be applied to all. There are six of these universal rules or conditions that are summarized below, in the historical sequence of their initial formulation:

- *Personal virtues* (Aristotle, 384–322 BC). The argument here is that we can do as we like, and follow our own self-interests, as long as we adopt a set of standards for our "right," "just," and "fair" treatment of one another. We have to be honest, open, and truthful, for example, to eliminate distrust, and we should live temperately so as not to incite envy. In short, we have to be proud of our actions and of our lives, for it is hard to be proud of actions that exploit or oppress others. The principle, then, can be expressed as "Never take any action which is not honest, open, and truthful, and which you would not be proud to see reported widely in national newspapers and on network television programs."

- *Religious injunctions* (St. Augustine, 354–403 and St. Thomas Aquinas, 1225–1274). Honesty, truthfulness, and temperance are not enough; we also have to have some degree of compassion and kindness towards each other to form a truly "good" society. Compassion and kindness are best expressed in the Golden Rule, which is not limited to the Judeo-Christian tradition, but is part of almost all of the world's religions. Reciprocity and compassion together build a sense of community. The principle, then, can be expressed as "Never take any action that is not kind, and that does not build a sense of community, a sense of all of us working together for a commonly accepted goal."

- *Utilitarian benefits* (Bentham, 1747–1832 and Mill, 1806–1873). Compassion, kindness, and a sense of community would be ideal if everyone were compassionate and kind and worked for the community rather than for themselves; but everyone won't and so we need a means of evaluating self-centered acts rather than eliminating them. An act, then, is "right" if it leads to greater net social benefits than social harms. This is the rule that is often summarized as "The greatest good for the greatest number," though in reality the society, not the majority, has to benefit. The principle can be summarized as "Never take any action that does not result in greater good than harm for the society of which you are a part."

- *Universal rules* (Kant, 1724–1804). Net social benefit is elegant in theory, but the theory does not say anything about how we should measure either the benefits or the harms—what is your life or health or well-being worth?—nor does it explain how we should distribute those benefits and allocate those harms. What we need is a rule to eliminate the self-interest of the person who decides in any given situation, and we can do that by universalizing the decision process. The principle, then, can be expressed as "Never take any action that you would not be willing to see others, faced with the same or a closely similar situation, also be free and even encouraged to take."

- *Distributive justice* (Rawls). The problem with the "willingness to see others be free and even encouraged to take" rule for actions that allegedly come from a good intent to promote social interest rather than a selfish desire to advance self-interest is that people differ in their social and economic situations. People have different social and economic wants. We need a rule to protect the poor and the uneducated who lack the power and position to achieve those wants. If we did not know who among us would be poor and uneducated—the Social Contract—everyone would be in favor of such a rule. The principle, then, can be expressed as "Never take any action in which the least among us will be harmed in any way."

- *Contributive liberty* (Nozick). Perhaps liberty, the freedom to follow one's own self-interest within the constraints of the law and the markets, is more important than justice, the right to be protected from extremes of that law and those markets. If so, then the only agreement that could be made under the conditions of the Social Contract—in which people do not know who would be rich or poor, who powerful or weak—would be that no one should interfere with the rights of anyone else to improve their legal abilities and marketable skills. The principle, then, can be expressed as "Never take any action that will interfere with the rights of others for self-development and self-improvement."

The method of moral analysis recommended in this text is that you look first at *your* moral standards of behavior—what do you intuitively believe to be "right" and "wrong," "fair" and "unfair," "just" and "unjust," based upon *your* goals, norms, beliefs, and values? Then look at the situation that you have encountered. Who will be benefited and who will be harmed? Who will be able to exercise their rights and who will be denied an equally free exercise of their rights? If those conditions in that situation

FIGURE 1.4   Analytical Process for the Resolution of Moral Problems

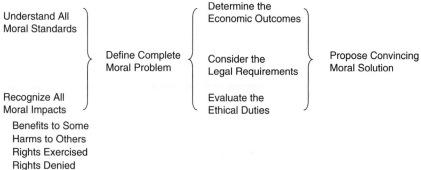

conflict with your moral standards, then you have a moral problem. Express that moral problem as clearly as you can, so that *everyone* involved will understand your concerns. Then analyze that moral problem through the perspectives of economic outcomes, legal requirements, and ethical duties to arrive at *your* moral solution. This process was earlier expressed in graphic form, which is repeated in Figure 1.4 for emphasis.

Chapter 2 will discuss in greater detail the analytical procedure of economic outcomes. Chapter 3 will deal with legal requirements. Chapter 4 will describe the ethical duties. Chapter 5 will focus on the reasons to be moral: the trust, commitment, and effort that frequently develop among all of the participants within an extended organization in response to decisions and actions that they perceive to be "right" and "just" and "fair." Chapter 6 will consider the managerial and organizational changes needed to achieve exactly those results, and the resultant cooperation, innovation, and unification that are needed for success in a competitive global environment.

Case 1-1

Merck Corporation and the Continued Sale of Vioxx

Merck Corporation is a large (61,500 employees) pharmaceutical firm headquartered in Whitehouse Station, New Jersey. For years the company was known primarily for the productivity of its research department, the restraint of its marketing plan, and the profitability of that unusual combination. Literally hundreds of prescription drugs had been conceived by their scientists, formulated in their labs, improved through their testing procedures, guided through governmental approval processes, and then manufactured and marketed worldwide. This marketing tended to be very low key and very doctor focused. Company research scientists would write articles for medical journals read by doctors. Company sales representatives would visit medical offices to speak directly to doctors. This combination of advanced research and restrained marketing—there was at this time no costly advertising of Merck products on television, no continual exhortations to "ask your doctor" about the alleged benefits of any of those products—proved to be exceedingly successful. Merck, as a result, was one of the most profitable firms in the United States, with a return on owner's equity that averaged 43 percent over the five-year period 1996 to 2000.

Merck Corporation was also one of the most respected companies in the United States over this same five-year 1996 to 2000 time span. Part of that respect came from an open and avowed focus of the firm upon the well-being of patients, not upon the growth in profits, as evidenced by a statement from the founder, George Merck, which became a major part of the firm's folklore and culture:

> We try never to forget that medicine is for the people, it is not for the profits. The profits follow, and if we have remembered that, they have never failed to appear.

Another part of the respect for Merck clearly felt by medical practitioners and everyday patients alike came from the willingness of the company to develop what were termed "orphan drugs." These were pharmaceutical prescriptions with little or no commercial potential. Usually they were used to treat a very rare disease where the market size was too small or the insurance coverage too low to enable the firm to recover their costs of development, testing, approval, manufacturing, and marketing. Occasionally they were needed to treat a very prevalent disease where the afflicted patients were far too poor and the affected nations far too undeveloped to make any meaningful payments to offset those costs of development, testing, approval, manufacturing, and distribution. Most pharmaceutical companies, under either of those two conditions, simply abandoned any orphan drugs they discovered in their research efforts.

Merck did not. They were willing to devote considerable effort and money to bring those discovered drugs not to the market but to the need. This was illustrated by Merck's development of the drug Mectizan for a frightful illness known as "river blindness," or onchocercias. This was a disease that afflicted some 18 million people in the mountainous areas of Central Africa. It was caused by the bite of a tiny black fly which bred in the fast-moving rivers and streams of that region. This was the reason for the restricted geographic location; the small black fly needed heavy rainfall and mountainous terrain. That was also the reason for the limited treatment options; aerial spraying—the usual remedy for malarial mosquitoes which breed in stagnant ponds and pools—was ineffectual in fast-flowing rivers and streams.

River blindness is a horrid disease. When a black fly bites a human being to draw blood, it frequently enables the larvae of a small parasitic worm carried by the fly to enter the human bloodstream. The parasitic worm by itself is not overly harmful, but when those worms reach maturity they release millions of microscopic offspring, known as microfilariae, which swarm throughout the body tissue. They tend to cluster in the skin, where they cause terrible itching and eventually lead to lesions, infections, and permanent sores. The itching is so severe that some victims resort to suicide. But even worse, after several years of skin torment the microfilariae invade the eyes, and the patient becomes blind.

In the mid-1980s researchers in a special veterinarian drug unit of Merck were working with a range of microbiotic cultures in an attempt to develop a treatment for the parasitic worms that affect cattle, hogs, horses, and other farm animals in the United States. One of these new cultures, code-named Mectizan, had been written off as a failure. It seemed to have no potential as a cure for any major animal diseases, though it was remarkably effective when used against the microfilariae of an exotic and relatively harmless gastrointestinal parasite found in horses.

One of the researchers, Dr. William Campbell, noticed a marked genetic similarity between the microfilariae found in horses that seemed to cause little damage and the microfilariae found in humans that led to river blindness. At the time Merck had a scientific-freedom policy that enabled him to spend up to $500,000 of company funds and invest up to a year of his own time to pursue a prescription drug concept before any formal evaluation of the commercial potential of the drug would be required. He quickly, within a very few months, was able to show that the new microbiotic drug, Mectizan, worked, and worked well, on the river blindness microfilariae growing in a tissue culture derived from human beings. There was, however, no guarantee that it would work equally well on the parasites growing in an actual human being without adversely affecting the health of that human being.

Members of the scientific review committee at Merck clearly understood that there was no commercial potential to this drug, but they promptly gave Dr. Campbell permission to conduct limited human tests on persons in Central and West Africa already afflicted with advanced stages of the disease, who—it was felt—could not be made worse off and might well be helped by the treatment. The drug exceeded benefit expectations, with no adverse side-effects. Members of the board of directors at Merck then approved, in sequence: (*a*) full-scale testing at a cost of $50 million, (*b*) governmental registration at a further cost of $50 million, (*c*) manufacturing start-up at an additional cost of $50 million, and then (*d*) free distribution at an annual cost of $100 million each year. The annual cost was required because the antimicrofilariae drug did not stay in the human bloodstream, and people who had been cured one year were susceptible to reinfection the next.

Merck had spent $150 million for the development, testing, and manufacturing of Mectizan, and then committed to spend $100 million per year over the foreseeable future, all for the distribution of a drug which had huge benefits for large numbers of people living in a depressed region of the world, but absolutely no profit potential at all for the firm. Dr. Campbell was lauded for his scientific insight, and Merck for their social conscience. Both received numerous awards and widespread publicity.

At about this time, however, Merck was changing. Some of their best-selling, blockbuster drugs such as Singulair (for asthma), Zocor (for cholesterol), Vioxx (for arthritis), Fosamax (for osteoporosis), Prinivil (for blood pressure problems), Prilosec (for gastrointestinal ills), and Crixivan (for HIV/AIDS illnesses) were coming off patent, which meant that they could soon be produced by competitors (often abroad) at far lower costs, and eventually sold as generics in the United States at far lower prices. Merck's drug "pipeline," which refers to the lineup of pharmaceutical compounds going through the development, testing, and approval procedures, had become far less productive. A new chairman was brought in, who proposed that the company emphasize marketing rather than science and—despite the far earlier admonition of George Merck, the founder—focus on profits rather than people. Television ads for Merck products began to dominate the air waves, particularly on the programs primarily watched by older viewers who were the principal consumers of pharmaceutical drugs. Prices on those drugs were increased, particularly in the United States, where there was no national health plan that could bargain extensively for the purchase of those drugs from a dominant position of economic strength (as there is in Canada and most of Europe, for example). As a result of all these changes, sales went down substantially, from $47.7 billion in 2001 to $22.0 billion in 2005, though profits as a percentage of sales increased almost equally substantially, from 15.3 percent in 2001 to 25.3 percent in 2005.

Vioxx was one of the Merck blockbuster drugs that was widely advertised on consumer television sets, and highly priced to make up for falling retail sales, as a result of the deliberate change in Merck strategy. Vioxx was a type of pharmaceutical drug known as a COX-2 inhibitor; it helped to control what can be the severe pain of rheumatoid arthritis (inflammation of the joints that tends to occur in many older people as they age). Vioxx had been developed in company labs and had gone through the standard medical testing and governmental approval procedures, but there turned out to be an underlying problem with the drug that became known with startling clarity in September 2004.

Merck withdrew Vioxx from the market in September 2004 after, it was claimed, company executives had just learned as a result of a follow-up clinical trial—that is, a clinical trial designed to examine the treatment effectiveness or pharmaceutical side-effects of a given compound *after* governmental approval had been fully granted by the Food and Drug Administration—that Vioxx might be the cause of heart attacks and strokes observed among patients who took it for more than 18 months.

There was immediate concern because Vioxx was a drug that had been prescribed for well over a million patients. Sales plummeted, as might have been expected. Law suits were filed, as also might have been expected. But then calm appeared to be restored, and some commentators began to praise Merck for having acted so forcefully, in totally removing the drug from the market rather than just attempting to warn patients by changing the label or to advise physicians by providing more data. An assumed parallel between Merck and Johnson & Johnson, another pharmaceutical company, which had promptly and totally removed Tylenol from the market when vials of that product had been found to have been tampered with and poisoned, was quickly noted by some of the news media.

Within a very few months, however, the furor erupted again, and all the earlier praise was quickly disavowed. Early results from the "discovery" process—in civil lawsuites the plaintiffs' attorneys are permitted to examine company records to determine what company executives knew about a given problem and when they first knew it—revealed that Merck executives had not been overly frank. They had not "just learned" about the problem of the increased risk for heart attack and stroke brought about by Vioxx when the product was withdrawn from the market in September 2004. Instead, they had received a series of warnings about the dangers inherent in this product starting in February 1997. At that time, while the governmental approval process was still ongoing and before Merck had begun selling the drug, one of their senior scientists expressed "great concern" about cardiovascular risks, and that initial warning was repeated, at intervals, over the subsequent seven years. The following time line is drawn from the *Wall Street Journal,* August 22, 2005, p. A1f., supplemented by the *Wall Street Journal,* December 9, 2005, p. A1f.:

> February 1997. Alise Reicin, senior research scientists at Merck, wrote in an e-mail that "the possibility of increased CV [cardiovascular] events is of great concern," and that this possibility, if confirmed by further study would "kill" the drug.

May 1999. The Food and Drug Administration formally approved Vioxx for the treatment of rheumatoid arthritis short-term pain, and Merck quickly started producing and marketing the drug, despite the earlier warning.

March 2000. Merck reported the preliminary results of a large test of Vioxx in comparison to naproxen, an over-the-counter remedy. In a footnote the company admitted that 0.5 percent of those taking Vioxx had heart attacks compared to 0.1 percent of those on naproxen.

Also in 2000. Dr. Edward Scolnick, chief of research at Merck, said in an e-mail that it was a "shame" that the study had linked Vioxx with an increased risk of heart attacks and strokes, and added an unclear statement that "it is a low incidence and it is mechanism based as we worried it was."

September 2001. The Food and Drug Administration apparently heard of this "comparative test" vs. naproxen, and warned Merck for improper marketing of Vioxx, saying that the company had misrepresented the drug's safety profile and minimized its potential risks.

October 2003. A Merck-funded study from Brigham and Women's Hospital in Boston, and coauthored by two Merck scientists amongst others, found that Vioxx did increase the risk of heart attacks and strokes compared with Pfizer's Celebrex (a competitive drug that was also a COX-2 inhibitor).

One year later, in September 2004, Merck formally stopped all sales of Vioxx. By August 2006, the company faced 14,000 individual and group claims covering 27,000 plaintiffs. These numbers had been higher, but some plaintiffs were forced to withdraw after their lawyers found that they could not produce adequate evidence (that is, prescription records) that they had actually taken the drug. This latter news produced a gleeful response from a financial analyst in New York City:

> "The plaintiffs are failing in the effort to extort money from Merck. The plaintiffs are just trying to get a quick buck out of Merck, and I think they'll go chase another ambulance once they figure out that Merck's not paying." (Statement of financial analyst, quoted in *The New York Times,* August 4, 2006)[1]

That attitude was quickly countered by a statement from an attorney for one of the plaintiffs, who said:

> The risks of Vioxx were known and known early. Merck could take the high road to patient safety or the low road to [corporate] sales.

Merck had vowed to contest each case and never agree to a settlement outside of court. That resolution must have been shaken, however, when the company lost the first Vioxx case, for the death of a 59-year-old man in Texas who participated regularly in triathlons. The jury awarded his widow $24 million in compensatory damages (in lieu of future earnings and for loss of future companionship) and $229 million in punitive damages (a penalty for past actions by the company in failing to notify the victim or his physician of the dangers of the drug). The $229 million in punitive damages by Texas law had to be reduced to $2 million, but the total was still $26 million for the first of 14,000 filed claims. Merck planned to appeal both awards.

[1]Copyright © 2005 by The New York Times Co. Reprinted with permission.

Merck won three of the next five cases, so the verdicts were split evenly between "guilty" and "not guilty" outcomes, but the "not guilty" ones often seemed based more upon the apparent ill health of the plaintiffs than upon the alleged poor effect of the drug. One of those plaintiffs was a 68-year-old woman who had survived her heart attack; she stood 5 feet 3 inches tall, weighed 265 pounds, and had diabetes, high cholesterol, elevated blood pressure, and clogged arteries. Interviews with jurors after many of these early trials indicated that (1) they felt that the victims bore some responsibility for not having taken better care of their own health conditions; (2) they believed that these victims and/or their families had not received adequate information from Merck about the health risks; (3) they disliked the direct-to-consumer marketing, particularly the frequent TV commercials, which they thought deliberately downplayed the health risks; and (4) they accepted as truthful the testimony of many of the plaintiffs' physicians, who frequently stated that they had received little or no information about possible medical risks to their patients.

Jurors evidently had been particularly impressed by the videotaped testimony of a doctor who said he never would have prescribed the painkiller for his patient, a plaintiff in the trial, if Merck sales representatives had warned him of its safety problems in one of their more than 22 visits to his office. This physician said that his patient was male, in his 70s, and diabetic, all of which increased the risk of a heart attack, and that his job as a doctor was to try to prevent heart attacks. Why, he asked, would I give him another risk factor? He ended by explaining that when he had specifically asked about risks, the Merck drug representative showed him a risk profile that claimed that taking Vioxx had less risk than aspirin.

Class Assignment

Assume that you had started working for Merck, perhaps in either marketing or finance, during the "people before profits" era that apparently ended in the mid- to late 1990s. Assume that you were concerned about the changes that you saw taking place within your company—the heightened emphasis upon consumer marketing and the increased reliance upon higher prices—but that you thought you understood the industrywide reasons for those changes: the decreased productivity of the R&D efforts at most domestic drug companies and the expanded competition with the generic drugs produced by many foreign firms. Assume that you learned, entirely by accident, about the alleged risks of heart attack and stroke that came with the use of Vioxx, and the apparent efforts by senior executives within Merck to conceal those risks. Let us say that your father had been diagnosed with severe rheumatoid arthritis, his physician had prescribed Vioxx, and your parents, who are retired and barely getting by on his pension and their Social Security, had come to you and asked if you could get them free samples without compromising either your integrity or your position. Let us lastly say that you had gone to the head of the department that conducted consumer tests at Merck, whom you knew reasonably well and whom you also knew had free access to an almost unlimited number of sample pills, but that he or she had told you, "Man, I wouldn't give him Vioxx under any circumstance; your father would be much better off if you went to the drugstore, and paid full price for some Celebrex, from Pfizer." You are surprised and ask why and get the full explanation that has been given in this case.

1. What would be your view of what Merck has done: economically, legally, and ethically? Assume that all this has occurred before September 2004, when the senior executives at Merck removed Vioxx from the market, and while the risks of Vioxx were still not public knowledge. Would you approve, or disapprove, of the continued sale of the drug by your firm?

2. If you disapprove of what Merck has done, would you go to the head of your division—the vice president of marketing or the chief financial officer—and attempt to convince him or her of your viewpoint? Even if you would not personally go to your superior at Merck (due to career risks), think about how you would word your explanation in order to be convincing to others.

3. If you approve of what Merck has done, would you then just tell your friend in charge of consumer tests at Merck, "Oh, that's OK. I'll be glad to take all the free Vioxx you can spare for Dad." Let us assume that you would not. Let us now further assume that the pills come in dissolvable capsules with the company name—Merck or Pfizer—printed on the side of each one. Your father probably will not care very much—he'll be glad to get either one—but let us lastly assume that your mother will be curious. She'll want to know why you changed the prescription. What would you tell her, and how would you now word your explanation in order to be fully convincing to her that this is the right thing for you to do?

4. Lastly, do you agree with the belief of George Merck, the founder, that if a company puts people ahead of profits, the profits will come. Or do you think that is far too simple a prescription for corporate health? What, if anything, would you add to his statement?

Case 1-2

Cruise Ships and the Disposal of Waste at Sea

Vacation cruises have become very popular. Approximately 85 cruise ships, primarily based in Miami, Florida, offer three-, five-, or seven-day trips to Bermuda, the Bahamas, the Caribbean, and the Yucatan Peninsula in Mexico. Some of these cruise ships are very large, carrying 2,000 to 3,000 passengers and 500 to 700 staff, the equivalent of a medium-sized town. The large size is a major cause of the pollution problem.

The large cruise ships are essentially floating hotels, but unlike land-based hotels they are not connected to municipal water and sewer systems. They carry the fresh water needed for drinking, washing, laundry, and kitchen use in huge tanks. Human wastes from toilets are stored in large tanks that are pumped out when the ship returns to the home port. Nonhuman wastes are stored in much smaller tanks that are discharged each night, at sea.

The nonhuman wastes are called "gray water," a euphemism that brings to mind the soapy water from baths and showers. That is certainly included, but also included is wastewater from the clothes washers for sheets and towels in the ship's laundry, from the dishwashers for plates, utensils, and pans in the ship's kitchen, and from the many garbage disposals. It is an unsavory, smelly mess that is discharged at night in order not to concern or disturb the guests.

Officials in the companies that own the cruise ships, such as Royal Caribbean Cruises, say that they cannot afford to carry tanks large enough to store all of the nonhuman wastes until they return to their home port. The ships add fresh water to their tanks when they stop at islands in the Caribbean or at ports in the Bahamas or Bermuda. But those ports do not have waste treatment plants large enough to accept either the human or nonhuman wastes for processing. The space needed for much larger tanks to store non-human wastes would, company officials claim, substantially take away from the space available for the accommodation of paying passengers. No one is hurt, they add, by disposal at sea because these are chemical (soap) and biological materials that quickly disperse in the wave actions of the sea. It is true that marine life has declined severely in this area, but company officials say this is due to poor waste treatment practices on the islands themselves and to overfishing by ships from many foreign countries.

The island nations don't like gray water dumping just off their coasts, but they are de-pendent upon the dollars brought by tourists shopping for souvenirs, gifts, and clothing at the ports of call during the cruise. Island nations that objected too strongly in the past have been told that the cruise ships would simply find a different port of call. Internation-al maritime law provides no assistance to those nations; it is not illegal for ships to dump wastes "at sea," which is usually defined as three miles from the nearest point of land.

Some of the smaller Caribbean nations appealed to the World Health Organization. They claimed that nutrients from the garbage and chemicals from the detergents had greatly increased the growth of viral and bacterial agents throughout the Caribbean. Now, they added, dense clouds of these tiny organisms can be found in the seawater, and many sea creatures, such as fish, turtles, and dolphins, are showing signs of external rashes and internal tumors. The World Health Organization said in reply that it had no authority to act as long as it could not be proven that human health was affected.

Senior executives at the major cruise lines were concerned, but they believed that there was little they could do. Ship designers had estimated that it would decrease pas-senger accommodations by 15 percent to 20 percent to add the much larger tanks need-ed to store the gray water wastes. Those tanks, due to their weight when full, would have to be built below the waterline in space currently used for the crew's quarters. The crew, now housed in very crowded conditions that cannot be further compressed, would have to be moved into new facilities built where passenger cabins now exist. Those same executives believed that, if those changes in the physical layout of the ships were made, ticket prices would have to be increased by an equivalent 15 percent to 20 percent to make up for the lost revenue. This, it was feared, would decrease customer demand. Now, because of their huge economies of scale and the scenic attractiveness of the region they visit, cruise ships offer highly desired and relatively inexpensive vaca-tions. On the other hand, the executives admitted that the quality of the seawater had apparently deteriorated to some extent, and that at least part of the responsibility for that deterioration might be due to the waste-dumping practices of the cruise lines.

Class Assignment

What should be done? What recommendations should you, as a leading member of the board of directors, make to the other members of the board, and how should you convince them to adopt those recommendations? The first chapter of this text suggested that you use the following pattern of analysis:

1. What groups will be benefited from continuing the present "dump at sea" policy?
2. What groups will be harmed from continuing the present "dump at sea" policy?
3. What groups will be able to fully exercise their rights if the present policy is continued?
4. What groups will be denied many of their rights if the present policy is continued?
5. How would you express the moral problem (if you believe this to be a moral problem) so that everyone involved will believe that you fully recognize and truly understand their particular problems and concerns?
6. What are the economic benefits? The rule is that you should always take the action that will generate the greatest profits for the company because this will also generate the greatest benefits for the society, provided it can be shown that all markets are fully competitive, all customers are fully informed, and all external and internal costs are fully included.
7. What are the legal requirements? The rule here is that you should always take the action that most fully complies with the law because the law in a democratic society represents the combined moral standards of all of the people within that society, provided it can be shown that the goals, norms, beliefs, and values of all of the various individuals, groups, and organizations have been equitably combined in the formulation process.
8. What are the ethical duties? The rule here is that you should always take the action (1) that you would be proud to see widely reported in national newspapers, (2) that you believe will build a sense of community among everyone associated with the action, (3) that you expect will generate the greatest net social good, (4) that you would be willing to see others take in similar situations in which you might be the victim, (5) that you believe does not harm the "least among us," and (6) that you think does not interfere with the right of everyone to develop their skills to the fullest.
9. What is your recommendation, and how would you explain your recommendation to the other individuals, groups, and organizations that are going to be affected by that decision or action if it is adopted?

Case 1-3

Whirlpool Corporation and the Sale of Dish Antennas

The Whirlpool Corporation is the world's largest manufacturer of major home appliances such as washers, dryers, ovens, stoves, refrigerators, dishwashers, freezers, trash compactors, and air conditioners. It is a global firm. Manufacturing plants and marketing divisions are located in North America, Central and South America, Southeast Asia, the Near East, Europe, Africa, and Japan. Company headquarters are in Benton Harbor, Michigan. Sales in 1998 totaled $10.3 billion, profits were $325 million, and 62,000 persons were employed.

Whirlpool, as do many other manufacturers of "long life" consumer products such as appliances, has a customer finance division that was started to provide financing to the retailers who stocked the company's products and to the customers who purchased those products. Whirlpool had a good credit rating; it was able to borrow money at low market rates and then lend that money at higher commercial rates to their distributors for inventory support and to their customers for installment purchases.

Over the years the customer finance division expanded beyond its original mission of supporting company sales through inventory financing for dealers and installment loans for customers, and began offering leases on heavy equipment for highway contractors, mortgages on real estate for mall developers, and contracts on "open end" notes for sales agents. Sales agents are companies or even individuals who may or may not have a store location but do most of their business by seeking out and direct selling customers. They frequently rely on telemarketing to get leads and then visit those potential customers to get orders.

All of these new forms of financing developed by Whirlpool carried higher interest rates, and consequently generated larger profits, than did their regular inventory support loans and installment purchase contracts. The open-end notes were particularly profitable. They were a form of credit card debt and carried the high interest rates—18 to 22 percent—associated with credit cards, and yet were used to finance single-item purchases of the type sold by the direct sales agents, such as roofing repairs, aluminum siding, and complete furniture suites.

An open-end note is essentially a credit card that is issued for a single sale. Little or no down payment is required, and the customer agrees only to make a minimal payment each month. The interest rates are high, and there are penalties for missing the minimal payment each month, but money is made available for people with low income and poor credit to purchase products that they otherwise could probably not afford. The problem is that these loans are on the edge of legality.

Under traditional, or closed-end, financing, the seller is required by the Federal Truth-in-Lending Act to disclose in a simple, clear written contract the amount of the total loan, the size of the monthly payment, and the number of months before the loan will be fully repaid. Under credit card or open-end financing there are far fewer disclosure requirements. The interest rate has to be stated on the contract (though this can be in small type at the bottom of the page), and the full amount of the loan has to be included. The monthly payment, however, is only a minimal amount, generally just large enough to cover the interest. Consequently, the number of months for full repayment cannot be computed and that figure is never disclosed. The lack of full disclosure has led in many instances to customer confusion and legal action. It did in this instance.

The Whirlpool Financial National Bank was one of two defendants, along with a Mr. Don Gantt, d/b/a Gulf Coast Electronics, named in a lawsuit filed by Barbara Carlisle and George and Velma Merriweather alleging that they had been misled by the defendants concerning the terms for the open-ended financing of the dish antennas they had purchased to improve television reception at their homes in rural Alabama. The abbreviation d/b/a/ means "doing business as"; it refers to an individual who operates under a company name that in reality is a proprietorship, not a corporation. Mr. Gantt, the individual in this case, was the sales agent whose proprietorship had sold the dish antennas. By the time of the trial Mr. Gantt was bankrupt, and he could not be located to appear either as a defendant or as a witness (trial transcript, p. 163, lines 4 to 6).

Television reception tends to be poor in much of rural Alabama. The broadcasting stations are in the major cities—Birmingham, Huntsville, Montgomery, and Mobile—and operate with low to medium power. Their signals do not carry throughout the state, and the rural regions lack the alternative of cable transmission. During the 1970s and 1980s persons living in those areas relied upon tall antennas, often attached to the roof or chimney of a home, with a directional control so that the receptor could be positioned to catch the signals from a specific station. It was not a totally satisfactory solution; the number of channels that could be received was very limited.

In the 1990s satellite dish antennas became available. They could receive an almost limitless number of channels, rebroadcast from satellites orbiting the earth. The problem was that the early models of the satellite dish antennas were expensive, and many of the persons living in the rural regions were poor and unable to afford the full purchase price, or even to make a substantial down payment upon that purchase price. Consumer financing was needed, and Gulf Coast Electronics—together with approximately 10 other sales agents within the state—used the open-end consumer financing provided by Whirlpool Financial National Bank to sell satellite dish antennas to poor customers in the rural regions of Alabama.

These sales agents generally had an office, not a store. They would use telephone calls to establish customer contacts, and then make home visits to get customer orders. Gulf Coast Electronics employed 10 persons who performed both functions. They were paid substantial commissions depending upon their number of completed sales, and they tended to be very aggressive. They were trained to demonstrate the advantages of the new antenna system, quote a total price of $1,124 that included delivery and installation, and then offer "nothing down" financing from Whirlpool Financial National Bank with minimal payments of $34 per month.

The primary issue at trial was the verbal description of the terms of that "nothing down" financing agreement given to the potential customers within their homes by sales agents working for Gulf Coast Electronics. The plaintiffs claimed that those sales agents had promised that payments of $34 per month for 36 months would totally pay for the antenna, delivery, and installation. In reality that would occur only if no interest were charged. According to the sales contract that was signed prior to installation, interest at the rate of 22 percent per year was to be added to the unpaid balance at the end of each month, which meant that total repayment—given that no late charges or other penalties were added to the total—would take five years.

Underlying the primary legal issue of whether the terms of the sales contract had been accurately revealed was a secondary concern over the equitable nature of the full sales transaction. The total sales price, with tax and installation, for the 19-inch RCA satellite dish antenna, termed a DSS system, sold by Gulf Coast Electronics was $1,124.24. Apparently the same system, prior to the sales tax and without the system installation, could have been purchased at a major electronics retailer such as Radio Shack or Circuit City for about $400. Thomas Methvin, attorney for the plaintiffs, questioned David Carroll, a witness for the plaintiffs, early in the trial:

Q: Today, how much can you go to a store and buy a DSS satellite dish for?

A: $199, and in some places.

Q: Back in 1995 when these victims bought theirs, how much did the same DSS satellite dishes by themselves cost in the store, not the package [tax and installation], but just the DSS [digital satellite system]?

A: In '95, to the best of my recollection, as far as I remember, they were $199. I know. I don't know what date. But at one time you could buy them for close to $400. So no more than $400. (Trial transcript, p. 48, line 17 to p. 49, line 1)

The $1,124 charged by Gulf Coast Electronics also included sales tax and installation. The sales tax would have been $32 (8 percent of $400), and installation was described as very simple. The complete DSS system came with a stand, the antenna, a length of coaxial cable, and a control box. It was necessary only to position the stand close to the house, set the antenna on the stand, drill a hole through the wall of the home, connect the antenna to the control box, and then the box to the television set. Witnesses testified that this installation took no more than 30 minutes.

Mr. Carroll, the witness who testified to the much lower cost of the DSS system when purchased at a retail store rather than through a sales agent, had been in charge of training for Centevision. Centevision was a sales agent similar to Gulf Coast Electronics; it also sold TV antennas and financed them through Whirlpool Financial National Bank. Mr. Carroll testified that he had trained between 10 and 20 new salespeople each week for Centevision, during a period of peak demand, and then the following exchange took place between Mr. Carroll and Mr. Methvin, attorney for the plaintiffs:

Q: And between the several, I believe you said two hundred or so salespeople that you trained yourself, was there a target market when you were selling these satellite dishes and home theater packages?

A: Yes, sir. We were trained to basically target the blacks, you know, any type of people living in trailers. People like that.

   Tripp Haston [for the defendants]: Judge, could we have an objection for relevancy. This man worked for a company named Centevision and not Gulf Coast Electronics. He didn't train anyone from Gulf Coast Electronics, who was the merchant in this case.

   Mr. Methvin [for the plaintiffs]: Judge, we think it's evidence to show not only was Gulf Coast Electronics one dealer that was doing it, but it came from the very top, that Whirlpool had lots of bad dealers. And we're going to have testimony from other witnesses that dealt with other dealers. And so that's why it's relevant. (Trial transcript, p. 28, line 21 to p. 30, line 19)

Two of the plaintiffs then testified that they had been told that payments of $34 per month would pay off the entire debt in three years. The first plaintiff, Mrs. Barbara Carlisle, explained that she had not only gotten an antenna for herself, but also arranged for her parents, Mr. and Mrs. Merriweather, the second plaintiffs, to have one installed at their home. After paying on the debt for two years she grew concerned that the balance on her monthly statements was not going down as rapidly as she had expected and, after talking with others at her church, found that she had been misled:

Q: Mrs. Carlisle, how did it make you feel when you found out you had been flim-flammed by these people?

A: It made me angry. It made me worry. I mean upset, very hurt. I got my parents involved in it, and I knew they were hurting from it. I've had headaches, sleepless nights, worrying, because I knew they were worried. And we're not rich people. We work hard for the little that we have. And we just don't deserve to be treated like that. And I think they should be punished for what they did.

Q: Mrs. Carlisle, as you sit here today, are you certain that February, 1995, when you were on the phone with those individuals from Gulf Coast, that you were told your payments would be $34.00 a month for three years and it would be paid for?

A: I'm positive.

Q: And when you called back for your parents, are you certain that you were told that their payments would be $34.00 a month for three years?

A: Yes. (Trial transcript, p. 127, line 21 to p. 128, line 12)

Mrs. Merriweather, the second plaintiff and Mrs. Carlisle's mother, also testified that she felt that she had been cheated by the company:

Q: When they told you that these people came in your house, and you trusted them because you couldn't read the papers yourselves, your husband couldn't read the papers, that you trusted to be telling you the truth. And when that lawyer told you they lied to you, were you upset?

A: I was sick, and I couldn't sleep. [Mrs. Merriweather continued with a graphic description of her various illnesses.]

Q: You think it was right for those people—ma'am, do you know how much the satellite costs today? Did you know you can buy a satellite for less then $300 today?

A: No. I didn't know it.

Q: When those people sold you that satellite—well let me ask you this way, how do you feel paying over a thousand and something dollars for a satellite you can buy for $300.00?

A: Huh, I don't feel right.

Q: You feel mad about that?

A: Sure is.

Q: You ever talk to your husband about this?

A: Yeah, I talk to him. He was just walking saying, "I'm tired of these folks doing us like this." (Trial transcript p. 184, line 13 to p. 185, line 20)

The final witness was a senior executive in the Whirlpool National Financial Bank, Brian Chambliss. The following exchange took place between Mr. Methvin, attorney for the plaintiffs, and Mr. Chambliss:

Q: Let me just ask a question that's very simple. If what the jury has heard from this witness stand from Mr. David Carroll and several of these witnesses, from Mrs. Carlisle and the Merriweathers, if what they heard is the truth, Whirlpool is a pretty sorry company, aren't they?

Mr. Haston (attorney for the defendants): Judge, I'd object to that question as argumentative.

Mr. Methvin (attorney for the plaintiffs): Well, let me just strike and ask it this way. [Mr. Methvin then continued the examination.]

Q: Will you stand behind what Whirlpool is selling, back them up one hundred percent? You're proud to be a part of this company?

A: Yes, I am.

Q: You're proud of what they did?

A: I'm proud to be a part of that company.

Q: Are you proud of what they did in this case?

A: I don't think we've done anything wrong.

Q: Nothing wrong. So if somebody goes into people's homes, sometimes unsophisticated people, armed with your documents, get them signed up, and they make payments to y'all and you find out they've been lied to, you say there's nothing wrong with that?

A: At this point I don't think we've done anything wrong. I think that there probably could have been a misunderstanding.

Q: Misunderstanding?

A: In what was presented to them.

Q: How about those roughly two hundred people that Mr. Carroll talked to? You reckon all two hundred of them had a misunderstanding?

Mr. Haston [attorney for the defendants]: Objection to the question as argumentative, Judge.

Class Assignment

Clearly Mr. Chanbliss, the executive from Whirlpool Financial National Bank, believes that his company has done nothing wrong. Another executive at Whirlpool, Christopher Wyse, reiterated that position in the following e-mail received by the case writer:

> As we have recently reached a confidential, out-of-court, settlement in this litigation, we will not be able to speak to your class on January 19. While we were looking forward to providing our views on these matters, the unreasonable risk associated with litigating in front of improperly impassioned juries and the potential cost in time and money in litigating such meritless claims made settlement an option the Bank had to consider. I'm sure you understand our position. (E-mail message from Whirlpool, dated December 7, 1999)

Do you agree that the case is a matter of "misunderstanding" and that the claims are "meritless"? Assume that the facts are reasonably as stated in the case; they were not disputed by the attorneys for the company at the trial except one stated that a competitive price for the DSS system at the time of the original transactions was $499 rather than $400. One of the concepts of this course is that, if you disagree with someone about the social and moral implications of their actions, you have to be able to logically convince them by arguing from some basic principles as to what is best for society. You can't just say, "This is my opinion." You have to be able to say, "This is my opinion, and these are the reasons why I think that it is right. If you disagree, tell me the reasons why you think it is wrong." This chapter's text suggested that you use the following method of analysis to fully explain your decisions:

1. What groups were benefited from the "antenna sales and financing" program?
2. What groups were harmed from the "antenna sales and financing" program?
3. What groups were able to fully exercise all of their rights with the use of that program?
4. What groups were denied some of their rights by the use of that program?

5. How would you express the moral problem so that each of the individuals and groups will believe that you fully recognize and completely understand their particular situation?

6. What are the economic benefits? The rule is that you should always take the action that will generate the greatest profits for the company because this will also generate the greatest benefits for the society, provided it can be shown that all markets are fully competitive, all customers are fully informed, and all external and internal costs are fully included.

7. What are the legal requirements? The rule here is that you should always take the action that most fully complies with the law because the law in a democratic society represents the combined moral standards of all of the people within that society, provided it can be shown that the goals, norms, beliefs, and values of all of the various individuals, groups, and organizations have been equitably considered in the formulation process.

8. What are the ethical duties? The rule here is that you should always take the action (1) that you would be proud to see widely reported in national newspapers, (2) that you believe will build a sense of community among everyone associated with the action, (3) that you expect will generate the greatest net social good, (4) that you would be willing to see others take in similar situations in which you might be the victim, (5) that you believe does not harm the "least among us," and (6) that you think does not interfere with the right of everyone to develop their skills to the fullest.

9. What is your recommendation, and how would you explain your recommendation to the other individuals, groups, and organizations that are going to be affected by that decision or action if it is adopted?

Chapter 2

Moral Analysis and Economic Outcomes

We are concerned in this book with ethical dilemmas: decisions and actions faced by managers in which the financial performance (measured by revenues, costs, and profits) and the social performance (stated in terms of obligations to individuals and groups) of the organization are in conflict. These are the moral problems in which some individuals and groups to whom the organization has some form of obligation—employees, customers, suppliers, distributors, creditors, stockholders, local residents, national citizens, and global inhabitants—are going to be hurt or harmed in some way outside their own control while others are going to be benefited and helped. These are also the moral problems in which some of those individuals or groups are going to see their rights ignored or even diminished while others will see their rights acknowledged and even expanded. The question is how to decide: how to find a balance between economic performance and social performance when faced by an ethical dilemma, and how to decide what is "right" and "just" and "fair" as the solution to the underlying moral problem.

In the previous chapter it was suggested that you first recognize the moral impacts—the mixture of benefits and harms, the contrast between rights and wrongs—and compare those impacts with the moral standards of the various individuals and groups who will be affected by the managerial decision or action. People's moral standards are bound to differ due to differences in their religious and cultural traditions and their economic and social situations. Everyone will not agree with your intuitive viewpoint. To get widespread understanding, you will have to address their moral concerns. It was suggested that you do this by first clearly stating the moral problem in a way that recognizes the concerns of all and then examining those concerns through the analytical methods of economic outcomes, legal requirements, and ethical duties. The intent is to reach a decision, or strike a balance, that can be understood and—hopefully—accepted by all. The process of reaching this decision, or striking this balance, is shown in Figure 2.1.

"Economic outcomes" in moral analysis do not refer just to the net balance of revenues over costs for the company that has proposed a given decision or action. Economic outcomes in economic theory refer to the net balance of benefits over harms for the full society as a result of that decision or action. This, as was described very briefly in the prior chapter, is the concept known as Pareto Optimality. It forms the moral basis of economic theory.

31

FIGURE 2.1   **Analytical Process for the Resolution of Moral Problems**

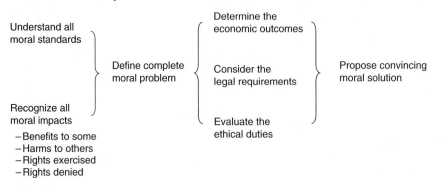

The Moral Basis of Economic Theory

For many persons, the concept of a moral basis for economic theory is a contradiction in terms. They learned economic theory as a logical and mathematical approach to markets, prices, and production, devoid of moral substance. As a result of this education, most noneconomists, and perhaps a few economists as well, appear to focus almost entirely on profit maximization. They view the theory of the firm as descriptive, designed to rationalize the behavior of business managers, and believe that such single-minded pursuit of profit automatically excludes any consideration of environmental health, worker safety, consumer interests, or other side issues.

Overconcentration on profits doubtless has resulted in these and other problems within our society, but that is neither a consequence nor a corollary of economic theory. Economic theory, in its more complete form, addresses these issues and includes ethical as well as economic precepts. Economic theory in its complete form is more a normative theory of society than a descriptive theory of the firm. Profit maximization is a part of the theory but only a part, certainly not the central focus, though it must be admitted, and this adds to the lack of understanding, that techniques for profit maximization occupy a central portion of the curriculum at most schools of business administration.

The central focus of the larger theory of society is the efficient utilization of resources to satisfy consumer wants and needs. At economic equilibrium—and an essential element in reaching equilibrium throughout the entire economic system is the effort by business managers to balance marginal increases in revenues against marginal increases in costs, which automatically results in maximum profits for the firm within market and resource constraints—it is theoretically possible to achieve Pareto Optimality.

Pareto Optimality refers to a condition in which the scarce resources of society are being used so efficiently by the producing firms, and the goods and services are being distributed so effectively by the competitive markets, that it would be impossible to make any single person better off without harming some other person. Remember this phrase: "It would be impossible to make any single person better off without making some other person worse off." This is the ethical substance of economic theory encapsulated in Pareto Optimality: Produce the maximum economic benefits for society, recognizing the full personal and social costs of that production, and then broaden the receipt of those benefits if necessary by political, not economic, actions.

Pareto Optimality provides the ethical content of economic theory. Without this concept of maximum social benefit at minimal social cost, the theory deteriorates into a simple prescription for individual gain and corporate profit. With this concept, however, the theory becomes a means of achieving a social goal: maximum benefits of most wanted goods and services produced at minimum costs of least wanted resources.

The theory requires that every business manager attempt to optimize profits. Consequently, the decision rule that an economist would propose for finding the proper balance between the economic and social performance of a business firm would be to always be truthful (don't mislead), honorable (observe contracts), and competitive (set prices and costs at marginal levels), and always decide for the greater financial return. The question of this chapter is: Can we use this decision rule when faced with an ethical dilemma?

For many economists, the concept of Pareto Optimality excludes any need to consider ethical dilemmas in management. This view is very direct and can be summarized very simply. "Ethics are not relevant in business, beyond the normal standards not to lie, cheat, or steal. All that is necessary is to maintain price-competitive markets and recognize the full costs of production in those prices, and then the market system will ensure that scarce resources are used to optimally satisfy consumer needs. A firm that is optimally satisfying consumer needs, to the limit of the available resources, is operating most efficiently and most profitably. Consequently, business managers should act to maximize profits, while following legal requirements of noncollusion and equal opportunity and adhering to personal standards of truthfulness and honesty. Profit maximization, according to economic theory, leads automatically from the satisfaction of individual consumer wants to the generation of maximum social benefits. Profit maximization, again according to management, is the only moral standard needed for management."

Is this summary an overstatement of the microeconomic view of ethics and management? Probably not. The belief that profit maximization leads inexorably to the well-being of society is a central tenet of economic theory and has been stated very succinctly and very clearly by both James McKie of the Brookings Institute and Milton Friedman of the University of Chicago:

> The primary goal and motivating force for business organizations is profit. The firm attempts to make as large a profit as it can, thereby maintaining its efficiency and taking advantage of available opportunities to innovate and contribute to growth. Profits are kept to reasonable or appropriate levels by market competition, which leads the firm pursuing its own self-interest to an end that is not part of its conscious intention: enhancement of the public welfare. (James McKie, "Changing Views," in *Social Responsibility and the Business Predicament,* Washington: Brookings Institute, 1974, p. 19)
>
> The view has been gaining widespread acceptance that corporate officials . . . have a "social responsibility" that goes beyond serving the interest of their stockholders or their members. This view shows a fundamental misconception of the character and nature of a free economy. In such an economy, there is one and only one social responsibility of business—to use its resources and engage in activities designed to increase its profits, so long

as it stays within the rules of the game, which is to say, engages in open and free competition, without deception or fraud. . . . Few trends could so thoroughly undermine the very foundations of our free society as the acceptance by corporate officials of a social responsibility other than to make as much money for their stockholders as possible. (Milton Friedman, *Capitalism and Freedom,* Chicago: University of Chicago Press, 1962, p. 133)

The statement by Milton Friedman was expanded in an article, "The Social Responsibility of Business Is to Increase Its Profits," that was published in the *New York Times Magazine* a number of years ago (September 13, 1970, p. 32f.). This article is often assigned for students at business schools in classes on business ethics or business and society. It is a frustrating article to read and then to discuss in class because it never makes clear the theoretical basis of Pareto Optimality; Professor Friedman assumed that readers would recognize and understand that basis of his contention.

The Moral Objections to Economic Theory

What is your opinion? Can we accept the microeconomic premise that maximum profits for a firm lead directly to maximum benefits for society? The response of people trained in other disciplines is often much more pragmatic than theoretical, and it too can be summarized very simply. "Yes, we know the theory, but look at where the blind pursuit of profit has led us: foreign bribes, environmental problems, unsafe products, closed plants, and injured workers. We need something more than profit to measure our obligations to society." This view, I think, has been most sensibly expressed by Manuel Velasquez of the University of Santa Clara:

> Some have argued that in perfectly competitive free markets the pursuit of profit will by itself ensure that the members of society are served in the most socially beneficial ways. For, in order to be profitable, each firm has to produce only what the members of society want and has to do this by the most efficient means available. The members of society will benefit most, then, if managers do not impose their own values on a business but instead devote themselves to the singleminded pursuit of profit, and thereby devote themselves to producing efficiently what the members of society themselves value.
>
> Arguments of this sort conceal a number of assumptions. . . . First, most industrial markets are not "perfectly competitive" as the argument assumes, and to the extent that firms do not have to compete they can maximize profits in spite of inefficient production. Second, the argument assumes that any steps taken to increase profits will necessarily be socially beneficial, when in fact several ways of increasing profits actually injure society: allowing harmful pollution to go uncontrolled, deceptive advertising, concealing product hazards, fraud, bribery, tax evasion, price-fixing, and so on. Third, the argument assumes that by producing whatever the buying public wants (or values) firms are producing what all the members of society want, when in fact the wants of large segments of society (the poor and the disadvantaged) are not necessarily met because they cannot participate fully in the marketplace. (Manuel Velasquez, *Business Ethics: Concepts and Cases,* New York: Prentice Hall, 1982, pp. 17–18)

This pragmatic response, which can obviously be supported by many examples within our society, is not compelling to most economists. They believe that the issues cited—the lack of competitive markets, the presence of injurious practices, and the exclusion of some segments of society—are part of economic theory and would be prevented by its strict application. How would they be prevented? Here, it is necessary to provide an explanation of the extensive structure of economic theory and of the logical interrelationships that exist among the components in that structure: the individual consumers, product markets, producing firms, factor markets, factor owners, and public institutions. The "factors" in that listing above are the scarce resources of labor, capital, and material used in the production of goods and services.

Doubtless an explanation of this structure and these interrelationships will be dull for those with a good grasp of economic theory, and trying for all others, but this explanation is necessary to deal with the ethical problems in the theory on a meaningful basis. If you truly are bored with economic theory, and willing to accept the rationality of the structure, skip ahead a few pages and dive directly into the section entitled, "The Moral Claims of Economic Theory."

The Logical Structure of Economic Theory

Economic theory is complex. Perhaps, to make this brief explanation more comprehensible, we should start with an overall summary. The focus of the theory, as stated previously, is the efficient utilization of scarce resources to maximize the production of wanted goods and services. The mechanism of the theory is the market structure: Each firm is located between a "factor" market for the input factors of production (labor, material, and capital) and a "product" market for the output of goods and services. The demand for each good or service is aggregated from the preference functions of individual consumers, who act to maximize their satisfactions from a limited mix of products. The supply of each good or service is aggregated from the production schedules of individual firms, which act to balance their marginal revenues and marginal costs at a limited level of capacity.

The production of goods and services creates derived demands for the input factors of labor, material, and capital. These factors are substitutable—they can be interchanged—so the derived demands vary with the costs. These costs, of course, reflect the constrained supplies in the different factor markets. A firm attempting to minimize costs and maximize revenues will therefore use the most available resources to produce the most needed products, generating not only the greatest profits for itself but the greatest benefits for society. The components of the theory and the relationships among these components, which together produce corporate profits and social benefits, may be more understandable in graphic form, as shown in Figure 2.2.

Now it is necessary to work through each of the six sections in Figure 2.2 in greater detail so that the relationships between revenues, costs, and social benefits will be clear. Those relationships, and their consequent outcomes, constitute the ethical content of economic theory.

Individual Consumers

Each consumer has a slightly different set of preferences for the various goods and services that are available, and these preferences can be expressed as "utilities," or quantitative measures of the usefulness of a given product or service to a specific customer. The "marginal utility," or extra usefulness, of one additional unit of that product

FIGURE 2.2 **Graphic Summary of Microeconomic Theory**

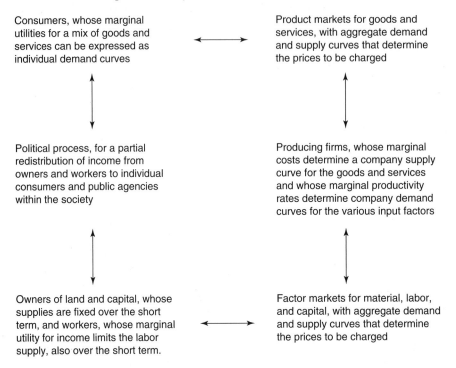

or service to that customer tends to decline, for eventually the person will have a surfeit of the good. The price that the person is willing to pay for the good also declines along with the marginal utility or degree of surfeit. Price relative to the number of units that will be purchased by a given person at a given time forms the individual demand curve, as shown in Figure 2.3.

Price can also be used to compare the relative usefulness of different goods and services to an individual. It can be expected that a person selecting a mix of products will choose an assortment of goods and services such that marginal utility per monetary unit would be equal for all the items at a given level of spending for this individual. Each good would be demanded up to the point where the marginal utility per dollar would be exactly the same as the marginal utility per dollar for any other good. If a customer had a higher marginal utility relative to price for any particular good, he or she would doubtless substitute more of that good for some of the others to achieve a better balance among his or her preferences. The final balance or mix, where the marginal utilities per monetary unit are equal for all products and services, can be termed the point of equilibrium for that customer.

The concept of consumer equilibrium is an important element in the structure of the economic condition termed Pareto Optimality. A customer with balanced marginal utilities per monetary unit for all available goods and services cannot be made better off at his or her level of spending, according to his or her standards of preference. The customer may buy hamburgers, french fries, and beer, and we may think that he or she

FIGURE 2.3 **Personal Demand Curve**

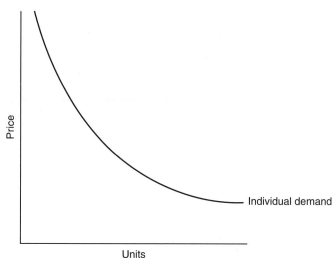

should be buying fish, fresh vegetables, and fruit, but that person is satisfying his or her standards, not our own, and they are being satisfied up to the limits of his or her ceiling on expenditures. Consequently, that person cannot be made better off without an increase in disposable income. Let us now look at the determination of the level of disposable income in microeconomic theory. This is more complex than the determination of the mix of desired purchases, but the logical structure can be followed through the product markets, the producing firms, the factor markets, the private owners of those factors, and the public processes for redistribution of factor income.

Product Markets

A product market consists of all the individual customers for a given good or service, together with all the producing firms that supply that good or service. The demand curves of all those customers can be aggregated to form a market demand curve. This market demand curve reflects the total demand for a good or service, relative to price. If price is the vertical axis and demand the horizontal axis, the market demand curve will generally slope downward and toward the right, indicating increased potential purchases at the lower price levels.

Crossing this market demand curve is a market supply curve that portrays the total available supply, again relative to price. The market supply curve generally slopes upward and toward the right, for the higher the price, the more units in total most companies can be expected to produce, until they reach a short-term limit of capacity. The market price, of course, is set at the intersection of the curves representing aggregate demand and aggregate supply, as shown in Figure 2.4.

Producing Firms

The aggregate supply curve, the other half of each product market relationship, is formed by adding together the individual supply curves of all the producing firms. These

FIGURE 2.4 **Market Demand and Supply Curve**

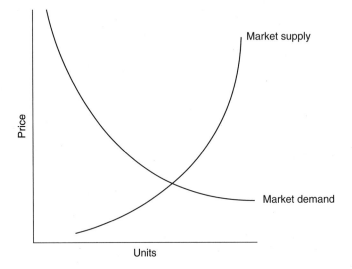

individual supply curves are generated by the cost structures of those firms at different levels of production, while the actual level of production for each firm is determined by a comparison of marginal revenues and marginal costs.

The marginal revenue of a producing firm is the extra revenue that the firm would receive by selling one additional unit of the good or service. To sell that additional unit in a fully price-competitive market, it is necessary to move down the aggregate demand curve to a slightly lower price level. To sell that additional unit in a non-price-competitive market, it is necessary to spend greater amounts on advertising and promotion to differentiate the product from those manufactured by other firms. Under either alternative, the marginal revenue from selling the last unit will be less than the average revenue from selling all other units. Marginal revenues inevitably decrease with volume.

The marginal cost of the producing firm is the obverse of the marginal revenue. Marginal cost is the extra expense that the firm would incur by producing one additional unit of the product or service. Marginal costs initially decline with volume due to economies of scale and learning curve effects, but they eventually rise due to diminishing returns as the physical capacity of the plant is approached. The rising portion of the marginal cost curve forms the supply curve of the firm; it represents the number of units that the firm should produce and supply to the market at each price level, as shown in Figure 2.5.

The producing firm achieves equilibrium when marginal costs are equal to marginal revenues. At the intersection of the marginal cost and marginal revenue curves, the profits of the firm are maximized. The firm can increase profits only by improving its technology; this would change the marginal costs and consequently the supply curve. However, over the long term, all firms would adopt the new technology and achieve the same cost structure. Production equilibrium would be reestablished at the new intersections of the marginal cost and marginal revenue curves for all firms within the industry.

FIGURE 2.5 **Marginal Cost Curve**

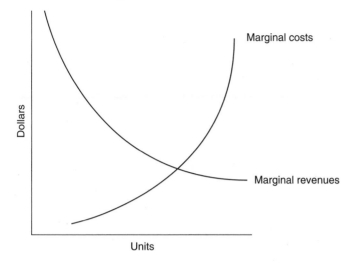

All the costs of production have to be included in computing the marginal cost curve for a firm. This is the second of the ethical constructs in microeconomic theory, along with the individual selection of goods and services according to private preference standards, or utilities. The internal personal costs (e.g., hazardous working conditions) and the external social costs (e.g., harmful environmental discharges) have to be computed, so that customers pay the full costs of production. The technology, of course, can be changed to improve working conditions and reduce environmental discharges, and this should be done to bring marginal costs down to marginal revenues at a new, nonhazardous and nonpolluting equilibrium, but it is an essential element in economic theory that product-market prices reflect the full costs of production.

Factor Markets

The technology of the producing firm determines the maximum output of goods and services that can be achieved for a given mix of input factors. The input factors of production are land (an apparently obsolete term that instead refers to all of the basic raw materials), labor, and capital. Charges for the input factors are rents for the land and other basic resources, wages for the labor, and interest for the capital. These charges are interdependent because the factors are interrelated; that is, one factor may be substituted for others in the production function.

The relationships among these input factors, and the amount of one that would have to be used to substitute for another, are determined by the technology of the production function and by the marginal productivity of each factor for a given technology. The marginal productivity of a factor of production is the additional output generated by adding one more unit of that factor while keeping all others constant. For example, it would be possible to add one additional worker to a production line without changing the capital investments in the line or the material components of the product. There should then be an increase in the physical output of that production line, and that increase, measured in units or portions of units, would be the marginal productivity of that worker. To maximize profits, a company should increase the use of each factor of production until the value of its marginal product (the increase in unit output, or productivity, times the price of those units) equals the cost of the input factor.

Factor Owners

The aggregate demand for each factor of production is equal to the proportion of that factor used in the production function of each firm times the output of those functions supplied to meet the product market demand. The demand for each factor of production is therefore derived from the primary markets for goods and services.

The aggregate supply of each factor of production, however, is limited. Over the long term, stocks of the basic materials may be expanded by bringing into production marginal agricultural lands, oil fields, and ore mines, while the reserves of investment capital may be increased by raising the rate of capital formation. Over the short term, however, the supply amounts are fixed. Aggregate supplies of labor are also limited, though for a different cause: Each worker has a marginal utility for income that decreases and becomes negative as his or her desire for greater leisure exceeds his or her preference for further work. This negative utility function creates a backward-sloping supply curve for labor and sharply limits the amounts available at the higher wage rates, as shown in Figure 2.6.

The price system in the different factor markets therefore ensures that the limited factors of production will be used in the most economically effective manner to produce the goods and services to be sold in the product markets, and that the rents, wages, and interest paid for these factors will reflect both the productivity of the factor and the derived demand of the goods.

FIGURE 2.6   Factor Supply Curves

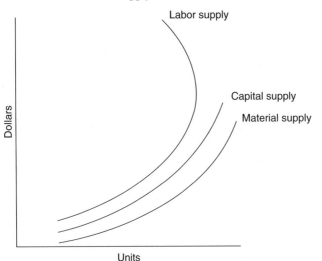

Political Processes

The owners of the factors of production, within a capitalistic society, are also the customers for the products and services generated by the production functions at the various firms. The owners receive the rents, the wages, and the interest payments for the use of the resources they want to sell and then purchase the goods and services they want to buy, following their personal preferences or utilities.

A political process for the redistribution of the rents, wages, and interest payments works through both tax provisions and welfare allocations, so that all individuals and groups within a given society have a minimal ability to participate in the product markets for the various goods and services to the extent determined by the members of that society. This political process is the third ethical construct in microeconomic theory. It ensures that the distribution of the revenues for material, capital, and labor will be equitable, following a democratically determined definition of equity.

The Moral Claims of Economic Theory

Now that there is a common understanding of the basic structure of economic theory, or the logical system of relationships among individual customers, product markets, producing firms, factor markets, resource owners, and political processes, it is possible to look at the claims of that theory relative to the social welfare. There are five explicit assertions:

- *Effective use of resources.* The price mechanisms of the factor markets allocate the scarce resources of society to their most effective uses. The marginal productivity of each factor, together with the cost (reflecting supply versus demand), determines the relative usage of the factors by the producing firms. At factor equilibrium, it would be impossible to expand total production without an increase in resource supply.

- *Efficient conversion of resources into products.* The production functions of the producing firms convert the limited input factors into the wanted output goods and services by the most effective methods (process technologies) and at the most efficient rates (output amounts). A firm's technology and capacity are long-term decisions, while the operating rate is a short-term choice, but all are based upon the balance between marginal revenues and marginal costs. Internal personal harms and external social damages are included in the marginal costs. At process equilibrium, it would be impossible to convert resources into products more efficiently and with less personal harm or social damage without an advance in technology.

- *Effective distribution of products.* The price mechanisms of the product markets distribute the wanted goods and services of society to their most effective uses. The marginal utilities of each customer, together with the prices (again reflecting supply versus demand) for the various products, determine the relative consumption of the goods and services. At market equilibrium, it would be impossible to improve consumer satisfaction without an increase in personal income.

- *Political adjustment of inequalities.* The political processes of the national society determine the personal income of each consumer through democratic means. The income may be distributed according to ownership of the factors of production or according to an individual's need, effort, contribution, or competence. Distribution of the overall benefits of the economic system is a political, not an economic, process.

*   *Managerial responsibility for profits.* Provided that the managers of the producing firms act to maximize profits, the customers for the goods and services act to maximize satisfactions, and the owners of the resources act to maximize revenues, the economic system will operate as efficiently as possible, producing the greatest output of wanted goods and services for the least input of scarce labor, capital, and material. If the revenues to the owners of the factors of production are equitably redistributed to the customers of the producing firms through a democratic decision process, it would be impossible to improve the life of any member of the system without harming the life of another member, because the system would have reached Pareto Optimality. Consequently, the social responsibility of the managers of the producing firms is to maximize profits and leave the redistribution of economic benefits to the political process.

Pragmatic Objections to Economic Theory

The usual objections to microeconomic theory are pragmatic in nature, based upon very obvious problems in our national society, and they generally include the three issues discussed by Professor Velasquez in the statement quoted earlier in this chapter.

*   *Exclusion of segments of society.* It is alleged that the minorities and the poor, because they lack ownership of any of the factors of production beyond their unskilled labor, receive inadequate income to participate in the product markets and consequently cannot maximize their own satisfactions in any meaningful way. The microeconomic response is quite obvious: "We grant you that this happens, but it is the fault of the political process and not of the economic system. You develop logically attractive political decision rules for the more equitable division of the benefits, and we will work to economically maximize the production of those benefits within market and resource constraints."

*   *Presence of injurious practices.* It is also alleged that managers of productive firms, because of an excessive concern with maximizing profits, have permitted or even encouraged some practices that are injurious to some members of society through workplace dangers or environmental pollution, or that are destructive to the market system through purchase bribes or employment discrimination. Here the response of most economists would be that these problems occur, but that they would not occur under the strict application of the theory. Let us look at five of these claimed moral problems and their presumed theoretical solutions.

    Purchase bribes. Personal payments to influence purchase decisions are evidently common overseas and not unknown within the United States. In an efficient market, however, bribes would be futile; they would raise the cost function by an amount equivalent to the payment so that nonbribing competitors would have an obvious price advantage. The microeconomic response is obvious: Insist that purchase decisions be open and subject to public comparison of the bids to ensure the selection of the lowest-priced proposal to supply needed goods and services. The lowest-priced proposal would necessarily come from a nonbribing competitor.

Process pollutants. Many industrial processes result in toxic residues and inert materials as by-products, which are either discharged as air or water pollutants or buried as liquid or solid wastes. The toxic by-products have an obvious social cost, both immediate and long-term. The microeconomic response has been clearly stated many times: Companies should recognize these nonfactor costs that are external to the productive process and include them in the pricing function. It might be expected, were these external costs accurately computed, that investments in proper disposal equipment would become clearly beneficial for the firm, or if they were fully included in the price, the product would become overly expensive for the customer to buy. Under either alternative, the amount of pollution would be substantially reduced.

Workplace hazards. It would appear that many of the mechanical hazards of industrial processing have been eliminated. Forty years of state and federal labor laws have removed most of the unprotected belts, open gearing, and nonshielded presses. Chemical risks still remain, however, and physiological and psychological problems will probably always be a part of mass manufacturing, due to the repetitive nature of the tasks and the time constraints of the process. The microeconomic response to workplace hazards is similar to that for process pollutants: The nonfactor costs of production should be recognized and included in the final price. Certainly, if the market is to operate efficiently to allocate resources within the society, customers have to pay the full costs of production, not partial costs subsidized by the physical or mental health of the workers.

Product dangers. The press has recently reported numerous instances of unsafe products, particularly in the automobile industry. Gas tanks poorly located, radial tires poorly fabricated, and automatic transmissions poorly designed have all been mentioned, together with such nonautomotive products as hair dryers (containing asbestos), teddy bears (containing sharp objects), and packaged foods (containing nonnutrients). I think it is safe to assume that the economic response would be that a product offered for sale within a competitive market should perform the function for which it was designed, and that many of the reported failures and hazards come from decisions to differentiate products in slight or artificial ways to avoid the discipline of price competition. Whatever the cause of product failures and hazards, the costs of improper design are now being charged back against the manufacturing firms through liability suits and jury awards. It can be assumed that product safety will soon be improved as a result of objective economic analysis.

Minority employment. Racial or sexual discrimination in employment, in an efficient labor market, would be self-defeating; a workforce limited to young or middle-aged white males would raise the cost of labor in the productive function and provide the nondiscriminating employer with a cost advantage. It is assumed in economic analysis that all groups are equal in performance capabilities. Training might be needed to justify that assumption, but the microeconomic response would be that training to correct social injustices should be provided as a public investment, determined by the political processes. Cost–benefit analysis would—in the view of most economists—assuredly show an economic return on that investment, as well as a social gain.

- *Absence of competitive markets.* Lastly, it is often claimed that the product markets for consumer goods and services are not price competitive because of oligopolistic (dominance by a limited number of large companies) practices among the producing firms serving those markets. Companies have become much larger recently, doubtless due to economies of scale and scope in production and distribution, while products have become more "differentiated," marked by slight distinctions in performance and design but supported by heavy promotion. The dominance of large firms in each market, and the inability of customers to judge the relative worth of products in those markets, is said to lead toward administered rather than competitive prices. "Administered pricing," where the price level is set by the company to provide a set return above costs without reference to either supply or demand, of course destroys the efficiency of the market. The economic response, however, is very simple: "Oh, we grant you that market structures are not truly competitive, and that market processes are not actually efficient under current conditions. However, no one is advocating limited competition or inadequate information. Public policy changes to restrict competitor size and to ensure consumer information are needed to reestablish the discipline of the market."

Theoretical Objections to Economic Theory

Economic theory is awesomely complete. There are few operating decisions in business to which it could not be applied—from hiring workers, purchasing supplies, and borrowing money to selecting technologies, establishing capacities, and setting prices. Likewise, there are few ethical problems to which microeconomic theory is not applicable, whether purchase bribes, process pollutants, workplace hazards, product dangers, or racial discrimination. It is very difficult to say, "Here is a managerial decision or action with definite ethical implications that is not included in the theory."

Economic theory is also enviably unified. All the managerial decisions and actions work together, through a system of explicit relationships, to create a socially desirable goal: maximum output of the wanted goods and services at a minimum input of the scarce material, capital, and labor. It is very difficult to say, "Here is a managerial decision or action following microeconomic theory that does not lead to a socially beneficial outcome."

Where does this discussion lead us? Are we forced to accept economic theory as an ethical system of belief for business management because of the complete and unified nature of the paradigm? Should we always act to maximize profits, as long as we are truthful, honest, and competitive, and use the concept of Pareto Optimality as the means of resolving our moral concerns? Or is there a theoretical problem with that paradigm?

Most noneconomists are intuitively distressed by the proposal that business managers have no moral responsibilities to other members of society, outside of fiduciary duties to a small circle of corporate owners. Most noneconomists are equally distressed by the proposal that business managers are governed by no moral requirements of behavior beyond adhering to personal standards of honesty and truthfulness, observing legal statutes for contracts and against collusion, and computing accurate costs for personal harms and social dangers. Why is this distressing, and what are the arguments against the microeconomic model that can be expressed on a theoretical rather than a pragmatic or intuitive basis? There are two major arguments: One pertains to the assumptions about human nature and the second centers on the beliefs about human worth that are part of economic theory.

Assumptions about the Nature of Human Beings

The economic model is utilitarian; that is, it is a philosophical system of belief that focuses on outcomes rather than duties, with the understanding that larger outcomes are invariably better than lesser ones. Utilitarianism has often been roughly translated as "the greatest good for the greatest number." The economic model follows this doctrine. It takes the position that the ultimate end is the greatest general good, and it defines that good as the maximum benefits of consumer products and services at the minimum costs of labor, capital, and material. The problem, as with all utilitarian theories, is that the distribution of the benefits and the imposition of the costs may be unjust. Consequently, it is necessary to add a political process to the economic paradigm to ensure justice in the distribution of benefits and the imposition of costs.

But "justice" is defined in the theory as a democratically determined pattern of distribution and imposition. This pattern does not follow a rule such as to each person equally, or to each according to his or her need, to his or her effort, to his or her contribution, to his or her competence, or even to his or her ownership of the factors of production. Instead, the pattern varies with the collective opinions of the members of society. This requires all members of society to be generously concerned with the charitable distribution of social benefits and the considerate imposition of social costs at the same time as they are selfishly concerned with the personal maximization of material goods and services in the product markets and of financial wages, rents, and interest payments in the factor markets.

I think that we can safely say that human nature exhibits both selfish and generous traits. We can doubtless go further and accept that human beings can perform selfish and then generous acts alternately. But it would seem an extreme assumption to believe that people can concurrently be generously attentive to others in all political decisions and selfishly attentive to themselves in all economic activities, and never confuse the two roles. The microeconomic model would appear to be based upon an exceedingly complex and unlikely view of the nature of human beings.

Assumptions about the Value of Human Beings

The microeconomic model is impersonal, for it requires that everyone be treated as a means to an end and not as an end in and of himself or herself. Customers for goods and services are people who maximize material satisfactions as a means of determining product demand curves. Owners of land, capital, and labor are people who maximize financial revenues as a means of determining factor-supply curves. Company managers are people who maximize corporate profits as a means of balancing market demands and factor supplies. No one acts as an individual human being, pursuing personal goals that move beyond economic outcomes to personal desires for liberty, opportunity, dignity, and respect.

This denial of worth can be seen particularly clearly in the position of the manager of the firm, who must act solely as an agent for the financial interests of the stockholders. What does this do to managers' self-esteem and self-respect? How can they live worthwhile lives when always being treated as a means to other people's ends or, perhaps even worse, when always treating other people as means to their own ends? Even though the society as an economic system may have achieved Pareto Optimality with maximal benefits at minimal costs, does the individual develop any sense of dignity and pride? The microeconomic model would appear to be based upon an exceedingly low and narrow view of the worth of human beings.

Conclusion

Where does this discussion of the moral content of economic theory lead us? There would seem to be two major conclusions. If we look at economic theory as a structured pattern of relationships explaining the optimal uses of scarce material, capital, and labor to produce the optimal numbers of consumer goods and services, then it is a logically complete and intellectually satisfying view of the world. But if we look at economic theory as the sole means of reaching a decision when confronted with a moral problem—a problem in which some individuals and groups will be hurt or harmed, or have their rights ignored or abridged—then it seems incomplete because of the unlikely assumptions about human nature and the unsuited beliefs about human worth. Most people want something more out of life than just being automated participants in a consumption–production cycle.

We have to respect the theory—particularly with the provisions that all markets must be competitive and all costs must be included—but we have to add to it. We have to add the legal requirements and ethical duties that are further means of resolving moral problems in ways that will be understandable to all because they appeal to the nature and worth of all. The next two chapters will look specifically at the moral claims of those two doctrines—legal requirements and ethical duties—as a further means of determining what is "right" and "just" and "proper" in the decisions and actions of business management.

Case 2-1

World Bank and the Export of Pollution

The World Bank is a transnational organization that provides funding for economic development projects throughout the world. It was started in 1946 to help in the rebuilding of Europe following the Second World War, with 14 member nations led by the United States. By 1990 it had grown to 125 member nations, and the focus had shifted to assisting Third World countries in their efforts to escape from poverty. It grants loans to governmental agencies and public institutions to build the physical infrastructure needed for global modernization.

The World Bank is not small. It has $30 billion in basic equity capital, subscribed by the member nations, but it can also borrow much greater amounts from capital markets in New York, London, Frankfurt, Singapore, and Tokyo at reduced rates because all of their borrowings are guaranteed by the member nations. The bank then lends those funds at increased rates for development projects that appear to hold the promise of economic progress for the recipient country. About one-third of those loans are for hydroelectric dams, power plants, and transmission lines to generate electricity. Another third are for roads, railroads, bridges, port facilities, and pipelines to extend transportation. The last third are for rural irrigation systems to improve agriculture, urban water and sewer projects to improve health, and factory modernization programs to improve productivity.

The World Bank is headquartered in Washington, D.C. Voting power among the member nations is proportional to their capital subscriptions, and consequently the board of directors is dominated by Western countries. Many of the upper-level employees are American citizens. In 1991 the chief economist at the World Bank was Lawrence Summers, who had previously been a professor of economics at Harvard. In December of that year he sent the following memorandum to some colleagues and friends:

> Just between you and me, shouldn't the World Bank be encouraging more migration of the dirty industries to the LDCs [less developed countries]? I can think of three reasons:
>
> 1. The measurement of the costs of health-impairing pollution depends on the forgone earnings from increased morbidity and mortality. From this point of view a given amount of health-impairing pollution should be done in the country with the lowest cost, which will be the country with the lowest wages. I think the economic logic behind dumping a load of toxic waste in the lowest wage country is impeccable and we should face up to that.
>
> 2. The costs of pollution are likely to be non-linear as the initial increments of pollution probably have very low cost. I've always thought that under-populated countries in Africa are vastly under-polluted; their air quality is probably inefficiently low compared to Los Angeles or Mexico City. Only the lamentable facts that so much pollution is generated by non-tradable industries (transport, electrical generation) and that the unit transport costs of solid waste are so high that they prevent world-welfare-enhancing trade in air pollution [prevent this dumping].
>
> 3. The demand for a clean environment for aesthetic and health reasons is likely to have very high income-elasticity. The concern over an agent that causes a one-in-a-million change in the odds of prostate cancer is obviously going to be much higher in a country where people survive to get prostate cancer than in a country where under-5 mortality is 200 per thousand. Also, much of the concern over industrial atmospheric discharge is about visibility-impairing particulates. These discharges may have very little direct health impact. Clearly trade in goods that embody aesthetic pollution concerns could be welfare-enhancing. While production is mobile the consumption of pretty air is a non-tradable.
>
> The problem with the arguments against all of these proposals for more pollution in LDCs (intrinsic rights to certain goods, moral reasons, social concerns, lack of adequate markets, etc.) could be turned around and used more or less effectively against every Bank proposal for liberalization [of trade]. (Memo from Lawrence Summers, cited

in Hausman and McPherson, *Economic Analysis and Moral Philosophy,* Cambridge: Cambridge University Press, 1996, p. 9)

This memo to friends and colleagues was somehow obtained by *The Economist,* a British news magazine with a worldwide audience. Its publication, in the words of Hausman and McPherson, "caused an uproar" and as a result, in the words of an author to be quoted later, environmentalists "went ballistic." Apparently, many people were offended by the blatantness of the proposal to export pollution-causing processes to Third World nations, where they would do less harm in monetary terms. They would do less monetary harm, Summers argued, because people's lives were worth far less in those low-wage countries (human life was valued as the discounted sum of the annual earnings to be expected by each individual over time), and because amenities ("pretty air" and attractive views) were far less appreciated. Some of the subsequent letters to the editor, and to Professor Summers, were said to be vitriolic. There was, however, also substantial and forthright support from other economists:

> Economics is the science of competing preferences. Environmentalism goes beyond science when it elevates matters of preference to matters of morality. A proposal to pave a wilderness and put up a parking lot is an occasion for conflict between those who prefer wilderness and those who prefer parking. In the ensuing struggle, each side attempts to impose its preferences by manipulating the political and economic systems. Because one side must win and one side must lose, the battle is hard-fought and sometimes bitter. All of this is to be expected.
>
> But in the 25 years since the first Earth Day, a new and ugly element has emerged in the form of one side's conviction that its preferences are Right and the other side's are Wrong. The science of economics shuns such moral posturing; the religion of environmentalism embraces it.
>
> Economics forces us to confront a fundamental symmetry. The conflict arises because each side wants to allocate the same resource in a different way. Jack wants his woodland at the expense of Jill's parking space and Jill wants her parking space at the expense of Jack's woodland. That formulation is morally neutral and should serve as a warning against assigning exalted moral status to either Jack or Jill.
>
> The symmetries run deeper. Environmentalists claim that wilderness should take precedence over parking because a decision to pave is "irrevocable." Of course they are right, but they overlook the fact that a decision not to pave is equally irrevocable. Unless we pave today, my opportunity to park tomorrow is lost as irretrievably as tomorrow itself will be lost. The ability to park in a more distant future might be a quite inadequate substitute for that lost opportunity.
>
> A variation on the environmentalist theme is that we owe the wilderness not to ourselves but to future generations. But do we have any reason to think that future generations will prefer inheriting the wilderness to inheriting the profits from the parking lot? This is one of the first questions that would be raised in any honest scientific inquiry.
>
> Another variation is that the parking lot's developer is motivated by profits, not preferences. To this there are two replies. First, the developer's profits are generated by his customers' preferences; the ultimate conflict is not with the developer but with those who prefer to park. Second, the implication of the argument is that a preference for a profit is somehow morally inferior to a preference for a wilderness, which is just the sort of posturing that the argument was designed to avoid.
>
> It seems to me that the "irrevocability" argument, the "future generations" argument, and the "preferences not profits" argument all rely on false distinctions that wither before

honest scrutiny. Why, then, do some environmentalists repeat these arguments? Perhaps honest scrutiny is simply not a part of their agenda. In many cases, they begin with the postulate that they hold the moral high ground, and conclude that they are thereby licensed to disseminate intellectually dishonest propaganda as long as it serves the higher purpose of winning converts to the cause.

In the current political climate, it is frequently taken as an axiom that the U.S. government should concern itself with the welfare of Americans first; it is also frequently taken as an axiom that air pollution is not always and everywhere a bad thing. You might, then, have expected a general chorus of approval when the chief economist of the World Bank suggested that it might be a good thing to relocate high-pollution industries to Third World countries. To most economists, this is a self-evident opportunity to make not just Americans but everybody better off. People in wealthy countries can afford to sacrifice some income for the luxury of cleaner air; people in poorer countries are happy to breathe inferior air in exchange for the opportunity to improve their incomes. But when the bank economist's observation was leaked to the media, parts of the environmental community went ballistic. To them, pollution is a form of sin. They seek not to improve our welfare, but to save our souls. (Landsburg, *The Armchair Economist: Economics and Everyday Life,* New York: Free Press, 1993, pp. 224–27)

Class Assignment

What is your view? Should polluting industries that affect both human health and environmental quality be exported to poorer countries where people's lives and preferences are less valued? For that matter, should wilderness areas be paved with asphalt for parking lots as long as their operations will be profitable? Remember, you must be able to defend your position, whether yes or no. How would you argue either for or against Professor Summers, Professor Landsburg, or both?

Case 2-2

Green Giant and the Move to Mexico

The Green Giant Company is a food products firm that specializes in canned and frozen vegetables. Started as the Minnesota Valley Canning Company in 1903, it was one of the earliest to adopt a memorable advertising character, the Jolly Green Giant who, together with his friend Little Sprout, appeared first in magazines and then on radio and eventually television. The company's name was changed in 1950 to reflect the popularity of the advertising symbol and slogan.

Green Giant was also one of the first to adopt the new technology of freezing rather than canning vegetables, which helped greatly to preserve their taste and texture. Growth was steady during the 1950s and 60s, and the company expanded from southern Minnesota to central California where there was a much longer growing season. A large facility for freezing fresh vegetables was built at Salinas, California, about 120 miles south of San Francisco, in 1964.

The Green Giant Company was acquired, in a friendly takeover, by the Pillsbury Company of Minneapolis, Minnesota, in 1978. Pillsbury produced flour, baking products, and packaged cake/cookie/brownie mixes. The food industry segments of the combined firms did not overlap, so the acquisition gave Pillsbury a much broader product line with customer appeal and a much larger output with economies of scale and scope.

In 1987, Pillsbury itself was acquired, in an unfriendly takeover, by the Grand Metropolitan Company of Great Britain. Grand Metropolitan produced alcoholic beverages and owned strings of pubs and betting parlors in England, Scotland, and Wales. It was said that the senior executives of that company were concerned about the decline in the consumption of alcoholic beverages as watching television at home replaced the traditional British practice of going out in the evening for a pint of beer and a game of darts at the neighborhood pub. They were determined to enter the consumer products market, and picked Pillsbury because they felt that those products, frozen fresh vegetables and packaged baking mixes, would fit other social changes, such as the growing employment of women outside the home, that were then taking place in Britain.

Pillsbury and Green Giant, together, were acquired by Grand Metropolitan when the Pillsbury stockholders agreed to accept a payment of $5.6 billion. Soon after the acquisition was completed, executives at Green Giant were told that they must increase the profits at that division "substantially" to help pay off debt arising from the acquisition. The executives at Green Giant were reminded that Grand Metropolitan's style of management had always been characterized as "a light but firm hand upon the throat." Failure to increase profits quickly and substantially, it was implied, could have severe career implications.

The problem with increasing profits either quickly or substantially in the canned and frozen vegetable industry is that these products have become close to commodities, with little brand recognition or consumer loyalty. Green Giant had the best-known trademark in the industry and held the largest market share, but it still controlled only 14 percent of total industry sales. The remaining 86 percent was held by Birdseye, Del Monte, Dole, Heinz, and "house brands" produced for the various supermarket chains. Further, the per capita consumption of frozen vegetables in the United States was steady, not growing, and canned vegetable consumption was falling as fresh produce was brought from distant nonseasonal growing regions by direct truck or even air shipment. Consequently there was little opportunity to raise sales through consumer advertising or to increase prices through product differentiation.

It was possible, however, to decrease costs by moving from California to Mexico. Green Giant had, since 1984, operated a small freezing plant in Irapuato, Mexico. Irapuato is in central Mexico, 500 miles south of the U.S.–Mexico border. The plant had been built in this area because the hot, sunny climate and dry, fertile soil produced excellent crops of cauliflower and broccoli year round, given adequate water for irrigation. Green Giant had drilled a number of deep wells and found adequate water.

The growing, processing, and packaging of frozen vegetables for export to the United States from Mexico also turned out to be very inexpensive. The average wage in Irapuato was 65 cents per hour. The average wage in Salinas, California, was $7.50 per hour. There were, of course, additional costs for transportation of the finished products north to the United States and for supervision of the untrained workers in Mexico, but the overall impact upon the profits of Green Giant could be very substantial and very quick if all of the California operations were moved to Mexico. It was estimated that such a move would save Green Giant $13,200 per worker per year.

In 1988, soon after the acquisition of Green Giant and Pillsbury by Grand Metropolitan, there were 1,400 workers working in the company's processing plants in the Salinas area. Salinas was a small city, almost totally dependent upon agricultural products for its livelihood. The prosperity of Silicon Valley, only 70 miles to the north in San Jose and Sunnyvale, had never reached Salinas primarily, it was said, because the population lacked the high degree of education needed for high-technology electronics manufacturing.

The question, in 1988, was whether Green Giant should move all of its growing, processing, and packaging operations from Salinas to Irapuato. There were a number of factors that would affect this decision beyond the obvious savings in costs:

1. The gain of jobs and the resulting industrial development would be welcomed in Irapuato. Even though Green Giant paid only 65 cents per hour, this was still above the minimum wage for the area, set by the government at 55 cents per hour. People had lined up to get the early jobs offered at Green Giant—or Gigante Verde as the company was known locally—and it was expected that the same thing would happen if all 1,400 jobs were moved to the area. Mexican unions had tried, but failed, to organize the workers.

2. The loss of the jobs, and the resulting unemployment, would be devastating to Salinas. It was expected that the economy of the area would remain agricultural, due to the excellent soil and weather conditions, but most of the jobs actually growing and harvesting the vegetables were considered to be too hard—bending and stooping under a very hot sun—for the people who had worked in the processing plants for Green Giant, many for the nearly 30 years the company had operated in Salinas. Most of the vegetables grown in the area would be shipped fresh to consumers in the rest of the country. There would be few job opportunities for the laid-off plant workers.

3. The movement of operations from Salinas to Irapuato would have substantial environmental impacts upon the area. Central Mexico is an arid region. Water is in short supply. Green Giant has drilled wells over 450 feet deep to get adequate amounts of clean water for washing and blanching (lightly boiling for about 30 seconds) the vegetables. With increased production following the move it was expected that the deep wells would dry up the 20-foot and 30-foot wells of the local population, who would then be forced to get water for cooking and washing from the river. No money was available for a municipal water system that would extend beyond the commercial center of the town. The river water could not—according to U.S. law—be used for processing vegetables destined for export to the United States because it is polluted by bacteria in untreated sewage from towns that are farther upstream and by pesticides that are in the runoff from the agricultural fields.

   > Green Giant and the U.S. government are both saying that the river water is not good enough for those of us who are so fortunate as to live in the United States, but that it is plenty good enough for Mexicans. (Verbal statement of environmental activist contacted by the case writer)

4. The movement of operations from Salinas to Irapuato would also have some social impacts upon the area. It can be assumed that Green Giant will pay taxes on their property in Mexico, though at a rate below that paid previously in California. These taxes will help to pay for needed improvements in the educational system and the

physical infrastructure of the community. It can also be assumed, however, that converting about 6,000 acres of land from growing corn and beans—the local subsistence crops—to growing broccoli and cauliflower for export will increase prices for corn and beans and thus increase the local cost of living.

Mexico does not have an efficient distribution system for food from one region to another. People are dependent upon what is grown locally. Water and food, of course, are the two most basic needs of life. Green Giant is going to take both of them. (Verbal statement of environmental activist contacted by the case writer)

Green Giant officials did not respond to the charge that growing broccoli and cauliflower for export in frozen form to the United States in the limited land areas suitable for farming within the Central Mexican region would raise prices on corn and beans needed for local consumption. The officials did say, however, that they would be willing to "work with" community leaders in Irapuato to build new water purification and sewage treatment plants, but did not specify exactly what percentage of the capital costs and operating of those plants their company was willing to shoulder.

5. The movement of operations from Salinas to Irapuato will, lastly, have an economic impact upon both countries. The jobs, though manual, repetitive, and dull, will be the first step in industrialization. Some of the workers will have to be selected and trained in machine repair, quality control, cost accounting, and workforce supervision. The wages, though low, will bring increases in living standards and the start of a middle class. The United States will benefit from the export of goods designed for that middle class and from improved competitiveness in the world economy, as low-cost labor in Mexico can be combined with capital and technology in the United States to counter firms from Japan and Southeastern Asia who are making extensive use of the low-cost labor in parts of the Orient.

Everyone benefits from freer trade. Mexico will export more to the U.S. The U.S. will export more to Mexico. Both countries will do what they are good at doing; this is the doctrine of comparative advantage, and the standards of living in each country will rise over time. (Statement of financial economist contacted by the case writer)

Numerous economists disagree with the doctrine of comparative advantage in international trade, particularly in the global markets for agricultural products where all producers appear to rely upon lower skilled and poorly paid workers, and where improved technologies and larger investments don't seem to bring a promise of better skills, higher wages, and lower costs.

Class Assignment

Put yourself in the position of the president of Green Giant in 1988. What action would you recommend, and why? If you decide to move, how would you explain your decision to the Green Giant employees, many of whom are older—the case says that some have been working at Green Giant since the frozen food plant opened in Salinas, 30 years ago—and no longer have the stamina to work in fields harvesting crops for shipment as fresh produce to markets in the United States, and certainly don't have the skills to work in the electronics plants about 40 miles to the north, in the Silicon Valley? If you decide not to move, how would you explain your decision to the senior executives at Grand Metropolitan who have demanded a "substantial and quick" increase in profits and have told you that their management style emphasizes a "light but firm hand upon the throat"? Do you agree with the economic doctrine of comparative advantage, which essentially states that it is in the best interests of every country to specialize in what they do best for the economies of scale that come from this specialization will drive down production costs and thus lower consumer prices for all countries?

Case 2-3

Public Utility Firms and the Need for Additional Electric Power

The consumption of electric power within the United States is growing at a compound rate of approximately 2 percent per year. This may seem low at first glance, but given the reluctance of many recently deregulated public utilities to make the very large investments needed for additional power generation and transmission capabilities, and given the spikes in demand brought about by both greater-than-normal variations in summer temperatures patterns and higher-than-expected increases in data processing and telecommunication usage rates, many regions within the country faces a coming shortage of electric power.

> Yesterday [August 17, 2006] Texas set a new record for electricity usage, exceeding last year's peak by 4.6%, a huge jump by industry measures. Most regions also have set records this summer, and some of the hottest weather may still be ahead. (*The Wall Street Journal,* August 18, 2006, p. A1)[1]

A shortage of electric power can bring severe difficulties. When demand exceeds supply the voltage declines, and a decline in voltage will—if permitted to continue for more than just a brief period of time—rapidly burn out industrial motors and process controls, commercial computers and storage devices, and residential heating and cooling units. The usual reaction by public utilities to a possible shortage of electric power is a series of rolling brownouts. Electric service is cut off for all users within a sequence of districts except for those organizations that provide such essential services as health care and police/fire protection. The problem is that these cut-offs, which may last three to four hours within a given area, frequently bring personal disruptions and—for some—considerable hardship. Think, for example, of elderly residents in a high-rise apartment complex deprived of elevator service, or of rush-hour commuters attempting to get home in an urban street system without working traffic lights. Most customers expect a utility to maintain a reliable surplus of generating capacity.

When public utilities were regulated by state commissions they were generally required by law to maintain a reliable surplus of generating capacity. But at that time the state commissioners set the rates that public utilities could charge for electric service to their various consumer groups—industrial, commercial, and residential—at levels that would guarantee a state-approved rate of return on all invested capital. The utilities did not then mind maintaining a safety margin of generating capacity because they were guaranteed an adequate return on their investments regardless of actual usage.

---

[1] *The Wall Street Journal.* Central Edition [only staff-produced materials may be used] by N/A. Copyright 2005 by Dow Jones & Company, Inc. Reproduced with permission of Dow Jones & Company, Inc. in the format Textbook via Copyright Clearance Center.

The major impact of the deregulatory legislation that was passed during the 1980s was a change in this guaranteed-rate-of-return pricing policy. Under the new rules utilities were expected to compete for customers, and prices were to be set by markets, not by regulators. The result was a natural tendency on the part of most public utilities to delay investing in additional base-load generating capacity that might not be used for a number of years, and to put off spending on system maintenance and upgrades until both were absolutely essential:

> Engineering experts now believe the nation is entering a period that could be marked by a dramatic increase in localized power outages unless considerably more is spent on replacing old and deteriorated lines. Replacing those old cables and equipment could add billions to utility spending (*The Wall Street Journal,* August 18, 2006, p. A1)

The decrease in maintenance spending and the delay in capacity investment created the well-known "external cost" problem in economics: the utilities benefited with higher profits, but the costs of downtime were pushed onto individuals and institutions outside each firm. The shortage of capacity investment also created the equally well-known "free loader" condition in economics: it was assumed that some other company would fill the void, and indeed for a limited period of time that did happen.

A number of companies outside the utility industry began to trade futures contracts, legally enforceable agreements to either purchase or sell electric power in set amounts for set prices at set times in the future. There were four underlying assumptions behind these futures contracts: (1) a shortage of electric power in one region of the country brought about by a peaking of demand within that region probably could be offset—or hedged—by a surplus of supply in another region; (2) a utility that was concerned about a shortage at a given time in the future would probably like to be protected against the ill effects of that shortage by purchasing a contract now for the delivery of the needed amount of electric power at a set cost and at a set time in the future; (3) a utility that expected a surplus at a given time in the future probably would like to be protected against the ill effects of that surplus by purchasing a contract now for the sale of the available amount of electric power at a set price and at a set time in the future; and (4) traders who were able to bring together the "shortage" buyers and the "surplus" sellers would be very well compensated for envisaging the potential offsets, marketing the hedged contracts, and absorbing the residual risks.

Enron was without question the prime example of a nonutility company that arranged and then marketed hedged contracts for both the purchase and sale of offsetting amounts of electric power. They attempted to protect themselves against the residual risks—the chances that the multiple contracts they arranged for the purchase and sale of electric power throughout the United States would not exactly offset themselves, that is, would not be precisely hedged—through their position as the owner and operator of the largest network of natural gas pipelines in the United States.

Natural gas at this time was a relatively inexpensive fuel source, and Enron built a number of what were then termed peak-load plants that had very low capital costs and very flexible operating characteristics. These peak-load generating plants consisted only of a gas turbine (similar to an aircraft jet engine, but designed to run on natural gas) and a direct-connected electric generator. They could be started or stopped easily, and run relatively inexpensively, to meet any high-demand levels, or peaks in usage, that were not covered by supply contracts. Many other companies and private investors built natural gas peaking plants as well, to take advantage of the combination of the high prices that could be charged for electric power in the event of a shortage and the relatively low costs of generating that power through the use of natural gas. Natural gas at that time was a resource that was not thought to be in short supply and thus not expected to swing widely in price.

The problem, of course, was that when serious shortages of electric power did occur, starting in California in 2000, prices of natural gas spiked also so that the operation of the peak-load plants was not nearly as profitable as the owners had expected, and many of the obsolete transmission lines failed so that distant supplies of peak-load power could not be delivered to fulfill the contract agreements. Enron and a substantial number of their imitators attempted to hide their resultant losses by innovative and in many instances improper accounting methods during 2001, but eventually those methods were discovered, and Enron and many of the others were forced to declare bankruptcy, starting in 2002. Then natural gas, along with crude oil, began to increase substantially in price throughout 2003 and both became questionable in supply during 2004. By 2005 it was generally accepted that public utilities could no longer rely on peak-load plants operated by firms outside the utility industry and had to begin planning for the construction of additional base-load generating capacity utilizing nonpetroleum fuels.

Ideally, natural sources—water power, wind power, and solar power—would be used to provide this additional base-load generating capacity using nonpetroleum fuels. Natural sources have very high capital costs but extremely low—almost nonexistent— fuel costs and frequently bring far-less-severe environmental impacts. The environmental impacts of natural sources used for power generation are not nonexistent, however. People frequently forget that hydroelectric dams block long sections of recreational rivers, wind turbines kill large numbers of migratory birds, and solar panels take substantial amounts of scenic land, while all raise immediate "not in my back yard" (NIMBY) objections from area residents. The extent of this NIMBY opposition can be illustrated by the following reaction of a prominent environmentalist to a proposal to construct a large wind power project in Nantucket Sound, within just a few miles of the expensive vacation homes and resort hotels that populate the south shore of Cape Cod:

> As an environmentalist, I support wind power, including wind power on the high seas. I am also involved in siting wind farms in appropriate landscapes of which there are many. But I do believe that some places should be off-limits to any sort of industrial development. I wouldn't build a wind farm in Yosemite National Park. Nor would I build one on Nantucket Sound, which is exactly what the company Energy Management is trying to do with its Cape Wind project. . . .
>
> Cape Wind's proposal involves construction of 130 giant turbines whose windmill arms will reach 417 feet above the water and be visible for up to 26 miles. These turbines are less than six miles from shore and would be seen from Cape Cod, Martha's Vineyard, and Nantucket. Hundreds of flashing lights to warn airplanes away from the turbines will steal the stars and nighttime views. The noise of the turbines will be audible onshore. A transformer substation rising 100 feet above the sound would house giant helicopter pads and 40,000 gallons of potentially hazardous oil.[2] (*The New York Times,* December 16, 2005)

[2] Copyright © 2005 by The New York Times Co. Reprinted with permission.

Despite the many problems, most utilities have experimented with natural sources for electrical generation, but those sources currently supply less than 1 percent of the electric power used within the United States. Other sources include heating oil (2%), biomass (7%), hydroelectric (7%), natural gas (14%), nuclear energy (20%), and coal (49%) (source of percentages is Environmental Protection Agency, "GHG Emissions Inventory," 2004, page number not given in electronic version).

Most public utilities have concluded that (1) natural sources are ideal from a public relations point of view when sited away from wealthy neighborhoods, but they create operating problems in that the solar panels do not work at night and wind turbines provide no power on calm days; (2) biomass (originally agricultural wastes and forestry residues that could be burned in boilers for steam generation, but now increasingly farm products—field corn, sugar cane, and switch grass—that can be biologically converted to alcohol-based fuels) is still very much in the experimental stage; (3) hydroelectric is no longer really an option because the good locations for storage dams have already been taken; (4) natural gas has become too expensive for all except very occasional peak-load usage; and (5) nuclear projects would be fraught with public concerns, regulatory delays, and waste disposal problems. That leaves coal as the probable energy choice.

Coal, from an economic perspective, is an excellent energy choice. It is still relatively inexpensive, and the United States has huge reserves. The state of Illinois alone, for example, has three times greater btu content (British thermal units, a standard measure of the energy potential in various fuels) in its coal than Saudi Arabia has from its oil. The problem is that coal, when mined, contains more than trace amounts of mercury and sulfur, and when burned, emits substantial amounts in fume form of mercury, sulfur dioxide, nitrous oxides, and carbon dioxide. Mercury (a heavy metal) is toxic and particularly harmful to young children. Sulfur dioxide, when combined with water vapor in the air, forms sulfuric acid, which then falls as acid rain, damaging life in rivers, lakes, and forests. Nitrous oxides and carbon dioxide are the so-called greenhouse gases that allegedly contribute to global warming.

The phrase "allegedly contribute" is used in the prior paragraph in reference to the perceived connection between greenhouse gases and global warming because, while there is near unanimous agreement within the scientific community that man-made emissions of these gases are the cause of observable temperature increases (polar ice caps and mountain glaciers are both clearly melting), the global weather system is so complex, with so many cause-and-effect interrelationships that cut across time periods and geographic regions, that no statistical proof has yet been offered.

The lack of statistical proof and the absence of regulatory control have together brought about a wide range of uncertainty in current utility planning for the expansion of electrical generating capacity based upon coal. There are two modern methods for the use of coal in the generation of electric power: (1) direct combustion single cycle and (2) integrated gasification combined cycle. The first (DCSC) provides the lowest cost for the customer; the second (IGCC) the highest benefit for the environment. The contrast between those two outcomes has generated extensive debate, argument, and even conflict within the utility industry, and between the utility industry and various public-interest groups. The following is a description of these alternative (DCSC versus IGCC) methods:

1. *Direct combustion single cycle.* In the DCSC method the coal is first crushed to form a fine powder, and is then blown into the firebox of a steam boiler. The coal powder granules (small, dustlike in nature) burn while still suspended in the incoming airstream—they do not form the bed of glowing coals on the grates of the firebox as is the case in older, more traditional coal-fired generating plants—and this airborne combustion is very complete, with limited smoke (few unburned bits of carbon) and high temperatures. The high temperatures produce what is termed "superheated" steam, steam considerably above the 212° F temperature at which liquid water turns into its gaseous form. This superheated steam is also superpressurized, and the high pressures very effectively spin the blades of a steam turbine which is direct connected to a rotary generator. The pressure in the steam dissipates as it comes from the combined turbine/generator set, having converted the heat energy of the coal to the mechanical energy of the turbine to the electrical energy of the generator. The spent (nonpressurized) steam at this point condenses back into water at a temperature just below 212° F, and that hot water is then reinjected back into the boiler.

   The modern DCSC use of coal is a highly efficient energy conversion process that provides low-cost electrical energy for public utility customers, but at some damage to the environment. The problem is that the high temperatures in the fire box vaporize the mercury and break down the sulfur in the coal and transform the nitrogen in the air to form mercury fumes and sulfur dioxide and a range of nitrous oxide emissions. These by state and federal law must be at least partially removed from the emission stream. Existing methods of separation do not permit complete removal at what is felt to be reasonable cost, however, and consequently there remains considerable discharge of these environmentally harmful contaminants. The carbon dioxide emissions are not considered environmentally harmful under current U.S. law (either federal or state), and consequently little or no effort is now made to remove them.

2. *Integrated gasification combined cycle.* In an IGCC process the input coal is again first crushed to form a fine powder, and then that powder is mechanically injected into an airtight steel pressure vessel, not into the firebox of a boiler. Carefully controlled amounts of oxygen are also injected into that steel pressure vessel. Only a portion of the coal burns, due to the careful control of oxygen, but that combustion is adequate to provide heat and increase pressure. Coal, of course, is a hydrocarbon, and the combination of high heat, high pressure, and limited oxygen causes the hydrocarbons to break down into hydrogen and carbon monoxide, both of which are highly combustionable gases.

   This mixture of hydrogen and carbon monoxide, termed "syngas" in industry parlance, is then used to fuel a gas turbine which is direct connected to a rotary electric generator. These gas turbines are water-cooled, unlike aircraft engines, which are air-cooled, or steam turbines, which do not have to be cooled. The high temperatures from the syngas combustion within the turbine create water temperatures within the cooling system that are considerably above 212° F, and consequently can be converted to steam to drive a secondary steam turbine and electric generator set. This secondary use of the output heat from the cooling system of the gas turbine to power a steam turbine and electric generator set is the reason this process is termed "combined cycle."

The construction costs for an IGCC electrical generating plant are estimated to be approximately 20 percent higher than those for a DCSC plant of the same megawatt capacity. The steel container for the integrated gasification process is considerably larger than the steel boiler for the direct combustion method, though both have to be built to withstand high pressures. The mechanical system for the injection of powdered coal (which is still a solid, and abrasive, despite the fine, granular, almost fluidlike form) into the pressure vessel for the integrated gasification method is far more complex—and expensive—than the relatively simple pump for the injection of the heated water (a fluid, and nonabrasive) into the boiler for the direct combustion process. Also, the combined cycle methodology requires two turbine/generator sets, each with its related switching panels and operating controls. A DCSC plant needs only one turbine/generator set and one group of switching panels and operating controls.

The operating costs for an IGCC electric-generating plant are also estimated to be approximately 8 percent higher than those for a DCSC plant of the same output capacity. This difference is due to the anticipated maintenance costs for the powdered coal injection mechanism. Powdered coal—as explained previously—is highly abrasive and will damage the injection mechanism, which has to be precisely machined to operate without leakage against the high gas pressures within the containment vessel. In a DCSC plant the coal is blown into the firebox, which is not pressurized but heats the water in the pressurized boiler through isolated flue tubes running the length of the boiler to the smokestack, and thus requires a far simpler mechanism.

The need for more frequent maintenance of the coal powder injection mechanism in an IGCC generating plant is also anticipated to lead to 10 percent greater downtime, though this is not expected to be too serious a drawback. It is presumed that the maintenance of the injection mechanism can be done during the early morning hours when the demand for electricity is at its lowest, and thus can be easily served by other generating plants within the overall utility system.

The 20 percent higher construction costs and the 8 percent higher operating costs of the integrated gasification combined cycle process, however, are serious drawbacks, for they will lead to higher customer prices. But there are also advantages to this IGCC process. The emissions of mercury, sulfur dioxide, and nitrogen oxides fumes will be substantially reduced because only 10 percent of the coal will be burned to provide heat for the gasification process. The balance of the coal will be converted to hydrogen and carbon monoxide during that process, but the chemical content of the mercury and sulfur will not change, due to the far lower temperatures in the pressure vessel of the IGCC process than in the firebox of the DCSC method. The mercury and sulfur will be left as solid residues within the containment vessel. Those residues can be removed, separated, and purified, and the mercury and sulfur sold as commercial products.

No outside air containing nitrogen will be introduced into the pressure vessel during the gasification process—the inputs are powdered coal and oxygen—so there will be no nitrogen oxides produced in the gasification process. And the emissions of carbon dioxide will also be substantially reduced. The syngas that will power the gas turbine/electric generator set is a mixture of approximately 75 percent hydrogen and 25 percent carbon monoxide. Hydrogen, when burned (oxidized), converts to water, while carbon monoxide converts to carbon dioxide; in this process the carbon dioxide will not be adulterated with the other emission fumes and gases, and can far more easily be sequestered and captured.

There is still some question about what to do with the carbon dioxide after capture; current thinking suggests that it be injected deep into the ground in aging oil fields to help drive out the remaining oil. When all the oil has been driven out, the surface wells could be capped—this current thinking continues—which would trap the carbon dioxide below the shale formations in the geological domes where for hundreds of thousands of years the oil and natural gas had been contained with very limited leakage.

3. *Quantitative comparisons of the generating processes.* The gasification of coal is chemically a well-established process. A version of this methodology was widely used in both the United States and Europe during the late 1800s and early 1900s to provide coal gas for the illumination of homes and businesses prior to the invention of the electric light bulb by Edison about 1895. It was further used for residential heating and cooking within the United States before the construction of the natural gas pipelines during the 1950s. The early gasification processes, however, were mechanically far simpler than those envisaged today. The earlier ones were not continuously operated. Coal in lump form was loaded, often by hand, through an open hatch into a steel pressure vessel; compressed air was injected, combustion was started, and the coal gas, very similar in composition to the present syngas, was drawn off. When all of the coal gas had been drawn off, the pressure vessel was allowed to cool, the residues were scrapped out, and the loading process started once again. It required hard, hot, dirty work, and involved an inefficient method in that the pressure vessel had to be first heated and then cooled for each gasification cycle.

The modern coal gasification process (IGCC) has far fewer workers, far better conditions, and far higher efficiencies, but all these advantages depend upon the complete automation of the process and the continuous operation of the plants. Chemically, the process is known to work; mechanically, the judgment is not as secure. Only two modern IGCC fully automated and continuously operated generating plants are now functional. Both were built with federal assistance, both have been deemed generally successful by their utility owners, but both are only about half the size of the 1,000 megawatt generating plants that are now being planned to meet the expected shortage of generating capacity. Consequently the future construction costs for a standardized version of the full-sized IGCC plants that are felt to be needed are not known with certainty. Additionally, neither of the two existing IGCC plants has been generating electricity long enough to provide absolutely reliable information on operating costs, particularly for the maintenance of the coal powder injection mechanisms. A summary that compares the construction and operating costs of DCSC versus IGCC plants can be found in Table 2.7, but it should be understood that this information is not fully accepted within the industry. It is known that a DCSC plant will have lower construction and operating costs, but it is not known exactly how much lower.

TABLE 2.7   **Quantified Comparisons of DCSC and IGCC Coal Based Electrical Generating Processes**

	DCSC Plants	IGCC Plants	Source
Proven technology	Yes, multiple plants now operating	No, only two experimental plants now operating	
Construction costs	Lower construction, costs known with certainty	Uncertain, but probably 20% higher than DCSC	*Wall Street Journal*, 5/5/06. p. C8
Operating costs	Lower operating costs known with certainty	Uncertain, but probably 8% higher than DCSC	*Wall Street Journal*, 5/5/06. p. C8
System reliability	Lower unplanned downtime	Uncertain, but probably higher downtime	*Megawatt Daily*, 6/27/06, p.10.
Thermal efficiency current method	33% to 35%	40% to 43%	*Megawatt Daily*, 6/27/06, p. 10.
Thermal efficiency future goal	40% to 43%	45% to 48%	*Megawatt Daily*, 6/27/06, p. 10.
Input coal costs due to type used	Higher due to need to use low sulfur coal	20% lower due to ability to use local coal	Managerial estimate
Customer prices due to differences	18% to 25% lower as result of all differences	Higher customer prices are major disadvantage	Managerial estimate
Mercury and lead emissions	Currently higher, though meet current standards	Uncertain, but believed to be 95% lower	*Megawatt Daily*, 6/27/06, p. 10
Sulfur dioxide emissions	Currently higher, though meet current standards	Uncertain, but believed to be 91% lower	*NYT*, 5/28/06, in electronic version only
Nitrous oxides emissions	Currently higher, though meet current standards	Uncertain, but believed to be 72% lower	*NYT*, 5/28/06, in electronic version only
Carbon dioxide emissions	Currently higher, no standards now exist within United States	Uncertain, but believed to be 40% lower	*Megawatt Daily*, 6/27/06, p. 10.
Cost to retrofit for full CO_2 control	Add 70% to cost of electrical generation	Add 25% to cost of electrical generation	*Megawatt Daily*, 6/27/06, p. 10.

The same uncertainty exists for comparisons of the mercury, sulfur dioxide, and nitrous oxides emissions between the two methods. The IGCC plants are known to generate lower amounts of mercury and sulfur dioxide than the DCSC plants due to their inherently different processes, but it is difficult to precisely measure how much lower a IGCC plant will be. Part of the problem is the relative lack of operating experience for the IGCC method. Another part of the problem is the ongoing development of that method; it is thought that the emission standards here can still be improved. But a major part of the problem comes from differences in the chemical content of the input coal. The IGCC process can use much cheaper forms of coal, with higher mercury and sulfur contents, and still achieve better emission results.

The cheaper forms of coal come from Appalachian and Midwestern sources; the more expensive forms come from Montana and Wyoming. IGCC plants in the East and Midwest can use local coals that require shorter and less expensive rail journeys, with far less consumption of diesel fuel for the hauling locomotives, but they are using coals with far higher mercury and sulfur contents. The question is whether the emission comparisons, to be truly meaningful, should be based upon similar coals, or upon different coals. The argument has been that the price advantage of the different coals has been included in the economic comparisons, and, therefore, that the impurity disadvantage of those different coals should also be included in the analysis. Similar to the cost comparisons, the emission comparisons listed in Table 2.7 have not been fully accepted within the industry.

Lastly, it is believed that the emission standards for mercury, sulfur dioxide, and nitrogen oxides will be substantially strengthened in the future, but the extent of those regulatory changes is not known with certainty. It is believed that the IGCC plants will meet those future emission standards without change. It is also believed that the DCSC plants will not meet those future emission standards without change, though that depends upon the degree of strengthening. However, it is assumed that the DCSC plants that exist at that time will be "grandfathered," or granted exemptions from complying with the revised standards so that expensive retrofitting will not be required.

4. *Possible regulation of carbon dioxide emissions.* The elephant in the room in the decision between the DCSC and IGCC processes for public utilities is the possibility of meaningful regulations on the emission of carbon dioxide, a major cause—it is believed, though not proven, as explained previously—of global warming. Here the differences can be measured with some precision. The IGCC process currently generates 40 percent less carbon dioxide than a DCSC plant of similar capacity and— due once again to the inherent nature of the gasification process that isolates the carbon dioxide from the other toxic waste products—can far more easily be retrofitted for full CO_2 control. It would add 25 percent to the cost of electrical generation to retrofit an IGCC plant, and 70 percent to the cost of electrical generation to retrofit a DCSC plant, a difference which would eliminate the present cost advantage of the DCSC process. It is not known, however, whether carbon dioxide restrictions will be imposed, the extent of those restrictions, or whether existing DCSC plants will again be grandfathered.

In summary, a new IGCC generating plant will probably cost 20 percent more to build, 8 percent more to operate, and require somewhat more downtime. Those higher capital, labor, and maintenance costs will be at least partially offset by the higher thermal efficiencies (the ability to extract more electricity from less coal due to the more complete combustion of the syngas in the gas turbine) and to the lower fuel costs (the ability to use less expensive coal with higher mercury and sulfur contents due to the lower emissions of those toxins in the IGCC process). The overall result of these economic factors is expected to be a price advantage of 18 percent to 25 percent for the customers of a DCSC plant in their purchases of electrical power.

Economic factors are not the only factors that enter into the decision process on the type of coal-fired generating plant—direct combustion single cycle or integrated gasification combined cycle—to be built. The 18 percent to 25 percent customer price advantage for a DCSC plant is at least partially offset by the environmental emission advantage for an IGCC plant. The problem is how to include that advantage in the decision process. It is not possible to put an exact economic value upon that environmental advantage, particularly given the expected grandfathering of DCSC plants. Essentially, the decision makers at public utilities are being asked to decide between two social goods—lower prices for the consumer versus lesser harms for the environment—with no way to directly compare those goods. Which process—DCSC or IGCC—do you think they should select, and how would you convince your opponents?

Class Assignment

Assume that you work for a public utility or for a consulting firm that has been asked to advise a public utility. Assume that you recently joined this company, directly out of your MBA or BBA program. Assume further that your employer has instituted some fairly advanced human resource management methods: they like to get younger employees directly involved in major decisions early in their careers to build competence and confidence. Assume lastly that these younger employees are evaluated, at least partially, on their willingness to take a stand, to frankly express an opinion, to actively participate in the decision. You've only been working for this company about a year and a half, but already you've heard some of the people who were hired only slightly before you encouragingly referred to "comers" (as in "up and coming") and others more derisively labeled as "blowers" (as in "wait to see which way the wind is blowing"). You clearly want to try to place yourself in the first group.

Assume that the public utility for which you work, either as an employee or as a consultant, plans to build six new 1,000-megawatt generating plants to meet expected increases in demand. At $1.2 billion for a DCSC plant or $1.5 billion for an IGCC installation, this will be a major capital investment decision. As both types of plants can operate for 50 or more years, this will be an investment decision with long-lasting consequences. It is also a decision that cannot be put off; it takes a minimum of four years to build a modern 1,000-megawatt generating plant of either type, and the current rate of increase in annual demand will create a probable shortage of generating capacity within that time frame. Lastly, it is a decision that cannot be subdivided; the equipment purchases will be far less expensive if all five plants are of the same design and ordered at the same time.

You have been invited, for the first time, to participate in one of these major planning sessions. You have heard, informally, that frequently the most junior person in the room is the first one asked to express his or her thoughts. Prepare the recommendation you would make if you were that most junior person.

Chapter 3

Moral Analysis and Legal Requirements

We are concerned in this book with ethical dilemmas: decisions and actions faced by business managers in which the financial performance (measured by the revenues, costs, and profits generated by the firm) and the social performance (stated in terms of the obligations to the individuals and groups associated with the firm) are in conflict. These are the moral problems in which some individuals and groups to whom the organization has some form of obligation—employees, customers, suppliers, distributors, creditors, stockholders, local residents, national citizens, and global inhabitants—are going to be hurt or harmed in some way while others are going to be benefited and helped. These are also the moral problems in which some of those individuals or groups are going to have their rights ignored or even diminished while others will see their rights acknowledged and perhaps expanded. The question is how to decide: how to find a balance between financial performance and social performance when faced by an ethical dilemma, and how to decide what is "right" and "just" and "fair" as the solution to the underlying moral problem.

In Chapter 1 it was suggested that you first recognize the moral impacts—the mixture of outcome benefits and harms, and the contrast between rights exercised and denied—and compare those impacts with the moral standards of the various individuals and groups who will be associated with or affected by the managerial decision or action. People's moral standards are bound to differ due to differences in their religious and cultural traditions and in their economic and social situations. Everyone will not view the same issues in the same way. To get widespread understanding and, hopefully, agreement, you have to address the moral concerns of all of those involved. It was suggested that you do this in stages. First, clearly state the moral problem in a way that explicitly recognizes the concerns of each of those individuals and groups, and then examine their concerns through the analytical methods of economic outcomes, legal requirements, and ethical duties. This approach will enable you to explain your moral solution in a way that will be understandable—and, hopefully, acceptable—to all. Explanation to reach agreement, in the view of this text, is fully as important as decision to reach closure. This approach has been portrayed as a graphic, which is repeated in Figure 3.1.

In Chapter 2 we looked at economic outcomes as a means of determining what is "right" and "just" and "fair" in order to resolve an ethical dilemma and reach an understandable and perhaps acceptable moral solution. Economic outcomes are not just the

FIGURE 3.1 **Analytical Process for the Resolution of Moral Problems**

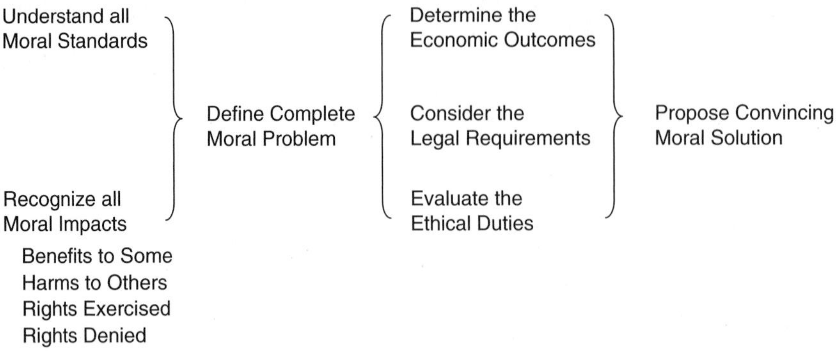

Understand all
Moral Standards

Define Complete
Moral Problem

Determine the
Economic Outcomes

Consider the
Legal Requirements

Propose Convincing
Moral Solution

Recognize all
Moral Impacts
   Benefits to Some
   Harms to Others
   Rights Exercised
   Rights Denied

Evaluate the
Ethical Duties

financial consequences of the company's decision or action for the firm. Instead, they are the financial consequences of that decision and action for all the members of the full society due to the economic relationships that exist between a producing firm, the product markets, and individual consumers on the demand side, and the factor markets and factor owners on the supply side. The political processes "in the middle" connect those two sides. According to economic theory, those relationships should distribute the benefits and harms of the corporate decision or action throughout society in a way that reflects everyone's utility preferences for both product purchases and factor sales, while the political processes should ensure that no one is left out. The result is greater output at lesser input for the full society, with that output distributed and that input allocated by impersonal market forces, supervised by impartial political processes. This condition, known as Pareto Optimality, should benefit all the members of the society.

The conclusion of Chapter 2 was that maximizing economic outcomes for the full society, and distributing those outcomes by impersonal markets, is a legitimate way of beginning to consider the moral problems of management. It is not, however, a complete and conclusive way of considering those problems. All of the product and factor markets have to be competitive and all of the external and internal costs have to be included, of course, but something more is still needed. That something more is a greater recognition of the nature and a fuller understanding of the worth of individual human beings. People don't live just to be product purchasers, factor sellers, and output determiners; they want something more in terms of justice, liberty, dignity, and respect. Part of that something more will be addressed in this chapter through the analytical method of legal requirements.

The analytical method of legal requirements can be summarized very simply in the statement that everyone should always obey the law. The law in a democratic society can be said to represent the minimal moral standards of that society, and those minimal moral standards should recognize the nature and understand the worth of individual human beings. You may or may not agree with the extent of those standards or the degree of that recognition and understanding, but you cannot really fault a person who obeys the law. You may feel that a person within an organization who faces a complex moral problem in which some people are going to be harmed and harmed badly, or have their rights eroded and eroded harshly, should go beyond the law. That person, however, may disagree with you. He or she may say, "We plan to optimize returns for our firm and benefits for our society. If you don't like that outcome, get together with a majority of your fellow citizens and pass a new law, which more fully recognizes the nature and understands the worth of other people, and we will obey the provisions of that new law. But until that happens please do not lecture us on the superiority of your moral standards. We see nothing wrong with what we are doing, and evidently other people don't either for what we are doing is currently legal and approved by a majority of the population."

This "always obey the law and be fully legal in your actions" method of moral analysis has a lengthy historical basis. Thomas Hobbes (1588–1679) was the originator of the proposal that the sole moral obligation of men and women was to obey the law, or the supreme governmental authority that sets the law. It is necessary to recognize that Hobbes lived during the end of the Middle Ages in England. This was a time of intellectual ferment as the feudal class structure was breaking down into a more open and equal society, but it was also an era of rebellion, conflict, and crime. Homes of the nobles had to be protected by deep moats and strong walls. Travels of the merchants had to be escorted by armed guards. Hobbes explained that this was a natural outcome of every person looking after his (at this time there was little gender equality, and consequently an added "or her" would have been considered superfluous) self-interests. This, he said, led to a presence of chaos, a lack of security, and a block to progress. There are four major points in his reasoning:

- *Equal ability.* Men, he wrote, are equals in their strength of body and mind despite their differences in class and position. Equality of ability leads to an equality of ambition, and therefore to a constant struggle by everyone for material gain and personal safety.
- *Continual war.* The individual struggles eventually become a war, and here there is a famous quotation: "And such a war as is every man against every man." This war, he wrote, was continual like bad weather, not intermittent like a shower.
- *Depressed economy.* This continual war where "every man is enemy to every man" resulted in a lack of security, and the lack of security led to a decline in industry, and here again there is a famous quotation: "and the life of man, solitary, poor, nasty, brutish, and short."
- *Proposed solution.* To stop this continual war, Hobbes said it is necessary to think of a "state of nature," a free association of equal individuals living before any self-serving institutions were put in place. He proposed that those people would reach two "Natural Laws":

> Men who are engaged in a continual war, to gain the benefits of an enforced peace, will seek it by all means available to them.
>
> The only means available to them is for all men to surrender all rights to a central authority who will establish peace by force and decree.

What does all this mean for the analytical method of legal requirements and the understood solution of moral problems? At the simplest level, the proposal from Hobbes comes across as the rule that everyone should always obey the law because it is in everyone's self-interest to have a stable and orderly society even though they have to give up their rights to obtain that stability and order. This, essentially, is very similar to the analytical method of economic outcomes in which Friedman proposed that everyone should always act to maximize returns because it is in everyone's self-interest to have a productive and efficient society. In Friedman's economic argument, you may not like the products that are produced or the resources that are consumed, but to get productivity and efficiency you have to accept them. In Hobbes's legal stance, you may not like the laws that are generated, particularly when those laws are established by autocratic dictums on the part of a governmental authority rather than by a democratic vote through the full society, but to avoid continual war once again you have to accept them. At this level, both the economic outcomes and legal requirements for a society are based upon the enlightened self-interests of members of that society.

At a more complex level, however, the proposal from Hobbes emerges as the legal requirement that all laws should reflect what people living in a state of nature would accept as the governing rules of society. This is not enlightened self-interest. This is impartial self-interest. This is the idea of the "Social Contract"; it is a very important and basic concept in moral analysis and needs to be further explained.

If you were to take 100 people, somehow separated from all prior economic, political, and social institutions, and put them on an island, would that society be idyllic or chaotic? Let us assume that it would be idyllic as long as there was enough food, fuel, clothing, and shelter for everyone. But suppose there was a shortage; then what would happen? You might well have the war of "every man against every man" that Hobbes predicted.

A "contractarian"—that is, a person who believes in the analytical worth of the concept of the Social Contract—would argue that whatever agreement those 100 people would make to stop the conflict and end the shortage would be the most rigorous definition you could find as to what was "right" and "just" and "fair" for that society at that time. This would then form a legal requirement for every member of that society to follow for the maintenance of their society and the production and distribution of their goods.

The contractarian would say that the people on the island, being free and equal but facing a shortage, would first discuss the distribution of benefits, the allocation of harms, the recognition of rights, and the imposition of wrongs. The agreement they then reached would have to be unanimous to be effective—one person holding out would make the agreement nonbinding in any Natural Law sense. This agreement would be totally without self-interest because people would not know their self-interest, and completely in the interests of the full society. It would be the way in which members of that society should distribute their benefits and harms, and should allocate their rights and wrongs, for this would be the way that had been determined by all to be best for all.

Obviously, you cannot put 100 people who are ignorant of their position in society on an island and record their decision on the distribution of the benefits and harms, and the allocation of rights and wrongs, that they would consider to be "right" and "just" and "fair." But you can imagine what would happen if you put everyone involved in a managerial dilemma—those benefited and those harmed, those with rights recognized and those with rights denied—in a room under conditions in which they did not know what position they held. They could be executives, employees, customers, suppliers, distributors, creditors, owners, or local residents. If they did not know what position they held, they would not know how they would be affected. If they did not know how they would be affected, they would not know their self-interests. They would then discuss the situation and attempt to find a solution that would be "fair" to all, for they would not know where within that "all" they would find themselves. This is the Social Contract concept that is also known as the "Veil of Ignorance." If no one knows what position they hold within an extended organization facing a moral problem, then they will not know how they will be affected by the various decisions or actions that are possible. Consequently, any resolution to that problem those people reach must be without known self-interest, and thus in the community interests of the citizens rather than the self-interests of the individuals.

The primacy of community interests is the reason that the concept of the legal requirements—always obey the law—can be used as a method of moral analysis. The idea is that there is a set of rules, established by the full society, that recognizes those community interests. Why not, then, fall back upon those rules when faced with a conflict between the financial performance of an organization and the social performance of that organization? Why not let the law decide, particularly in a democratic society where the argument can easily be made that the rules within the law represent the collective moral judgments made by members of the full society? Why not follow these collective moral judgments instead of trying to establish our individual moral opinions?

There are numerous examples of laws that do reflect collective moral judgments. Almost everybody within the United States would agree that unprovoked assaults are wrong; we have laws against assault. Almost everybody would agree that toxic chemical discharges are wrong; we have laws against pollution. Almost all of us would agree that charitable giving is right; we have no laws against charitable giving. Instead, we have laws—provisions within the tax code—that encourage gifts of money, food, and clothing to the poor and to organizations that work to help the poor. The question of this chapter is whether we can use this set of rules—often complex, occasionally obsolete, and continually changing—to form "right" and "just" and "fair" decisions when faced with a choice between our financial gains and our social obligations.

Numerous attorneys and business executives believe that you can base ethical decisions and actions on the requirements of the law. These people would say that if a law is wrong, it should be changed, but that until it is changed it provides a meaningful guide for action. It provides this guide for action, they would add, because each law within a democratic society represents a combined moral judgment by all the members of our society on a given issue or problem. They will concede that you and I might not agree personally with the combined judgment on a particular issue. But, they would add, if managers follow the law on that issue, those managers cannot truly be said to be wrong in any ethical sense since they are following the impartial moral standards of the majority of their peers.

How do we respond to those claims? And if it is not possible to respond logically and convincingly, are we forced to accept those claims that the rule of law should be determinant in resolving moral problems even though some people may be hurt or harmed, or have their rights ignored or restricted, in ways that they believe to be unfair? I think that it is necessary first to define the law, so that all of us will recognize that we are discussing the same set of concepts, and then to examine the processes that are involved in formulating the law. This examination will be generally the same as in Chapter 2, "Moral Analysis and Economic Outcomes," in which we looked at market forces as the determinants for managerial decisions in ethical dilemmas. However, compared to economic theory, legal theory is relatively incomplete, and there are numerous alternative hypotheses that will have to be considered. First, however, let us define the law and expand on what is meant by the rule of law.

Definition of the Law

The law can be defined as a consistent set of universal rules that are widely published, generally accepted, and usually enforced. These rules describe the ways in which people are required to act in their relationships with other people within a society. They are requirements to act in a given way, not just expectations or suggestions or petitions to act in that way. There is an aura of insistency about the law; it defines what you must do.

These requirements to act, or more generally requirements not to act in a given way—most laws are negative commandments, telling us what we should not do in given situations—have a set of characteristics that were mentioned briefly above. The law was defined as a consistent, universal, published, accepted, and enforced set of rules. Each of those terms needs to be further defined:

- *Consistent.* The requirements to act or not to act have to be consistent to be considered part of the law. That is, if two requirements contradict each other, both cannot be termed a law, because obviously people cannot obey both.
- *Universal.* The requirements to act or not to act also have to be universal, or applicable to everyone with similar characteristics facing the same set of circumstances, to be considered part of the law. People tend not to obey rules that they believe are applied only to themselves and not to others.
- *Published.* The requirements to act or not to act have to be published in written form so that they are accessible to everyone within the society to be considered part of the law. Everyone may not have the time to read or be able to understand the rules, which tend to be complex due to the need to precisely define what constitute similar characteristics and the same set of circumstances. However, trained professionals—attorneys—are available to interpret and explain the law, so that ignorance of the published rules is not considered to be a valid excuse.
- *Accepted.* The requirements to act or not to act in a given way have to be generally obeyed. If most members of the society do not voluntarily obey the law, too great a burden will be placed on the last provision, that of enforcement.
- *Enforced.* The requirements to act or not to act in a given way have to be enforced. Members of society have to understand that they will be compelled to obey the law if they do not do so voluntarily. People have to recognize that if they disobey the law, and if that disobedience is noted and can be proven, they will suffer some loss of convenience, time, money, freedom, or life. There is, it was said, an aura of insistency about the law; there is also, or should be, an aura of inevitability: It defines what will happen if you don't follow the rules.

This set of rules that are consistent, universal, published, accepted, and enforced— what we call law—is supported by a framework of highly specialized social institutions. There are legislatures and councils to form the law; attorneys and paralegal personnel to explain the law; courts and agencies to interpret the law; sheriffs and police to enforce the law. These social institutions often change people's perception of the law because the institutions are obviously not perfect.

The adversarial relationships within a trial court often seem to ignore the provisions of consistency and universality and to focus on winning rather than on justice. The enforcement actions of the police also often seem to be arbitrary and to concentrate on keeping the peace rather than maintaining equity. Let us admit that enforcing the law, on the street, is a difficult and occasionally dangerous task. Police do not always act in the interests of the full society. Let us also admit that interpreting the law, in the court, is a complex and frequently tempting activity. Attorneys, also, do not always act in the interests of the full society. But we are looking at the law as an ideal concept of consistent and universal rules to guide managerial decisions, not as a flawed reality.

The Law as Collective Moral Standards

If the law is viewed in ideal terms as a set of universal and consistent rules to govern human actions and management decisions within society, the question is whether we can accept these rules—flawed though they may be by pragmatic problems in interpretation and enforcement—as representing the collective moral judgments of members of our society. If we can, then we have the standards to guide managerial decisions and actions even though these standards may be at a minimal level. If we cannot accept the set of rules as representing the collective moral judgment of our society, then we will have to look elsewhere for our standards. In considering the possible relationship between moral judgments and legal requirements, there would seem to be three conclusions that can be reached fairly quickly:

Considerable Overlap

The requirements of the law overlap to a considerable extent but do not duplicate the probable moral standards of society. Clearly, a person who violates the federal law against bank robbery also violates the moral standard against theft. And it is easy to show that the laws governing sexual conduct, narcotics usage, product liability, and contract adherence are similar to the moral beliefs that are probably held by a majority of people in our society. I think that we can agree that in a democratic society, the legal requirements do reflect many of the basic values of the citizens, and that there is an area of overlap between the law and morality, as shown in Figure 3.2.

But the area of overlap is not complete. There are some laws that are morally inert, with no ethical content whatever. The requirement that we drive on the right-hand side of the road, for example, is neither inherently right nor inherently wrong; it is just essential

FIGURE 3.2   **Overlap between Moral Standards and Legal Requirements**

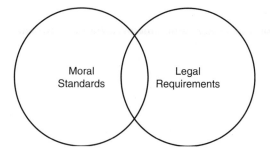

Moral Standards

Legal Requirements

that we all agree on which side we are going to drive. There are also some laws that are morally repugnant. Until the early 1960s, some areas of the United States legally required racial discrimination (segregated education, housing, and travel accommodations), and slavery was legally condoned just 100 years earlier. Finally, there are some moral standards that have no legal standing whatever. We all object to lying, but truthfulness is not required by law except in a court, under oath, and in a few other specific instances such as employment contracts and property sales.

People who believe in the rule of law and accept legal regulations as the best means of governing human conduct within society would respond by saying that it is not at all clear that racial segregation was deplored by a majority of the population prior to 1962, or even that slavery was considered unconscionable before 1862. In a much lighter vein, concerning lying, they might even claim that most people have become accustomed to, and perhaps are amused by, a reasonable lack of truthfulness in advertising messages and political discourse. Moral standards, they would say, are difficult to determine, and we must be careful not to imply that our standards represent those held by a majority of the population.

Negative Injunctions

The requirements of the law tend to be negative, while the standards of morality more often are positive. In the law, we are forbidden to assault, rob, or defame each other, but we are not required to help people, even in extreme situations. There is no law, for example, that we must go to the aid of a drowning child. Here, we do have a situation where the moral standards of the majority can be inferred, for doubtless 99.9 percent of the adult population within the United States would go to the aid of a drowning child, to the limit of their ability. People who support the rule of law, however, would say that this instance does not indicate a lack of relationship between moral standards and legal requirements; it only indicates the difficulty of translating one into the other when a positive compassionate or charitable act is needed. How, they would question, can you define in consistent and universal terms what is meant by assistance, the characteristics of the person who is to provide that assistance, and the circumstances under which it will be required? This, they would conclude, is just another illustration that the law represents the minimum set of standards to govern behavior in society and that actions beyond that minimum have to come from individual initiative, not legal force.

Lengthy Delays

The requirements of the law tend to lag behind the apparent moral standards of society. Slavery, of course, is the most odious example, but sexual and racial discrimination, environmental pollution, and foreign bribery can all be cited as moral problems that were belatedly addressed by legislation. Advocates of the rule of law would say, however, that the evidence of a delay between apparent moral consensus and enacted legal sanctions does not necessarily indicate a lack of relationship between legal requirements and moral standards. It only serves to confirm that relationship, they would claim, for laws controlling discrimination, pollution, and bribery were eventually passed.

None of these arguments—that legal requirements are not fully consistent with moral standards (they overlap rather than duplicate), or that the legal requirements appear in different forms (negative rather than positive) and at different times (sequential rather than concurrent) than moral standards—seems truly decisive. None of these arguments really helps to determine whether a given legal requirement does indeed represent a collective moral judgment by members of a specific society and consequently can serve as means to analyze the managerial decisions and actions of a company within that society. We can easily say that the law does not represent our moral judgment in a given situation, but how can we say that the law in that instance does not represent the moral judgment of a majority of our peers? For that, I think, we have to follow through the process by which our society has developed the law as a universal and consistent set of rules to govern human conduct.

Formation of the Law: Proposed Stages

Law is obviously a dynamic entity, for the rules change over time. Think of the changes that have occurred in the laws governing employment, for example, or pollution. This is essentially the same point that was made previously, that there seems to be a time lag between changes in moral standards and changes in legal requirements. Actions that 20 years ago were considered to be fully legal—such as racial and gender discrimination in hiring, or the discharge of chemical wastes into lakes and streams—are now clearly illegal. The question is whether these changes in the law came from changes in the moral standards of a majority of our population through social and political processes, and consequently whether the law does represent the collective moral standards of our society. The social and political processes by which the changing moral standards of individual human beings are alleged to become institutionalized into the formal legal framework of society are lengthy and complex, but a simplified version is shown in graphic form in Figure 3.3.

FIGURE 3.3   **Process by Which Individual Norms, Beliefs, and Values Are Institutionalized into Law**

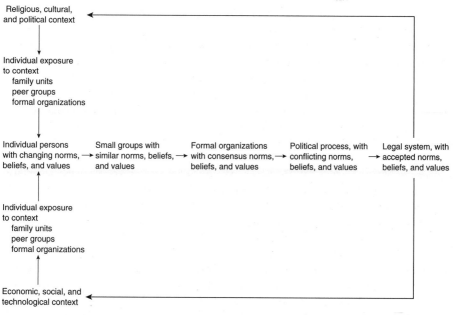

There are four stages in the proposed formation of explicit legal requirements through the inclusion of collective moral standards. These are the stages of (1) individual persons, (2) small groups, (3) formal organizations, and (4) political institutions. Each will be addressed in sequence. Some of the information about the first stage has been covered in an earlier chapter, but it is repeated here for emphasis and understanding.

Formation of the Law: Individual Persons

As Chapter 1 described, each individual within society has a set of goals, norms, beliefs, and values that together form his or her moral standards. Goals, also as described in that chapter, are what we want out of life. They include material possessions (cars, homes, boats, and vacations), lifestyle preferences (security, position, leisure, and power), personal goods (family, friends, health, and respect) and social aims (justice, equality, a clean environment, and a world at peace). Clearly, these goals differ between people. Equally clearly, they influence the norms, beliefs, and values that those individuals hold, and, consequently, the moral standards that they profess and allegedly the laws that they wish to see enacted.

Norms, once more as described in the earlier chapter, are criteria of behavior. They are the ways an individual expects others to act when faced with given situations. Foreign students from certain Asiatic countries, for example, bow slightly when addressing a university professor; the bow is their norm or expectation of behavior given that situation. University faculty members within the United States are generally somewhat annoyed when this occurs; their norm or expectation of behavior in that situation is considerably less formal and generally more egalitarian. The depth of the bow and the degree of annoyance both decline over time as the expectations of behavior on both sides are modified through learning.

Another example of a norm of behavior is far less facetious and much more relevant to the discussion of moral standards and the law. Most people expect that others, when they meet them, should not cause them injury. Norms are expectations of the ways people ideally should act, not anticipations of the ways people really will act. A person who holds a norm against assault and robbery—as most of us do—will not ordinarily walk down a dark street in the warehouse district of a big city at three in the morning; he or she feels that people should not assault and rob each other, not that they will not do so.

Norms are expectations of desired behavior, not requirements for that behavior. This is the major difference between a norm and a law; the norm is not published, may not be obeyed, and cannot be enforced except by the sanctions of a small group whose members hold similar norms and use such penalties as disapproval or exclusion. Norms also are often neither consistent nor universal. The person who actually commits a crime in the warehouse district at three in the morning, feeling it permissible to assault and rob someone else given his or her situation and need upon one night, doubtless would feel outraged and unfairly treated if assaulted and robbed in the same place and at the same time the following night. Norms are just the way we feel about behavior; often they are neither logically consistent nor universally applied because we have never thought through the reasons we hold them.

Beliefs are criteria of thought; they are the ways an individual expects other people to think about given concepts and to support specific norms. I believe in participatory democracy, for example, and I expect others to recognize the worth of that concept and support my norm of free elections. You may believe in environmental preservation and expect other people to recognize the importance of that idea and support your norm against burying harmful chemicals.

Beliefs are different from norms in that they involve no action—no overt behavior toward others—just an abstract way of thinking that tends to support an individual's goals and norms. Asiatic students who bow to American professors believe, it is alleged, in a hierarchical society based upon age, not position, with definite gradations between older faculty and younger students. People who hold the norm that others should not assault and rob them, even on darkened streets and in deserted neighborhoods, generally believe in the worth of human beings and the preservation of personal property. In one last example, the norm that a company should not bury toxic wastes in leaking 55-gallon drums is associated with beliefs about the public benefits of a clean environment and the adverse effects of chemical pollution upon family health.

Values, the fourth and last of this pattern of personal criteria that together form the moral standards of an individual, are the rankings or priorities that a person establishes for his or her goals, norms, and beliefs. Most people do not consider that all their goals, norms, and beliefs are equal in importance; generally, there are some that seem much more important than others. The important goals, norms, and beliefs are the ones that a person "values," or holds in high esteem.

Values, of course, are often controversial. Why? Because a goal, norm, or belief that one person holds in high esteem can conflict with a different goal, norm, or belief that another person holds in equally high esteem. Generally there will be little accommodation or compromise because each person attaches great importance to his or her goals of what people should want to achieve, to his or her norms of how people should want to act, and to his or her beliefs of why people should want to accept his or her goals and norms. We live in a pluralistic society, with numerous cultural traditions, and in a secular nation, with no accepted or endorsed religious doctrines; consequently, we have to live with the fact that goals, norms, beliefs, and values will differ among individuals. These differences can and do lead to conflicts. Similarities, however, can and do lead to associations. Those associations are important in the formation of the small groups that allegedly affect the formation of the law.

Formation of the Law: Small Groups

People with similar goals, norms, beliefs, and values tend to associate with each other. This is partially the result of those similarities; we all like to be with other people who tend to accept our views on the important issues of life. But it is also partially the result of the influence of our religious and cultural traditions and our economic and social situations upon our goals, norms, beliefs, and values. We also all like to associate with others who tend to share our traditions and situations. These associations, over time, lead to the formation of small and informal groups of like-minded individuals.

These small and informal groups of like-minded individuals do, through a process called accretion of power, have an apparent though delayed and indirect impact upon the legal requirements in a democratic society. People with closely similar goals, norms, beliefs, and values and from nearly identical traditions and situations tend to rely upon the groups to which they belong to forward their views and respect their backgrounds in their interactions with the larger formal organizations and political institutions.

It has to be admitted that these tendencies toward conformity can—and frequently do—lead to exclusion and discrimination. This, we will find, is one of the reasons that the legal requirements of a society cannot be said to be fully based upon the moral standards of all of the members of that society. There frequently has been some ostracism of people who hold diverse standards. But it also has to be admitted that these small and informal groups of people who share parallel views and compatible backgrounds do wield considerable influence through social and political processes upon the viewpoints of organizations and the requirements of societies. Groups of people, even though their numbers are small and their structures informal, are generally more powerful in changing organizational policies and social laws than are single individuals.

There are exceptions to this "groups are more powerful than individuals" dictum, of course. Some individuals are particularly articulate. Some individuals are exceptionally adept. And some individuals are unusually charismatic. But in general it can be said that coherent groups generate greater influence on organizational policies and social laws than do independent persons, for most of us are not "particularly articulate," "exceptionally adept," or "unusually charismatic."

Formation of the Law: Large Organizations

Small, informal groups are usually part of much larger formal organizations. These larger formal organizations can be of many different types: business firms, labor unions, political parties, charitable agencies, religious institutions, and veterans' associations. They all share—and this is the reason for the "formal" classification—accepted goals, stated policies, and structured positions. People know why they exist or claim to exist, how they act or claim to act, and who's in charge or claims to be in charge. There are exceptions here, too, of course. The accepted goals of some organizations tend to get lost over time. The stated policies ("policies" are explicit statements as to what should be done in given situations) tend to get forgotten, and the structured positions ("structure" refers to the hierarchical ranking, or authoritative power, of those positions) tend to become ignored. But generally the goals, the policies, and the positions are dominant in the management of large formal organizations.

The small, informal groups that are part of each large and formal organization tend to come into conflict with each other over their distinctive goals, norms, beliefs, and values. Over time the larger organizations and the small groups either achieve an acceptable compromise on these issues and their resultant standards, or split into smaller organizations that can achieve such a compromise. There are alternative theories on the means by which this compromise is formed: autocratic decision, bureaucratic adjustment, coalition bargaining, or collective choice. Doubtless all these methods are employed to different degrees in different organizations, but the outcome that can be observed is that many organizations do eventually display a culture of shared goals, norms, beliefs, and values that do lead to accepted standards. Organizations that display such a coherent culture—and remember that these are not just business firms, they include labor unions, political parties, charitable agencies, religious groups, and industrial associations as well—tend to have considerable power in the political institutions that formulate the laws and establish the legal requirements of the society.

Formation of the Law: Political Institutions

The political institutions—governmental units at federal, state, and local levels—are the means by which the goals, norms, beliefs, and values, and the resultant moral standards, of private individuals, small groups, and larger organizations are formalized into law. The political process by which this transmission occurs can, once again, be seen basically as a means of resolving conflict. Organizations, groups, and individuals obviously have different opinions on what should be achieved in the future (goals), what should be done now (norms), what should be the supporting rationale (beliefs), what should be the order of priority (values), and what are the standards that should be applied (morals). These different views have to be reconciled into a consistent, universal, published, accepted, and enforced set of rules (the definition of the law) to be effective. This is—or should be—the function of the political institutions.

Again, there are alternative theories on the ways by which this is done: presidential leadership, institutional compromise, congressional bargaining, and constituent pressure. The terms would differ at the federal, state, and local levels, but the process doubtless remains approximately the same. The important issue is that all of the participants in this process are influenced by votes, surveys, contributions, reports, messages, and—to some extent—threats from private individuals, small groups, and large organizations. The accretion of power means that the groups are more effective than the individuals, and the organizations more effective than the groups, in wielding this influence.

The actual process by which laws are enacted represents a complex series of interactions. Doubtless no one except a member of Congress or a representative in one of the state legislatures fully appreciates the extent and time demands of the formal hearings, office meetings, and committee reports, with their constant interruptions. There are also informal exchanges that occur in hallways, parking lots, and evening receptions, marked by both open efforts to summarize opinions from the general voters expressed in personal letters, telephone calls, and media reports, and closed efforts to include viewpoints of the special interests reinforced by campaign contributions. All of these help to form the opinions of the legislators. It is easy to be cynical when thinking of the political process, particularly when the high cost of election campaigns is considered and the need to raise money to finance those campaigns is included, but it is difficult to invent a better process than representative democracy.

Conclusions on Legal Requirements as a Method of Moral Analysis

The question now is whether this sequence of private individuals to small groups to large organizations to political institutions, lengthy and complex though it may be, truly does serve to combine the personal moral standards of our population, slowly and gradually, into the universal legal requirements of our society. That is, does the law actually represent the collective moral judgment of our citizens, or does this cumulative process break down at some point? The proposal that the law of a democratic society does indeed represent the collective moral judgment of the citizens of that society is certainly appealing. However, there would seem to be five major problems in the transfer from individual moral standards to universal legal requirements through the various stages of the social and political process:

- *Inadequate information.* The goals, norms, beliefs, and values, and consequently the moral standards, of the members of society may be based upon a lack of information relative to issues of importance. Many people in southern Quebec may have been unaware of the impact of the huge hydroelectric generating projects—described at the beginning of the first chapter of this book—upon the people of northern Quebec. Many people in the United States may be unaware of the magnitude of the toxic waste disposal problem; I certainly do not know the amount or the impact of that waste upon human health and the natural environment. It is difficult for personal moral standards to influence the law if some information is missing.

- *Incomplete participation.* The moral standards of some members of society may not be included in the formation of the small groups that subsequently influence the formal organizations and the legal institutions. People with similar goals, norms, beliefs, and values and from identical religious/cultural traditions and economic/social situations tend to become associated in small groups, but those similarities and identities also tend to exclude some members of society from different traditions and alternative situations. Goals, norms, beliefs, and values lead to conflicts as well as to associations. It is difficult for personal moral standards to influence the law if some individual viewpoints are excluded.

- *Inconsistent representation.* The moral standards of some groups within society may not be fully represented in the consensus of the formal organizations that subsequently influence the legal institutions. Many organizations do share goals, norms, beliefs, and values, but there is no evidence that each group within the organization has equal influence in determining that consensus. This can be seen in the goals, norms, beliefs, and values of many nonprofit organizations such as hospitals and universities; the standards of the professional personnel—the physicians and the faculty—often seem to predominate. It is difficult for personal moral standards to actively influence the law if some group standings are given prominence.

- *Inconsistent formulation.* The moral standards of some organizations within society may not be equally considered in the agreements of the political institutions that result, or should result, in the formulation of the law. This is the same point that was made above in shaping the consensus of an organization, though on a much larger scale. There is no guarantee that all organizations have equal influence, or even equal influence weighted by size or need, in determining the final provisions of the law. This can be seen in much tax legislation; certain organizations always seem to be favored. It is difficult for personal moral standards to eventually influence the law if some organizational considerations are preferred.

- *Inconclusive composition.* The moral standards of individuals, groups, organizations, and institutions that make it through the social and political processes that allegedly formulate the law are often incompletely or imprecisely stated and have to be supplemented by judicial court decisions or administrative agency actions. This can be seen in both product liability cases and equal employment reviews; the meaning and the application of legal requirements frequently have to be clarified outside of the legislative procedures. It is difficult for personal moral standards to influence the law if some provisions are interpreted by governmental bodies that are intentionally independent of those standards.

What can we say in summary? We can observe that there obviously is some overlap between the moral standards and the legal requirements of our society. The federal law against robbery and the moral standard against stealing serve as an example. And we can see that some changes in the goals, norms, beliefs, and values of individual members of society have eventually been reflected by changes in the law. The Foreign Corrupt Practices Act and the Federal Equal Employment Act are examples here. But we will have to admit that there is no direct relationship in all instances. The social and political processes by which the law is formulated are too complex and too cumbersome—and perhaps too subject to manipulation—for changes in people's goals, norms, beliefs, and values to be directly translated into changes in that set of universal and consistent rules that we call law. Consequently, we cannot view this set of rules as representing the collective moral judgments of our society, and therefore we cannot rely totally on this set of rules when confronted by an ethical dilemma.

Legal requirements can serve as a guide to managerial decisions and actions, but as in the case of economic outcomes, they are not enough. They don't include the full range of personal goals, norms, beliefs, and values and consequently—once again, as in economic outcomes—don't represent the true nature and actual worth of individual human beings. Legal requirements are useful. They provide an approximation of that nature, and they approach that worth by recognizing the value of liberty, opportunity, dignity, and respect. We need something more. In the next chapter we will look at the fundamental norms and absolute values of normative philosophy as a third possible means of providing that "something more."

Case 3-1

Sarah Goodwin and Impure Products

Sarah Goodwin was a graduate of an MBA program on the West Coast. She had majored in marketing, was interested in retailing, and had been delighted to receive a job offer from a large and prestigious department store chain in northern California. The first year of employment at this chain was considered to be a training program, but formal instruction was very limited. Instead, after a quick tour of the facilities and a welcoming speech by the president, each of the new trainees was assigned to work as an assistant to a buyer in one of the departments. The intent was that the trainees would work with five or six buyers during the year, rotating assignments every two months, and would make themselves "useful" enough during those assignments so at least one buyer would ask to have that person join his or her department on a permanent basis.

Buyers are critical in the management of a department store. They select the goods to be offered, negotiate purchase terms, set retail prices, arrange displays, organize promotions, and are generally responsible for the operations of the departments within the store. Each buyer acts as a profit center, and sales figures and profit margins are reported monthly to the senior executives. In this particular chain, the sales and profits were calculated on a "per square foot of floor space occupied by the department" basis, and the buyers contended, generally on a friendly basis, to outperform each other so that their square footage would be expanded. The buyers received substantial commissions based upon monthly profits.

Sarah's first assignment was to work for the buyer of the gourmet food department. This was a small unit at the main store that sold packaged food items such as jams and jellies, crackers and cookies, cheese and spreads, candies, etc., most of which were imported from Europe. The department also offered preserved foods, such as smoked fish and meats, and some expensive delicacies, such as caviar, truffles, and estate-bottled wines. Many of the items were packaged as gifts, in boxes or baskets with decorated wrapping and ties.

Sarah was originally disappointed to have been sent to such a small and specialized department, rather than to a larger one that dealt with more general fashion goods, but she soon found that this assignment was considered to be a "plum." The buyer, Maria Castellani, was a well-known personality throughout the store; witty, competent, and sarcastic, she served as a sounding board, consultant, and friend to the other buyers. She would evaluate fashions, forecast trends, chastise managers ("managers" in a department store are the people associated with finance, personnel, accounting, or planning, not merchandising), and discuss retailing events and changes in an amusing, informative way. Everybody in the store seemed to find a reason to stop by the gourmet food department at least once during each day to chat with Maria. Sarah was naturally included in these conversations, and consequently she found that she was getting to know all of the other buyers and could ask one of them to request her as an assistant at the next rotation of the assignment.

For the first five weeks of her employment, Sara was exceptionally happy. She was pleased with her career and her life. She was living in a house on one of the cable car lines with three other professionally employed women. She felt that she was performing well on her first job, and making sensible arrangements for her next assignment. Then, an event occurred that threatened to destroy all of her contentment:

> We had received a shipment of thin little wafers from England that had a crème filling flavored with fruit: strawberries and raspberries. They were very good. They were packaged in foil-covered boxes, but somehow some of them had become infested with insects.
>
> We did not think that all of the boxes were infested, because not all of the customers brought them back. But some people did, and obviously we could not continue to sell them. We couldn't inspect the package, and keep the ones that were not infested, because there were too many—about $9,000 worth—and because we would have had to tear the foil to open each box. Maria said that the manufacturer would not give us a refund because the infestation doubtless occurred during shipment, or even during storage at our own warehouse.
>
> Maria told me to get rid of them. I thought that she meant for me to arrange to have them taken to the dump, but she said, "Absolutely not. Call [name of an executive] at [name of a convenience store chain in southern California]. They operate down in the ghetto, and can sell anything. We've got to get our money back."
>
> I protested, but Maria told me, "Look, there is nothing wrong with this. The people down in the ghetto have never had luxury food items of this nature. These wafers will be sold very cheaply, and for most of the people who buy them it will be an opportunity to

try something really good. Only a few people will get an infested box. They won't be very happy, but down in the ghetto they expect that when they see a low price on an expensive product. They make the choice. We don't. (Verbal statement of Sarah Goodwin, a disguised name, to the case writer)

Class Assignment

What would you do in this situation? You can either ship the wafers or not. If you decide to ship the wafers, then be prepared to explain your action to the three housemates who probably will have the same initial reaction that Sarah had. If you decide not to ship the wafers, then be prepared to explain your action first to Maria and—if not successful there—to a senior executive in the department store chain to whom you might appeal. It is suggested that you use the following methods of analysis in (1) deciding what to do and (2) convincing other people that your decision is the "right," "just," and "fair" approach to the problem:

- *Economic benefits.* Always take the action that generates the greatest profits for the company because this will generate the greatest benefits for the society, provided that all markets are fully competitive, all customers are fully informed, and all external and internal costs are fully included.

- *Legal requirements.* Always take the action that most fully complies with the law, for the law in a democratic society represents the minimal moral standards of all of the people within that society, provided it can be shown that the self-interests of the various groups have been truly combined in the formulation process. The simple test of this prescription is "Would everyone accept this law under the conditions of the Social Contract or the Veil of Ignorance, where no one knew what their self-interests actually were and consequently how they would personally be affected?"

- *Ethical duties.* Always take the action (1) that you would be willing to see widely reported in national newspapers, (2) that you believe will build a sense of community among everyone associated with the action, (3) that you expect will generate the greatest net good for the full society, (4) that you believe all others should be free or even forced to take in roughly similar situations, (5) that does not harm the "least among us," and (6) that does not interfere with anyone's right to develop his or her skills to the fullest.

Case 3-2

H. B. Fuller and the Sale of Resistol[*]

Resistol is a fast-drying, solvent-based liquid adhesive used to glue paper, cardboard, wood, leather, plastic, rubber, and textile products. In essence it is an industrial-strength form of the familiar airplane glue or rubber cement, with the properties of rapid set, strong adhesion, and water resistance.

* *Note:* This is a shortened version of an earlier case written by Professors Norman Bowie and Stefanie Lenway, both of the Carlson School of Management at the University of Minnesota, and is used with their permission.

Resistol is widely used in Central and South America by the small shoe and clothing manufacturers, leatherworkers, woodworkers, carpenters, and repair shops that are typical of the region. It is also widely used by individual customers for the quick repair of shoes, clothing, and household goods. It is easily available from industrial suppliers in large containers and from retail shops in small tubes. The easy availability is a large part of the problem.

Fumes from the solvent in Resistol are a hallucinogenic, and street children in four of the poorest countries of Central America—Guatemala, Honduras, Nicaragua, and El Salvador—have started using those fumes as a mood-altering drug. The street children are a result of the extreme poverty of the region. Their parents are unable to support them; in many instances the parents are unable even to support themselves, or they may be dead or in jail. Consequently, the children roam the streets, begging for food, doing odd jobs, stealing small objects, getting by as best they can. They sleep in doorways at night. They live a miserable, squalid life.

Many of the street children try to escape their misery and squalor by turning to the hallucinogenic fumes of Resistol. Small tubes are available for a very few pesos from legitimate vendors in the local shops that dot both large cities and small towns; the glue is widely used for the household repair of broken articles and torn clothing. Small amounts are also available from illegitimate dealers who sell it even more cheaply in plastic bags strictly for inhaling. The problems is that the tolulene solvent used in Resistol, when inhaled, brings feelings of elation and escape from reality, but it also does irreversible brain damage and causes loss of motor control.

Foreign tourists often remark on the odd behaviors and uncoordinated movements of the street children, and regional newspapers frequently demand that their governments "do something," but there is little that can be done. There is no treatment that would be effective to counter this Resistol affliction, and no money is available for the better care and housing of these children.

Resistol is manufactured by H. B. Fuller Company, of St. Paul, Minnesota, a specialty chemical company frequently confused with the better known but much smaller Fuller Brush Company. The adhesive is marketed in Central America by Kativo Chemical Industries, S.A., a wholly owned subsidiary of H. B. Fuller.

Traditionally the H. B. Fuller Company has given regional executives in foreign subsidiaries a great deal of autonomy to respond quickly to currency fluctuations, political changes, and market needs. When numerous stories appeared in the Honduran newspapers under the title "Los Resistoleros" (the users of Resistol), Humberto "Beto" Larach, the manager of Kativo's Adhesive Division, quickly informed the editors that Resistol was not the only substance abused by Honduran street children and that the image of the manufacturer was being damaged by taking a prestigious trademark as a synonym for drug abusers. He threatened to sue the newspaper for defamation of character.

Señor Larach felt strongly that the glue-sniffing problem was not caused by the solvent in the product, but by the poverty of the region, for which he and H. B. Fuller were not responsible. He recommended to the St. Paul office that no action be taken to change the formulation or the distribution of the product. It was possible, for example, to use a much less volatile solvent that would decrease the hallucinogenic effect of the fumes but would also lengthen the drying time of the adhesive. Señor Larach said that in third world countries most industrial supply firms and retail stores would stock only one brand of a product and that if the product specifications were changed in an unsatisfactory way, the users would demand that their suppliers switch brands to a readily available competitor with the desired qualities. Resistol, at the date of the case, was by far the dominant quick-setting adhesive sold in the region, with a market share over 80 percent, but competitive products were readily available from companies in both France and Germany.

Señor Larach also explained that reducing the volatility of only the solvent of the adhesive sold through the retail stores (that is, keeping the adhesive sold through industrial suppliers at full "industrial" strength) would not solve the problem either. The street children currently obtained the glue in small tubes from the retail stores and in small jars from adults who either bought it through the industrial suppliers or stole it from the industrial users.

In 1986 a Peace Corps volunteer in Honduras, disturbed by the situation and angered by what he perceived as a lack of response on the part of Kativo, formed a committee of local religious and social leaders to attempt to reduce the use of the drug by the street children. The first act of this committee was to petition the government to pass a law dictating that allyl isothiocyanate (also known as "oil of mustard") be added to all quick-setting adhesives sold in the country to prevent their abuse. Allyl isothiocyanate is a chemical that irritates the mucous membranes of the upper respiratory tract; it can also cause burns to the eyes and skin. When used in full strength it is the "mustard gas" that caused horrendous casualties in World War I. Members of the committee had no intention that the chemical be used in full strength in Resistol; they conceded, however, that its presence even in diluted form would make the adhesive unpleasant to apply in normal industrial and consumer use but felt that this situation was better than its continued misuse by children. During the 1970s allyl isothiocyanate had been added to airplane glue in the United States to prevent a similar form of abuse.

The Peace Corps volunteer in Honduras also started a letter-writing campaign directed both to the senior executives at H. B. Fuller and to the trust officers and pension managers who held much of that company's common stock. The letters were accompanied by photographs of the street children, translations from news accounts, statements by the local clergy, and invitations to visit the region and observe the situation.

The senior executives at H. B. Fuller commissioned a study by a large international consulting firm which reached seven major conclusions:

1. Oil of mustard is not only a skin and lung irritant; prolonged exposure even in diluted form can cause nausea, dizziness, headaches, and asthma.

2. No less hallucinogenic solvent is readily available that will not severely detract from the present quick-setting, high-adhesion, and water-resistant qualities of the product.

3. No less harmful additive is readily available that will both decrease the use of the adhesive as a street drug and maintain the present desirable product qualities.

4. It would be possible to search for a less hallucinogenic solvent or a less harmful additive, but the search would be expensive and no guarantee of success could be offered.

5. Sales of Resistol in Central America amounted to over $12,000,000 per year; profits were not listed in the report released to the public, but they were assumed to be high.

6. Sales of Resistol in Central America were thought to be important to the industrial development of the region. Water-based adhesives are used in Europe, the United States, and Japan, but these require microwave dryers and presses for curing. Those dryers and presses are not available in Central America due to their capital cost.

7. Sales of Resistol in Central America were thought to be related to the sales of paint (the major product of both H. B. Fuller and Kativo); that is, if the suppliers and retailers purchased industrial adhesives from other sources, they were likely to purchase industrial finishes from those sources as well. Paint sales by Kativo were over $50,000,000 per year.

In 1987, two events occurred that forced the senior executives at H. B. Fuller to directly address the problem of Resistol sales in Central America. First, the National Assembly of Honduras passed a law mandating the use of allyl isothiocyanate in all solvent-based adhesives sold in that country. Señor Larach, however, reported that the National Assembly had included no mechanism for enforcement of the law, that he had been assured by members of the Assembly that the law had been passed to placate the committee for religious and social leaders, and that there was no intent to enforce it. Señor Larach also said that the National Assembly was likely to be dissolved in the near future (which would overturn all laws passed during its recent session) as part of the political instability that troubled the region.

Second, the president of H. B. Fuller Company received a telephone call from the editor of the largest statewide newspaper in Minnesota. The editor explained that his daughter was a member of the Peace Corps in Central America, had complained that "a company in St. Paul is selling a product that is literally burning out the brains of children down here." The editor also said that the paper had sent a reporter to Honduras and planned to run a story on the allegation if true, and that the call from the editor was a courtesy to alert the executives at H. B. Fuller and enable them to "tell their side of the story if they wished to."

Class Assignment

You are president of H. B. Fuller Company. What would you do? If you wish to stop the production, change the formulation, or alter the distribution of Resistol in Central America, do realize that—as the case describes—there were be severe marketing consequences. Current customers apparently like the product as is, and Señor Larach reports that they will respond to any changes by simply buying less of it. If your decision is likely to result in revenue—and consequently profit—decreases, be prepared to explain that decision to members of the board of directors. If your decision is to continue the production and marketing of Resistol with no changes in formulation or distribution, then be prepared to explain that decision to readers of the "largest statewide newspaper in Minnesota." One of the essential concepts of this course is that you have to be able to logically convince other people that your recommendation is "right" by arguing from the basic principles as to what is best for society. There are three of these basic principles:

- *Economic benefits.* Always take the action that generates the greatest profits for the company because this will generate the greatest benefits for the full society, provided that all markets are fully competitive, all customers are fully informed, and all external and internal costs are fully included.

- *Legal requirements.* Always take the action that most fully complies with the law, for the law in a democratic society represents the minimal moral standards of all of the people within that society, provided it can be shown that the self-interests of the various groups have been truly combined in the formulation process. The simple test of this prescription is "Would everyone accept this law under the conditions of the Social Contract or the Veil of Ignorance, where no one knew what their self-interests actually were and consequently how they would personally be affected?"
- *Ethical duties.* Always take the action (1) that you would be willing to see widely reported in national newspapers, (2) that you believe will build a sense of community among everyone associated with the action, (3) that you expect will generate the greatest net good for the full society, (4) that you believe all others should be free or even forced to take in roughly similar situations, (5) that does not harm the "least among us," and (6) that does not interfere with anyone's right to develop his or her skills to the fullest.

Case 3-3
KPMG and the Sale of Questionable Tax Shelters[*]

KPMG in 2005 was one of the largest of the public accounting firms, a member of the "Big Four." The other three, in order of size, were PricewaterhouseCoopers, Deloitte & Touche, and Ernst & Young. KPMG was fourth, but it still employed more than 100,000 people, including 6,700 active partners, 76,000 service professionals, and 21,000 administrative staff and support workers.

KPMG in 2005 was one of the oldest of the public accounting firms. It was the result of a series of mergers between William Peat and Company (founded in London in 1870), Marwick, Mitchell & Company (founded in New York in 1897), Klynveld Kraayerhof & Company (founded in Amsterdam in 1917), and Deutsche Treuhand-Gesellschaft, formed in Germany in the 1920s but led in postwar Europe for many years by Reinhard Goerdeler and now closely associated with his name. The KPMG abbreviation stands for Klynveld, Peat, Marwick & Goerdeler.

KPMG in 2005 was one of the most global of the public accounting firms, with offices and/or personnel in 144 countries. The clients of the KPMG were primarily the large industrial and service corporations and middle-market firms that are headquartered within the United States, Western Europe, and—to a lesser extent—Southeastern Asia, but that have manufacturing and marketing operations, direct subsidiaries, and joint ventures throughout both the developed and developing worlds. For many years the goal of KPMG was to provide these international clients with high-quality auditing, tax, and advisory services regardless of the multiple economic, political, and legal systems within which they operated. Obviously, government requirements, tax regulations, and market demands differ by country, and a truly global accounting firm has to have the detailed knowledge and professional expertise that can adjust for those

* *Note:* The author acknowledges the assistance of Martin Stuebs, Assistant Professor of Accounting, Hankamer School of Business, Baylor University, in the preparation of this case.

differences on a country-by-country basis and yet combine those differences into consistent reports and universal policies that can be relied upon by managers and investors worldwide.

KPMG in 2005 was one of the most independent of the public accounting firms. They have an unusual governance structure. KPMG is not a single firm. Instead, it is a network of separate partnerships that market and provide auditing, tax, and advisory services worldwide under the KPMG name through a Swiss cooperative—KPMG International—that has no ownership interests in any of those groups and that consequently serves far more as the coordinating than as the controlling entity. They also have an unusual professional outlook. Senior officials—particularly those within the U.S. group—do not hesitate to express their disagreements with governmental policies and agency decisions, from the viewpoint that professional accounting rules and procedures should take precedence over governmental decisions and regulatory actions:

> No major accounting firm was more certain of its own righteousness, or more scornful of government efforts to control it, than was KPMG.
>
> It told the [U.S.] Securities and Exchange Commission that the commission had no right to interfere in the firm's choice of business activities. [The issue here centered on the question of whether KPMG should continue to offer a wide range of management consulting services in addition to their more standard auditing, tax, and statement advisory work; for many years the partners refused to sell their management consulting division despite what were alleged to be conflicts of interest between that division and their auditing, tax, and advisory work.] The partners also argued that the SEC was wrong when it fined the Xerox Corporation for improper accounting that KPMG had earlier approved. [The issue here concerned the time at which Xerox, a long-time client of KPMG, based in Rochester, N.Y., should record as income a discounted estimate of the expected revenue stream from office copiers shipped to Central and South American dealers for eventual rental. This could be at the time of the copier shipments from Rochester, or at the time of their rental overseas. The decision was materially important to Xerox's financial statements because (1) Xerox dominated the market for office copiers in Central and South America; and (2) there was frequently a delay of over a year between the date of factory shipments and the start of rental payments overseas. KPMG had approved the recording of income at the time of shipment, which had the effect of substantially increasing Xerox's reported sales and profits for any given year. The I.R.S. declared that this approval was the result of a deliberate error, and also fined KPMG $23 million.]. . .
>
> Of all the major accounting firms, [KPMG] was the one with the strongest sense that it alone should determine both the quality of its work and the rules it should follow. Proud and confident, it brooked no criticism from regulators. . . .
>
> KPMG took the position that the commission had no right to control how it conducted its business. It viewed accounting as a self-regulated profession that should not face government control. (*The New York Times,* August 30, 2005, p. C1)[1]

Lastly, KPMG in 2005 was one of the most troubled of the public accounting firms. This numerically large, historically old, globally represented, professionally experienced, and independently minded accounting firm—the *New York Times* in the article cited above called it "a proud old lion"—had been forced to admit wrongdoing on a massive scale.

---

[1] Copyright © 2005 by The New York Times Co. Reprinted with permission.

The issue in this instance was the marketing of a proprietary series of tax shelters to wealthy individuals who had received substantial sums—usually in excess of $20,000,000—as the result of the sale of a private company or the receipt of a corporate bonus. KPMG had offered these tax shelters as personalized packages containing three elements: (1) newly developed accounting methods that could either generate reportable losses to offset the income receipts or convert those higher-taxed income receipts to lower-taxed capital gains, (2) opinion letters from KPMG partners supporting the legality of those newly developed methods, and (3) arranged contacts with either large investment banks or cooperative charitable organizations to generate the reportable losses or convert the income receipts. The Internal Revenue Service, a division of the U.S. Treasury, ruled that the accounting methods were abusive, that the opinion letters were fraudulent, that the operational means had no underlying economic rationale, and that the full personalized packages strayed far over the admittedly hazy line that separates lawful tax avoidance from illegal tax evasion.

Charges and countercharges, claims and counterclaims, followed this initial ruling with neither side giving way, but over time the Internal Revenue Service apparently grew weary of the ongoing dispute and threatened to bring criminal charges against KPMG for their sale of these newly developed tax shelters. Suddenly the situation became very serious, very fast. A public accounting firm, if convicted of criminal intent, is prevented from continuing to provide government-sanctioned auditing and tax work for their clients, and just the threat of potential criminal liability appears to drive away both corporate and individual clients very quickly. This had happened to Arthur Andersen and Company in 2002, at a time when that accounting firm was the largest and probably the most respected of what were then termed the "Big Five." Arthur Andersen had been threatened with criminal liability in connection with its approval of a number of enhanced-income-recognition and reduced-liability-inclusion accounting methods used in the preparation of the financial statements for Enron Corporation, after it became obvious that massive revisions of those statements were needed. Arthur Andersen was driven out of business by that threat of legal claims before they had been formally charged or legally convicted of any wrongdoing.

Faced with this threat of criminal prosecution, the senior partners of KPMG felt forced to negotiate a settlement. This settlement, termed a "deferred prosecution agreement," allowed the partners to avoid a criminal indictment which probably would have been a "death knell" for the firm, but required the U.S. group within KPMG International to essentially plead guilty to developing, marketing, and providing abusive tax shelters:

> In the statement of facts [that accompanied the settlement], KPMG acknowledged that the firm's partners "assisted high-net-worth United States citizens to evade United States individual income taxes on billions of dollars in capital gain and ordinary income by developing, promoting and implementing unregistered and fraudulent tax shelters." . . .
>
> [KPMG went on] to say that partners prepared false representations for purchasers of the shelters, then based opinion letters approving the transactions on those representations. Some opinion letters also were fraudulent in that they misrepresented the nature of the shelter transactions, according to the statement. (*The New York Times,* August 30, 2005, p. C1)[2]

---

[2] Copyright © 2005 by The New York Times Co. Reprinted with permission.

To achieve this settlement KPMG was required to (1) pay imposed penalties of $456 million without the benefit of offsetting liability insurance proceeds or income tax reductions, (2) accept a monitor to supervise an agreed-upon program of governance restructuring and organizational change, (3) severely limit its future income tax service offerings, and (4) provide no legal assistance or monetary payments in lieu of that assistance to the senior partners and professional employees who were expected to be later charged personally in this case. Mr. Timothy Flynn, the newly elected chairman and chief executive of KPMG, who had negotiated this settlement and accepted these terms, was contrite:

> "We regret the past tax practices that were the subject of the investigation," Mr. Flynn said in a statement. "The resolution of this matter allows KPMG to confidently face the future as we provide high-quality audit, tax and advisory services to our large multinational, middle market and government clients." (*The New York Times,* August 30, 2005, p. C1)[3]

Government officials at the nation's capital were exuberant. The settlement had been approved by a federal court, and these officials believed that they had demonstrated to the satisfaction of that court that the tax shelters were abusive because they had been based upon false premises and undisclosed methods:

> "The message we want to send is that if you engage in fraud, if you participate in providing false statements, you're going to be prosecuted," Alberto Gonzales, the attorney general, said at a news conference held in Washington, D.C. . . . "We want to be very, very clear: there is no company that is too big or industry too important that will escape prosecution if they in fact engage in wrongdoing." (*The New York Times,* August 30, 2005, p. C1)

> Mark W. Everson, the commissioner of the I.R.S., said in Washington, "The only purpose of these abusive deals was to further enrich the already wealthy and to line the pockets of KPMG partners. "(*The New York Times,* August 30, 2005, p. C1)

Others, however, were less sanguine. Attorneys for the nine KPMG partners who now expected to be charged personally without the support of their prior employer, and indeed after that employer had pleaded guilty to exactly the same charges upon which they were to be tried, were quick to point out that no U.S. court had ruled that the shelter transactions themselves were improper:

> "The government is attempting to criminalize the type of tax planning that tax professionals engage in on a daily basis," Robert S. Fink, a lawyer who is representing Richard Smith, one of the former KPMG partners, said in a statement. He added, "If the government wants to put an end to these types of transactions, the proper response is for Congress to change the law, not to scare professionals away with indictments." (*The New York Times,* August 30, 2005, p. C1)

All of the participants in the controversy, of course, tended to have self-centered views about the justice of the outcome of this preliminary case. There were, however, a number of aspects of the underlying situation that either surprised or startled independent observers:

1. *The extent of the tax savings.* This was not a smallish affair. Prosecutors claimed that the tax shelters covered by the agreement had permitted more than $11 billion in

---

[3] Copyright © 2005 by The New York Times Co. Reprinted with permission.

artificial losses, and enabled over 400 U.S. citizens to avoid paying some $2.5 billion in taxes (*The Wall Street Journal,* March 11, 2006, p. A9)

2. *The level of the participating employees.* These shelters had not been arranged by lower level tax professionals and/or administrative staff who senior officials might have been able to claim had acted individually, counter to strict partnership rules. The nine individuals who were indicted in August 2005 were all at the senior level. Jeffrey Stein had been deputy chairman of KPMG. Mr. Richard Smith, mentioned in the brief quotation directly above, had been vice chairman. John Lanning was the head of the Tax Department, and Jeffrey Eischeid had been in charge of the Personal Financial Planning Unit within that department that had first designed and then marketed the shelters. (*The Wall Street Journal,* August 30, 2005, p. C1)

3. *The extent of the recorded profits.* KPMG was reported to have recorded $124 million in profits over the full period of the marketing effort, from 1996 to 2002 (*The New York Times,* August 27, 2005, p. A1). The receipts apparently were so attractive that two of the nine indicted partners, Robert Pfaff and John Larsen, had resigned from KPMG to form their own sales agency, Presidio Advisory Services, to market the tax shelters. They received fees of $134 million during 1999 and 2000 (*The New York Times,* March 28, 2006, no page reference on the electronic version).

4. *The intensity—and crudity—of the sales effort.* KPMG aggressively promoted its new tax-saving products. A KPMG e-mail had been introduced in court despite earlier attempts to shield all these communications with attorney–client privilege— a judge had ruled that merely copying a lawyer and not requesting his or her input did not provide this time-honored protection—that urged its employees to "sell, sell, sell," and then continued:

> "We are dealing with ruthless execution, hand-to-hand combat, blocking, and tackling. Whatever the mixed metaphor, let's just do it." (E-mail from unnamed partner, quoted in *Tax Notes,* July 25, 2005, p. 432, and reprinted with permission)

> "Our reputation will be used to market the transactions. . . . I believe the time has come to s*** and get off the pot. The business decisions to me are primarily two: 1) Have we drafted the opinion with the appropriate limiting bells and whistles . . . and 2) Are we being paid enough to offset the risks of potential litigation resulting from the transaction?" (E-mail from Philip Weisner, at the time the head of the KPMG National Tax Office, quoted in *Tax Notes,* July 25, 2005, p. 432, and reprinted with permission)

> "I think that the expression is s*** *or* get off the pot. I vote for s***." (E-mail from Jeffrey Stein, then deputy chairman of KPMG, quoted in *Tax Notes,* July 25, 2005, p. 432, and reprinted with permission)

5. *The extent of the concealment plan.* The indictment of the KPMG partners went beyond the development, marketing, and provision of allegedly abusive tax shelters; the indictment also included what were said to be deliberate attempts to conceal the nature of these shelters. It claimed that KPMG: (*a*) had not registered the shelters with the IRS, as required by law, (*b*) had prepared tax returns for their clients that disguised the operations of those shelters, (*c*) had copied legal officers and outside attorneys on all e-mails and memos associated with the shelters in order to later claim attorney–client privilege, (*d*) had forced their clients to sign nondisclosure agreements to prevent them from revealing the nature and/or operation of the

shelters, and (*e*) lastly—it was alleged—had encouraged some of the defendants to lie both to investigators from the IRS and to members of a senate investigative panel that held public hearings in November 2003 (*The Wall Street Journal,* August 30, 2005, p. C1)

> According to the indictment, one defendant, Mr. Eischeid, gave "false, misleading and evasive" testimony to the I.R.S. in 2002 about certain tax shelters. The indictment cited an e-mail message from one KPMG partner who wrote that the firm's general counsel and outside lawyer "determined that 'the less said the better.'" As a result, this e-mail message continued, "the record will reflect repeated 'I don't knows,' 'I don't recalls,' and "I was out of the loops'—the rope-a-dope Enron defense." (*The New York Times,* August 30, 2005, p. C1)

It is important to understand, however, that these widely used, strongly supported, highly profitable, aggressively promoted and—apparently—deliberately concealed tax shelters had never been declared to be illegal in formal court proceedings. It is clear that the many officials at the IRS felt that they were illegal—indeed, those officials had classified these shelters as "potentially abusive" less than a year after they were first offered for sale by KPMG—but such a classification does not prevent taxpayers from using the shelters; it just exposes them to eventual penalties and interest payments if the shelters are later found in court proceedings to have been improper:

> Regulators have been clamping down on aggressive tax shelters, raising the stakes for taxpayers who want to operate legally but also don't want to give the IRS more money than is required.
>
> The new climate is a response to the federal government's vigorous push in recent years to curb questionable tax shelters—loosely defined as transactions with no real business purpose other than to avoid taxes.
>
> There is often a blurry line, however, between improper tax shelters and more legitimate strategies that take advantage of the intricacies of the tax code to lead to big tax savings. A number of strategies questioned by regulators are composed of well established, legal building blocks—such as using different types of trusts, partnerships, retirement plans, annuities and life insurance policies, all of which can have special tax advantages. However, these strategies are often pieced together in such a way that there ends up being little, if any, real economic purpose. (*The Wall Street Journal,* October 13, 2005)[4]

The issue, then, in determining the legitimacy of newly designed tax shelters is the existence of "real economic purpose," which can probably be interpreted as meaning an actual chance for growth and profit from an at-risk investment. To conclude this case, we will provide detailed descriptions, of two of the shelters, that were offered during congressional hearings that were held on November 18, 2003, by the United States Senate Permanent Subcommittee on Investigations. After opening statements by senior legislative members from both parties, Senator Carl Levin (D. MI) alternately read from and paraphrased a report prepared by the subcommittee staff. He began with an apology for planning to speak at greater length than was customary in an attempt to explain the technical features of two of these shelters, and then continued:

---

[4] *The Wall Street Journal.* Central Edition [only staff-produced materials may be used] by N/A. Copyright 2005 by Dow Jones & Company, Inc. Reproduced with permission of Dow Jones & Company, Inc. in the format Textbook via Copyright Clearance Center.

Unlike legitimate tax shelters, abusive tax shelters have no real economic substance. They are designed to provide tax benefits not intended by the tax code and are almost always convoluted and complex. . . . [They] are MEGOs—that means "my eyes glaze over." Those who cook up these concoctions count on their complexity to escape [government] scrutiny and public ire. (U.S. Congress, Senate Committee on Homeland Security and Governmental Affairs, *U.S. Tax Shelter Industry: The Role of Accountants, Lawyers and Financial Professionals,* 108th Cong., 1st sess., November 18, 2003, p. 4)

Senator Levin explained that the staff of the subcommittee had conducted extensive studies of four of the allegedly faulty tax products designed, marketed, and sold to wealthy individuals by KPMG. He identified these four products by their acronyms of BLIPS, FLIPS, OPIS (pronounced "oh-pees"), and SC2 (pronounced "see-twos"), but said that he planned to explain the operations of only two: the BLIPS and the SC2.

The BLIPS Tax Shelters

Senator Levin noted that the term BLIPS stood for "bond linked issue premium structures," and he explained the way in which these structures worked, which he had warned would be found by many to be "convoluted and complex," through a series of steps using a hypothetical example. The following is not a direct quotation of that hypothetical example; the case writer has simplified, and attempted to amplify where that might be needed, Senator Levin's more detailed description.

Senator Levin started by asking listeners at the hearing and readers of the transcript to imagine that an individual taxpayer had a gain or profit of $20 million that came about from a well-publicized retirement bonus or performance award. That taxpayer would receive a telephone call from one of the KPMG tax partners or tax professionals who had been—as noted earlier—strongly encouraged to engage in the marketing effort. The partner or professional would offer to shelter a substantial portion of the taxpayer's gain or profit by creating a $20 million capital loss.

Senator Levin also asked interested listeners and/or readers to further imagine that the individual taxpayer, presumably impressed by the reputation and experience of KPMG, agreed to this shelter proposal. KPMG quickly proceeded to the next step, which was to establish a limited liability company, or LLC, in that person's name. A "limited liability company" is essentially a corporation with a small number of owners, frequently just the taxpayer or members of the taxpayer's family, who will then be protected from any personal liabilities or direct legal claims by the corporate form.

At the same time KPMG introduced the taxpayer to an investment banking firm, which had previously agreed to provide financing for these tax shelter LLCs under the terms and conditions proposed by KPMG, and to a private investment counselor, who had agreed to provide financial advice for the tax shelter LLCs under those same terms and conditions. Now all the parts were in place, and the following sequence of eight actions took place, all as graphically displayed on Figure 3.4:

1. *Provide equity of $1.4 million.* In the first action the individual taxpayer provided the LLC which had been created for that person by KPMG with an equity investment. This equity investment was always in an amount equal to 7 percent of the capital loss that the taxpayer wished to create; in the instance cited by Senator Levin this 7 percent investment would be $1.4 million.

FIGURE 3.4 Sequence of Eight Steps in the Operation of the Bond Linked Issue Premium Structure (BLIPS) Tax Reduction Plan Developed by KPMG

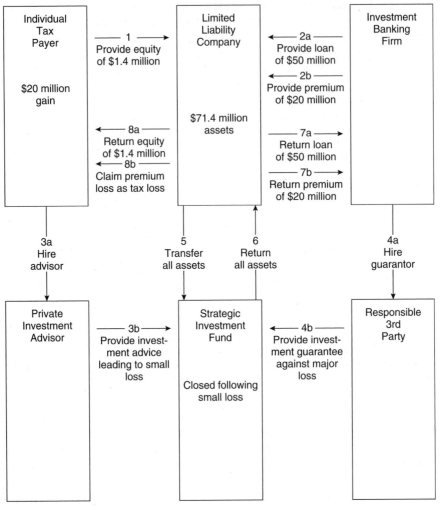

2. *Provide loan of $50 million and premium of $20 million.* The investment banking firm recommended by KPMG next provided the LLC set up by KPMG with a seven-year-term loan of $50 million, at a high rate of interest, 16 percent per year. Allegedly due to a desire to reward the taxpayer's willingness to have his or her LLC pay such a high interest rate, the investment bank also provided the LLC with an interest-free $20 million "premium." This premium was the key to the operation of the proposed tax shelter. The premium was clearly not a loan in that there were no expectations of repayment except under one very special and voluntary condition, so it could not be classified as a liability on the balance sheet of the LLC, and consequently had to be classified as equity. That very special condition, however, was that the premium had to be repaid if the bank loan was terminated before its seven-year expiration date, so the premium could not as yet be considered as corporate income for the LLC.

Senator Levin did not go into detail on this premium, or on the classification problems (debt versus equity) created by the premium. It appeared that no one in the past had ever thought about the use of a substantial premium to reward a borrower's willingness to pay a high interest rate, so it seemed to remain in an accounting "never-never" land, with its indefinite status explained by notes on the income statement and balance sheet. This premium, however, was in all cases exactly equal to the amount of the original gain that the taxpayer wished to protect, so its importance remained clear. It should also be noted that the investment bank was able financially to provide this uncertain $20 million cash advance to the taxpayer's LLC because the very certain $50 million dollar loan at 16 percent interest if held to maturity over the seven-year time period would result in actual interest payments to the investment bank of $71 million, far above the $20 million premium that had been paid and was to be forgiven.

The LLC now had an equity investment of $1.4 million owned by the taxpayer, a semi-equity advance of $20 million provided by the investment bank but apparently owned by the taxpayer, a seven-year-term loan of $50 million that was owed to the investment bank, for a total held in secure money market securities or short-term bonds of $71.4 million. There was a formal agreement, however, that none of this money, except for the original $1.4 million equity provided by the taxpayer, could be invested outside of the bank, or used as collateral for any investments outside the bank, without the formal permission of the bank. That permission was, in fact, given only following (*a*) the taxpayer's hiring of a private investment counselor approved by the bank to provide reliable advice on those investments, and (*b*) the bank's contracting with a responsible third party to provide a guarantee against any major loss in those investments.

3. *Hire private investor counselor.* The taxpayer in consequence hired the private investment counselor recommended by KPMG to provide professional advice for the management of the $71.4 million in assets held by the taxpayer's LLC. The private investor counselor promptly suggested that the LLC owned by the taxpayer and a similar LLC owned by the investment counselor jointly form a strategic investment company, or SIC, with $1.4 million contributed by the taxpayer's LLC and $140,000 contributed by the investment advisor's closely similar LLC. This SIC partnership then asked the investment banking firm for permission to actively manage the $70 million in assets (loan and premium) that had been provided by the investment bank to the taxpayer's LLC.

4. *Hire responsible third party.* The investment banking firm, before agreeing to the request from the jointly owned SIC to actively manage the funds the investment bank had provided to the taxpayer's LLC, hired a "responsible third party" to provide a guarantee against any major loss (generally interpreted as any loss above $250,000) brought about by the management of the $70 million represented by the loan and premium. This third party was frequently a wealthy individual whom the partners in the investment banking firm wished to reward with a low-risk, high-reward arrangement. It was low risk because the private investment counselor hired by the taxpayer was limited by the terms of his or her contract with the taxpayer as to the types of investments he or she could recommend, and it was high reward because the 16 percent interest rate on the loan provided by investment bank to the LLC generated sufficient funds to support a substantial payment.

5. *Transfer all assets from LLC to SIC.* The investment bank, reassured by the limitations on the types of investments that would be permitted under the terms of the contract between the taxpayer and the investment counselor, and fortified by the investment guarantee offered by the terms of the contract between the investment bank and the responsible third party, then gave permission for the $50 million loan and $20 million premium held by the LLC to be actively managed by the SIC. Those funds were transferred to the SIC, which soon began a cautious program of speculation in foreign currency exchange transactions.

6. *Return all assets from SIC to LLC.* Speculation in foreign currency exchange transactions can be quite profitable for knowledgeable investors, but they can also be almost guaranteed to eventually result in at least one loss, even for the most competent trader. Senator Levin somewhat caustically explained that eventually there would be at least one loss here, usually within 60 to 90 days of the start of foreign currency exchange trading, although he noted that those losses were inevitably under the $250,000 threshold of the guarantee provided by the third-party investor. That is, the third-party investor was never harmed by having to act on his or her guarantee. Despite the relatively small scale of the losses, Senator Levin continued, in 186 individual cases out of the 186 BLIPS examples examined, this was the signal for the taxpayer to pull out of the jointly owned SIC, which brought about the return of all remaining SIC assets—except for the $140,000 initially contributed as equity by the private investment advisor—to the taxpayer's LLC. The private investor counselor received that $140,000, plus agreed-upon salary payments from the individual taxpayer, and so he or she lost very little and was content with the outcome.

7. *Return of loan and premium from LLC to investment bank.* The individual taxpayer, allegedly disheartened by the financial losses suffered by the professionally managed though jointly owned SIC, decided to also close his or her LLC, and this triggered the automatic repayment of the investment bank loan and the return of the investment bank premium. The investment bank received all of the funds represented by their loan and their premium, plus accrued 16 percent interest on the loan for the period that the loan had been in place, so they lost nothing and were content with the outcome.

8. *Return of equity and claim of loss by the taxpayer.* The individual taxpayer who had established the LLP, and who had joined the SIC, bore all of the loss incurred by the foreign currency exchange trading, but he or she received most of the $1.4 million that had originally been invested as equity in the LLP, and given that this loss was small, he or she was content with the outcome. He or she was particularly content with the outcome because the individual taxpayer was able to claim that he or she had "lost" the $20 million premium provided by the bank under the tenuous accounting rules that permitted the treatment of such a premium as owner's equity. That alleged $20 million loss neatly offset the original $20 million income to the taxpayer, and consequently meant that no taxes would be due upon that income.

The SC2 Tax Shelter

Senator Levin next moved to a description of the SC2s. These, he said, were slightly simpler than the BLIPS; they appeared to generate an inflated charitable donation and an eventual capital gain rather than an alleged capital loss. Senator Levin explained here that the term SC2 stood for "S Corporation Charitable Contribution Strategy." He did not say why the acronym was not then a more apparent SC3S (perhaps to be pronounced "see-threes," instead of the usually employed "see-twos").

Again, Senator Levin asked listeners at the hearing and readers of the transcript to imagine a taxpayer who had received a bonus or payment of $20 million during the year. He also asked his listeners or readers to imagine that this taxpayer had been contacted by a partner from KPMG, and had agreed to purchase the SC2 tax-saving program to be provided by KPMG. The first step here was for KPMG to establish an S corporation that would be owned by the taxpayer and/or members of his or her family.

S corporations are commercial enterprises, again with a very limited number of shareholders, that provide all of the protections against personal liability and legal claims of the normal corporate form, but here the profits are assumed to flow directly to the individual shareholder or shareholders, and thus are taxed at personal rather than corporate rates. S corporations are frequently used for the start of new entrepreneurial ventures where it is assumed that profits will be nonexistent for the first few years, and thus expected losses can be used to offset actual profits provided by the more mature investments of the individual shareholder or shareholders. In the specific example recounted by Senator Levin, the S corporation was (*a*) to have 100 shares of voting stock, all to be solely owned by the taxpayer; (*b*) to have 900 shares of nonvoting stock, all to be eventually contributed to a charitable organization; (*c*) to have full investment authority over all the funds that that were to be deposited by the taxpayer, with that authority obviously controlled by the voting shares owned by the taxpayer; (*d*) to have a nondistribution agreement such that no shareholders, holding either voting or nonvoting shares, could expect to receive any dividends or interest from the investment income of the S corporation; and (*e*) to have a life expectancy of three years, long enough to establish the claim that, if the S corporation were sold, the revenues of such a sale represented a capital gain rather than personal income to the recipient or recipients. Such a capital gain, of course, would be taxed at much lower rates than personal income. Once this S corporation had been established, with these five specific conditions, Senator Levin described the process of sheltering the soon-to-be-received $20 million income from federal and state taxes in a series of steps, here graphically depicted in Figure 3.5.

1. *Deposit the $20 million check, when received, in the S corporation.* An individual taxpayer who had contracted with KPMG to shelter his or her expected gain of $20 million through a SC2 tax reduction plan was told to deposit the check representing his or her bonus or payout in the S corporation rather than in a personal account soon after that check was received. The 100 shares of voting stock would then be issued to the taxpayer.

2. *Donate all nonvoting stock to a charitable organization.* KPMG would then introduce the individual owning all 100 shares of voting stock in the S corporation to the head of a legitimate charity that has been prescreened by KPMG to be amenable to the following proposal. The individual owning the voting stock in the S corporation would offer to donate to the prescreened charitable organization all nonvoting shares. The charity, however, would in turn sign a redemption agreement permitting the S corporation to repurchase these nonvoting shares at a specific share price, just

FIGURE 3.5 Sequence of Five Steps in the Operation of the S Corporation Charitable Contribution Strategy (SC2) Tax Reduction Plan Developed by KPMG

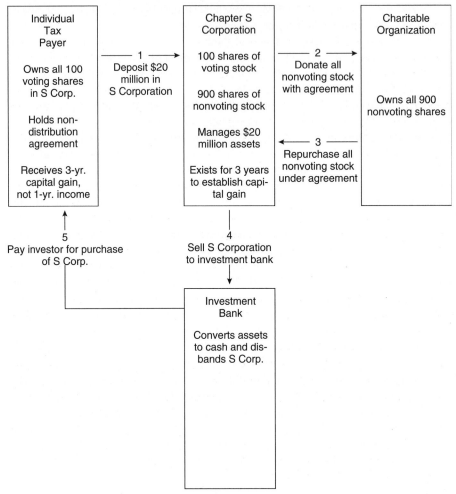

after the completion of a specific time period. Following this agreement, and after this donation, the ownership of the S corporation would be 90 percent held by the charity through the nonvoting shares and 10 percent by the taxpayer through the voting shares. This arrangement assured that only 10 percent of the $20 million check representing the individual taxpayer's gain or bonus would be subject to the income tax of that individual taxpayer; 90 percent would be exempt from taxation because it was understood to go to the charity which owned that balance of the shares. The nonvoting status of those shares, and the existence of the nondistribution agreement, did not affect the alleged ownership of the assets of the S corporation.

3. *Repurchase all nonvoting shares from the charitable organization.* The 90 percent of the $20 million check deposited in the S corporation and allegedly owned by the

charity did not actually go to the charity because of the nondistribution agreement passed by the S corporation prior to the donation and agreed to by the charity as a precondition of that donation. Instead, the funds were held by the S corporation, under the management of the taxpayer, and either earned money market interest or were otherwise suitably invested until just prior to the completion of the specified three-year time period, when the charitable organization was required to offer their 900 nonvoting shares to the S corporation for repurchase at the specified share price that had been agreed upon at the time of the donation of those nonvoting shares. The money used to repurchase the nonvoting shares, generally about half of the dividends and interest received on the $20 million investment over the three-year time period of that investment, went directly to the charitable organization, and was then used for the charitable purposes for which that organization had originally been founded.

4. *Sell the S corporation to an investment bank.* After the repurchase of the nonvoting shares, all of the holdings in the S corporation would be 100 percent owned by the individual taxpayer and controlled by his or her voting shares. With the expiration of the nondistribution agreement, all of the investment funds held by the S corporation, plus all of the dividend and interest income received by the S corporation, would be available for distribution to the individual taxpayer. But rather than making that distribution, and paying personal income taxes on that distribution, the individual taxpayer could now sell the S corporation, as an entirety, to an investment bank recommended by KPMG. That investment bank would then cash out all of the stocks, bonds, and money-market funds from their recently purchased S corporation, and close that corporation.

5. *Pay the investor for the purchase of the S corporation.* When the S corporation paid the taxpayer for the S corporation, that payment would qualify as a capital gain because the taxpayer would be selling an asset—in this case his or her interest in the S corporation—that had appreciated in value. When the S corporation was established the taxpayer owned just 10 percent of the capital stock of the company; when the S corporation was sold the taxpayer owned 100 percent of the stock. The sale of an asset that has appreciated in price is always treated as a capital gain for tax purposes, not as annual income, and capital gains are taxed at far lower rates.

Class Assignment

1. In your opinion, do the BLIPS and SC2 tax shelters as described within this case qualify as legitimate methods for tax avoidance rather than—as the government has claimed—illegitimate means for tax evasion? Assume that you had gone to work for KPMG immediately after graduation from your college or university, at the time when these tax shelters first came to the attention of the IRS in the late 1990s, which—as described previously in this case—had then labeled them only as "potentially abusive." Further assume that the chairman of KPMG, rather than the brusque and even crude person apparently revealed by his or her statements—also as described previously—was a friendly and thoughtful individual, who frequently came to some of the training sessions for newly hired employees. Assume that you are in one of those training sessions in the late 1990s, and that the instructor has told you that the chairman will be present on the next day, that the topic will be

the BLIPS and SC2 tax shelters, and you should be ready to discuss those two tax shelters using company-prepared descriptions of the shelters as your assignment. Assume lastly that the company-prepared descriptions were forthright, essentially similar in content to those presented a number of years later by Senator Levin.

Remember that all this is occurring early in the controversy, before KPMG found it necessary to admit wrongdoing to prevent being driven out of business, and before so many senior officials were indicted for criminal activity. All that you know are the details of the operations of the two shelters, and the fact that the IRS has labeled them "potentially abusive." Suppose this friendly and thoughtful chairman started the class discussion by asking the question, "Should we, at KPMG, continue to market and provide these particular tax shelters?" How would you respond? It is suggested strongly that you use the Analytical Process for the Resolution of Moral Problems that was initially described in Chapter 1, and portrayed in Figure 1.1 which has been reproduced in most of the subsequent chapters. The first theme of this text is that not only must you decide what you sincerely believe to be right and just and fair, but that you must be able to *logically* convince others. The second theme of this text is that it is important to your career to be able to logically convince others. How would you structure your argument in that class?

2. A lawyer who represented Richard Smith, one of the KPMG partners indicted by the government, was quoted in the case as saying, "If the government wants to put an end to these types of transactions, the proper response is for Congress to change the law, not to scare professionals away with indictments." How would you suggest that the law be changed in order to fully clarify what this case previously termed "the admittedly hazy line that separates lawful tax avoidance from illegal tax evasion"? Why, in your opinion, does the law not now provide that full clarification?

3. Lastly, what were the personal goals and organizational forces that brought about the near dissolution of KPMG? The actions of a small group of senior executives bought this "proud old lion" close to criminal charges and consequent dissolution, as had already happened to Arthur Andersen. In short, what should you learn from this example about the management of professional service organizations within a highly competitive economy?

Chapter 4

Moral Analysis and Ethical Duties

We are concerned in this book with ethical dilemmas: decisions and actions faced by business managers in which the financial performance (measured by the revenues, costs, and profits generated by the firm) and the social performance (stated in terms of the obligations to the individuals and groups associated with the firm) are in conflict. These are the moral problems in which some individuals and groups to whom the organization has some form of obligation—employees, customers, suppliers, distributors, creditors, stockholders, local residents, national citizens, and global inhabitants—are going to be hurt or harmed in some way while others are going to be benefited and helped. These are also the moral problems in which some of those individuals or groups are going to have their rights ignored or even diminished while others will see their rights acknowledged and often expanded. The question is how to decide—how to find a balance between financial performance and social performance when faced by an ethical dilemma, and how to decide what is "right" and "just" and "fair" as the solution to the underlying moral problem. The first chapter of this text suggested a formal analytical process for the resolution of these complex moral problems.

The analytical process described in Figure 4.1 proposed three alternative means of resolving these moral problems that mix benefits and harms and contrast the recognition and denial of rights. Let us assume that you want to reach a solution with which you can feel comfortable and believe to be as "right" and "just" and "fair" as possible. But let us also assume that you further want to reach a solution with which the other

FIGURE 4.1 **Analytical Process for the Resolution of Moral Problems**

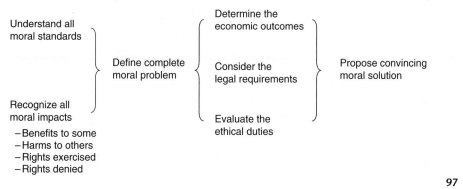

people associated with or affected by the problem can likewise feel comfortable, and agree to be as "right" and "just" and "fair" as possible. The argument of this text is that explaining your decision to reach an agreement on moral problems is fully as important as making your decision to reach a closure on those problems. How can you both make and explain your decision? There are three methods of analysis that should help you to decide and others to understand. They are summarized, once again, very briefly below:

- *Economic outcomes, based upon impersonal market forces.* This methodology was described in Chapter 2. The belief is that a manager should always act to maximize product revenues and minimize factor costs, given that all markets are competitive and all costs are included. The underlying rationale is that each firm is connected to the product markets and factor markets of the society, and individuals within the society can thus decide what products they most want to buy and what factors they least want to keep. Under those conditions, personal decisions on what is best for the individual should aggregate into market decisions as to what is best for the society. As we saw in the earlier chapter, however, there are both practical and theoretical problems with that approach. The most telling problem is that it does not fully recognize the nature or completely value the worth of individual human beings as expressed by their needs for liberty, opportunity, dignity, and respect. It certainly helps to know the economic outcomes to the society, but something more is needed.

- *Legal requirements, based upon impartial social and political processes.* This methodology was described in Chapter 3. The belief is that a manager should always obey the law, despite disagreements with some provisions of that law, for the law can be said to represent the collective moral standards of the members of our society. Each member has a set of goals, norms, beliefs, and values that are primarily derived from his or her religious and cultural traditions and his or her economic and social situations. Combined, those goals, norms, beliefs, and values form his or her moral standards. The moral standards of each individual are gradually aggregated into the legal requirements of the society through impartial social and political processes that move from informal groups to formal organizations to legal institutions. Again, there are both practical and theoretical problems with this approach; the most telling is that it does not combine all traditions and all situations equally, and some are excluded. It certainly helps to know the legal requirements of the society, but once again something more is needed.

- *Ethical duties, based upon rational thought processes.* This methodology will be described in the current chapter. Essentially the belief is that a manager should always act in accordance with a set of objective norms of behavior or universal statements of belief that are "right" and "just" and "fair" in, of, and by themselves. The norms and beliefs that all of us hold intuitively are based upon our religious and cultural traditions and our economic and social situations. They are subjective and personal; they vary among people. But there are some norms and beliefs that can be said to be objective and universal, to be based upon reason rather than emotion. These can be considered to be "right" and "just" and "fair" in, of, and by themselves because they can be logically seen to lead to a "good" society in which everyone will have liberty, opportunity, dignity, and respect. This is "moral reasoning": logically working from an objective and universal first principle through to a decision on the ethical duties we owe to others. There are some problems here also, though perhaps not as serious as in the other two approaches. Moral reasoning does recognize the nature and does value the worth of human beings as expressed by their needs for liberty, opportunity, dignity, and respect.

Moral reasoning—logically working from an objective and universal first principle through to a decision on the ethical duties we owe to others—requires an understanding of normative philosophy. It is not possible to summarize normative philosophy in a single chapter just as, quite frankly, it is not really possible to summarize economic relationships or social/political processes in a single chapter. But it is possible to convey some of the basic concepts and methods, provided the reader is interested and willing to think about them. I assume that you are interested and willing to think about these issues or you would not have gotten this far.

Definition of Normative Philosophy

Philosophy is the study of thought and conduct. Normative philosophy is the study of proper thought and conduct; that is, how we should think and behave. Normative philosophers have been looking at these issues of proper behavior for more than 2,400 years, since the time of Socrates, who lived from 470 to 399 BC. They have attempted to establish a logical thought process, based upon an incontrovertible first principle, that would determine whether an act is "right" or "wrong," "just" or "unjust," "fair" or "unfair." They have not been successful—otherwise all that would be needed would be to quote the sources and state the findings—but many of their concepts and methods can be used to expand the earlier concepts of economic outcomes and legal requirements. All hard ethical choices are compromises, between financial needs and social responsibilities in the case of a business firm, between material wants and personal duties in the case of an individual. Normative philosophy provides some help in making those compromises, but that help is not as extensive as one might wish. Here, however, is an introduction to the normative philosophy of morality and ethics.

First, there is a difference between morality and ethics. Morality refers to the standards of behavior by which people are judged, and particularly to the standards of behavior by which people are judged in their relationships with others. A person in the midst of a desert, isolated from everyone else, might act in a way that was immature, demeaning, or stupid, but he or she could not truly be said to have acted immorally since that behavior could have no impact upon others, unless it were to waste water or some other resource needed by travelers in the future.

Ethics, on the other hand, encompasses the system of beliefs that supports a particular view of morality. If I believe that a person should not smoke in a crowded room, it is because I have accepted the research findings of most scientists and the published statements of the surgeon general that tobacco smoke is harmful to health. My acceptance of those findings is my ethic for that particular situation. Ethics is normally used in the plural form because most people have a system of interrelated beliefs rather than a single opinion. This difference between morality and ethics is easy to remember if one speaks of moral standards of behavior and ethical systems of belief, and I will use those terms in this discussion.

The Concept of Ethical Relativism

The next issue to be addressed in this description of the techniques of moral reasoning is that of ethical relativism. The question here is very basic: Are there objective universal principles upon which one can construct an ethical system of belief that is applicable to all groups in all cultures at all times? Moral standards of behavior differ between groups within a single culture, between cultures, and between times. This is obvious. For example, within the contemporary United States, moral standards for decisions on environmental protection differ between the leaders of public interest groups and the executives of major industrial corporations. It is probable that these standards of environmental protection would differ even more greatly between the United States and third world countries, or between the contemporary period and the late 19th century.

The ethical systems of belief supporting the moral standards of behavior also differ; each group, in each country, in each time period, can usually give a clear explanation of the basis for its actions. To continue the earlier example, representatives of natural-resource interest groups can provide a perfectly logical reason for their support of a prohibition upon logging in old-growth forests. It preserves the recreational opportunities for future generations, they would say. Managerial personnel from a natural-resource company can offer an equally logical reason for their opposition to such a prohibition. We need the building materials for present-day housing, they would claim. Both sides base their arguments on a system of beliefs as to what is best for the national society, but unfortunately those beliefs differ. I think we can all agree that among the most irritating aspects of the debate over ethical issues such as environmental protection are the attitudes of personal self-righteousness and the implications of opponent self-interest that seem to pervade all these discussions. Both sides assume that their systems of belief are so widely held, and so obviously logical, that their opponents have to be small-minded and illiberal. They do not recognize the legitimate differences that can exist between ethical systems as to what is "right" or "just" and "fair" for the society.

The question in ethical relativism is not whether different moral standards and ethical beliefs exist; they obviously do, and we all have experiences to confirm that fact. The question is whether there is any commonality that overrides the differences. In the mixed chorus of competing moral standards and diverse ethical systems, can we discern any single principle that unifies them all? Or are we left with the weak and unsatisfactory conclusion that all ethical systems are equally valid, and that a person's choice has to be relative to his or her religious and cultural traditions and economic and social situations? If all ethical systems are equally valid, then no firm moral judgments can be made about individual behavior, and we are all on our own to do as we like to others, within economic limits and legal constraints.

Fortunately, there is one principle that does seem to exist across all groups, cultures, and times and that does form part of every ethical system: the belief that members of a group do bear some form of responsibility for the well-being of other members of that group. There is disagreement about the size of those groups and the nature of those responsibilities, but there is widespread recognition that men and women are social beings, that cooperation is necessary for survival, and that some standards of behavior are needed to ensure that cooperation. In one of the most famous statements in normative philosophy, Thomas Hobbes (1588–1679) argued (as was explained previously in Chapter 3) that if everyone acted on the basis of his or her own self-interest and ignored the well-being of others, life would be "solitary, poor, nasty, brutish, and short."

People in all cultures, even the most primitive, do not act solely for their own self-interest, and they understand that standards of behavior are needed to promote cooperation and ensure survival. These standards of behavior can be either negative—it is considered wrong to harm other members of the group—or positive—it is considered right to help other group members—but they do exist and can be traced in both sociological and anthropological studies. Consequently, the important question in moral relativism is not whether your moral standards are as good as mine; it is whether your moral standards that help other members of society are as good as mine that help other members of society.

That second question is very different from the first; it forces both of us to justify our standards relative to a principle that does extend over groups, cultures, and times. We can say that our definitions of what is "right" differ, and we can each act in accordance with those definitions and believe that we are morally correct. Yet the way in which we determine what is "right" has to be exactly the same, and has to come down to the benefit for our mutual society. That "benefit" is not necessarily material. It includes the achievement of economic outcomes, the observance of legal requirements, and the attainment of greater cooperation and cohesion. This latter benefit is the input of normative philosophy into ethical analysis and the determination of moral standards.

The fact that there can be two different moral standards, both of which can be considered to be "right," is confusing to many people. Let me try to clarify this apparent paradox with an example. We will use what I assume will be the familiar example of low-level corruption among South American import customs officials. Let us say that I am from Brazil, one of the countries in South America in which this problem is endemic, and I believe it is morally acceptable to pay small bribes to the customs agents in order to expedite import clearance and shipment to the customer. You, on the other hand, are from the United States, and you find the practice to be morally unacceptable. We differ, and though I work for you, in the same company, I don't dwell on the differences.

You come to Brazil; together we shepherd an important shipment through customs. You return to New York and tell your friends at lunch, "I had to pay." They are shocked, or would be if South American customs officials were not so notorious. I have dinner with friends that night, and tell them, "The man didn't want to pay." They are shocked, or would be if North American business practices were not often thought to be so bizarre. Both of us are right, as long as we base our standards on what we believe to be best for society. I think, "Customs agents need the money; our government sets their salary assuming that they make a small percentage." You think, "The system would work better if everyone were much more honest." Both of our standards are based upon what we believe to be best for our society; consequently both are "right."

Now, if we had the time and wanted to make the effort, we could search for a universal principle that would help us to define what we meant by "best" for our society.

And if we could measure that "best" in the achievement of economic outcomes, the observance of legal requirements, and the attainment of social cooperation, then we might be able to agree on which of our standards was more "right." We can't measure those goods in any comparable sense, so we can never really resolve that question. But we can come close.

What I am trying to explain, using this illustration, is that two different moral standards can both be believed to be "right." That is not the same thing as saying that the two different moral standards actually are "right." We have to accept the proposition that we bear some responsibility for other members of our society or life becomes very "solitary, poor, nasty, brutish, and short," for us as well as for others. That responsibility becomes the absolute upon which our ethical systems are based. The difficulty comes in defining the exact terms of that responsibility. That is the function and goal of normative philosophy. Normative philosophy can't do this, but once again it can come close because it does focus on the inherent human desires for justice, liberty, dignity, and respect.

This is somewhat in the nature of an aside, but the question of moral relativism—whether moral standards are valid across groups and cultures and times, or whether moral standards just depend upon religious/cultural traditions and economic/social situations—is sometimes applied to business firms. Albert Carr, in a famous article in the *Harvard Business Review* entitled "Is Business Bluffing Ethical" (January–February 1968), suggested that business was a "game" in which different rules apply than in everyday life. It was a game, he said, similar to poker in which no one expected the truth to be fully spoken or agreements to be completely honored. The game players know that some evasions are permitted in company statements; hearers have to be vigilant. The game players also know that some compromises can be made in company products; buyers have to be wary. There are rules that limit the evasions and compromises, but those rules are set by the players themselves and are not fully understood by the public.

It is not difficult to find evidence of this "game" approach to business. Company–union wage negotiations are seldom examples of verisimilitude. Public accountants would not be needed if all financial figures were accurately reported. There is a reason that gas pumps and grocery scales are inspected by a public agency and sealed to prevent tampering. The pictures of a product on the outside of a box frequently do not match the reality of the product on the inside of that box.

What do you think of this view of management as a game, in which almost any act is permitted that the other side does not detect and offset? This is a game in which the rules are set by the players, using their moral standards, which they then claim are "fully as good as anyone else's." How would you argue against this view? This text would suggest that you first come back to the objective and universal absolute that everyone has some responsibility for the well-being of other members of society. This is a moral standard that has been exhibited by every other culture at every other time.

You should then question whether the moral standards evidenced in the management-as-a-game approach would benefit society—as measured by the achievement of economic outcomes, the observance of legal requirements, and the realization of social cooperation—as much as would the moral standards of a different "tell the truth and don't compromise on quality" approach. It would strike me that the answer to that question was clear. We have to justify our moral standards by showing how they benefit society, not by saying that they benefit us.

Let us say that you accept the basic premise that both you and I bear some form of responsibility for other people within our society, and that our society cannot continue to exist without some standards of behavior between individuals, groups, organizations, and institutions that would benefit all of society. The question then becomes, how do we determine what those standards of behavior should be? We all have an intuitive understanding of what we believe to be "right" and "wrong." The problem is that we don't know exactly how to classify our own actions and those of our neighbors.

The universal recognition that we owe something to other people within our society and should be bound by some objective concept of "right" and "wrong" in our behavior to those people has to be made operational. That is, we have to establish some consistent analytical method to classify our actions as "right" or "wrong." If we can't, it's not for lack of trying. As mentioned before, intellectual history over the past 2,400 years has been filled with attempts to justify subjective and individual moral standards of behavior through objective and universal ethical systems of belief, or "principles." None work perfectly, but six major systems do have a direct relevance to managerial decisions: Eternal Law, Personal Virtue, Utilitarian Benefit, Universal Duty, Distributive Justice, and Personal Liberty.

The Principle of Eternal Law

The principle of Eternal Law can be summarized in the statement that we should act in the way that our Creator wanted us to act, with kindness and compassion towards others. Many church leaders and some philosophers (Thomas Aquinas and Thomas Jefferson among them) believe that there is an Eternal Law, incorporated in the mind of God, apparent in the state of Nature, revealed in the Holy Scripture or Sacred Writing of each religion, and immediately obvious to any man or woman who will take the time to study either nature or the Scripture and Sacred Writings. Thomas Jefferson, really the first of the secular humanists, believed that the truths of this law were "self-evident," in his famous phrase, that the rights were "inalienable," and that the duties could be easily derived from the rights. If people had rights to "life, liberty and the pursuit of happiness," then they had obligations to ensure those rights for others, even if this meant revolution against the British Crown. Religious leaders tend to emphasize the revealed source of the truth more than the reasoned nature, but they also believe that the state of the law is unchanging, and that the rights and duties are obvious: If we are loved, then we must love others. This reciprocal exchange is summarized in Christian theology by the Golden Rule: Do unto others as you would have others do unto you.

What is wrong with Eternal Law, or Natural Law, interpreted by either religious leaders or normative philosophers, as the basis for an ethical system in management? Nothing, except for the number of interpretations. No two Natural Law theorists, and very few religious writers, have ever been able to agree on the exact provisions of the revealed or reasoned truth. Each religion provides moral standards for its members, and many of the members observe those standards in daily life; but the standards differ between groups, and there is no way to determine which one is "right" or "just" or "fair" for the full society.

Even the Golden Rule, that simple, elegant, sensible guide to life, somehow can't be applied universally. If you were a wealthy man or woman, you would probably want to be able to retain your wealth, and you would be willing to let others retain their wealth as well. If I were a poor person, I would want others to share their benefits and income, and I in turn would be willing to share the little I had. Religious rules of conduct tend to be situation dependent; that is, our interpretation of them seems to vary with our personal circumstances. This may happen because most of our religious injunctions for moral behavior were developed many years ago in an agricultural society that had greater equality between individuals but less liberty for each person. The rules are not easily applied in an industrialized and global society where those conditions are exactly reversed.

Let me at this point add that the Golden Rule is not limited to Christianity. It is found in the Sacred Writings of almost all of the world's religions. The following is a very brief listing, in alphabetical order to ensure no preference or bias, of these totally sensible but not fully applicable statements:

- Buddhism (religious creed and ethical system of central and eastern Asia, founded about 460 BC). "Harm not others with that which pains yourself."
- Confucianism (ethical system added to the existing Chinese religious creed about 510 BC). "Loving kindness is the one maxim which ought to be acted upon throughout one's life."
- Hinduism (traditional religious creed and social system of the Indian subcontinent). "This is the sum of duty: do nothing to others which if done to you would cause you pain."
- Islam (religious creed of western and southeastern Asia, founded about AD 630). "Not one of you is a believer until you wish to everyone what you love for yourself."
- Judaism. "What is hurtful to yourself, do not do to others. That is the whole of the Torah, and the remainder is but commentary. Go and learn it."
- Taoism (religious creed and philosophic system of northern China, founded about 550 BC). "Regard your neighbor's gain as your gain, and regard your neighbor's loss as your loss."

What, then, can be said to be the ethical principle derived from Eternal Law? Obviously, it must be relevant to all religious, not just a select few. And equally obviously, it must be simple and direct. Act with kindness and compassion toward others. Create a sense of community, a belief that everyone is working together to achieve a common goal.

The Principle of Personal Virtue

The principle of personal virtue can be summarized in the statement that we should act in ways that convey a sense of honor, pride, and self-worth. We don't necessarily have to be kind and compassionate to others. We don't necessarily have to be concerned about the rights or benefits of others who are in some way beneath us on any economic, social, or political scale. We do, however, have to be honest, truthful, courageous, temperate, and high-minded. Why? Because the goal of human existence is the active, rational pursuit of excellence, and excellence requires those personal virtues.

The "rational pursuit of excellence"—a goal also often termed "knowledge of the good"—is the basis of ancient Greek philosophy. If you commit those two phrases firmly to your memory, all of the rest of the teachings of Socrates, Plato, and Aristotle will be absolutely clear to you.

Two thousand four hundred years ago in Athens, those three men began to address questions of duties and justice, and laid the foundation for the Western approach to both politics and ethics. Why in Athens, and why at that time? Greece is a mountainous peninsula, with limited agricultural land suitable for growing grain, but the climate is warm and mild, ideal for olives, grapes, and livestock. There were easy "along the coast" sea routes to Egypt, then the granary of the Eastern Mediterranean. Egypt had surplus wheat and barley for export, but needed olive oil and wine. A very prosperous trade developed between the two regions. The defeat of the invading Persian army at Marathon in 490 BC brought a period of peace in Greece that lasted for 140 years, a time that came to be known as the "Golden Age" of Athens.

Conflicts between the nobles (the ex-warriors), the merchants (the ex-sailors), and the citizens (the current residents) brought about an interest in government within Athens. An interest in government brought about schools, first to teach rhetoric (how to talk to the assembled groups), and then logic (how to convince the assembled groups). An interest in logic led to the question, "What is the good life?"

Socrates (470–399 BC) addressed this question, "What is the good life," for both individuals and societies (which, at the time, meant city-states such as Athens). Socrates wrote nothing, yet Plato recorded Socrates' discussions with other Athenians in the form of a set of dialogues soon after the death of the older man, and these can be assumed to be his thoughts if not his words.

The goal of Socrates was to develop the "first rule for a successful life." Successful then meant happy; it would probably now be translated as contented and prosperous. There could be no happiness in the pursuit of pleasure, Socrates continued, or the ownership of property, unless you knew how to use each one of those well. Knowledge of the "good" was then the goal of life. But knowledge of the "good" came from both the goodness/badness of the character and the wisdom/foolishness of the intellect. It was necessary to develop both so that everyone (nobles, merchants, and citizens) would recognize the "good" both for themselves (ethics) and for their society (politics). Ethics and politics were synonymous in Greek thinking; you could not have one without the other.

Plato (427–347 BC) focused on politics, on the need to have a "good" society in order to have a "good" life. He wrote *The Republic,* in which he focused on the concept of justice. Athens at the time, like the other city-states on the Greek peninsula, was divided into statesmen (the leaders of the citizens; they were men of thought), nobles (the warriors, who were men of courage), and merchants (the sailors, who were men of discretion). You needed all three for a "good" (again, contented and prosperous) society. "Justice" was said to be the harmonious union of all three groups of citizens, with each group excelling at what they did best and with no group interfering with the activities of any of the others.

Aristotle (384–322 BC) focused on ethics, on the need to have "good" men (and women, though women were not emphasized in the Greek philosophy nearly as much as in the Greek literature of the period) in order to have a "good" society. The goal of a society, he wrote, has to be happiness for all of the citizens. But what is happiness? Not pleasure, wealth, or fame. People are reasoning animals, he wrote, and thus happiness has to be associated with reason. Given that the active use of reason leads to excellence, then happiness has to be the pursuit of excellence. But excellence can occur on a number of different dimensions, such as openness, honesty, truthfulness, temperance (moderation), friendliness, courage, modesty, and pride. If everyone would strive for excellence on those dimensions, then all of the elements in the diverse society—statesmen, warriors, and merchants, each with different goals, activities, and interests—would work well together.

This ethical principle, that "we should be open, honest, truthful, moderate, and proud" of what we do, can be translated into very modern terms. Would you be willing to have your decisions and actions, relative to a moral problem in which some people are going to be hurt or harmed in some way, reported on the front page of a national newspaper or portrayed on the evening portion of a national news broadcast?

What is the problem with the ethical principle of personal virtue? Being "open, honest, truthful, moderate, and proud" in reality is not enough. Some people can be "open, honest, truthful, moderate, and proud" of decisions and actions that may seem to the rest of us to have been exploitive, mean, and self-centered. But these very specific dimensions of personal virtue do provide a different perspective from which to view complex moral problems, and they do seem to help in deciding when the question is, "What is the right thing to do?"

The Principle of Utilitarian Benefits

The principle of Utilitarian Benefits can be summarized in the statement that we should attempt to create the greatest net benefits for society. This is termed a teleological approach in normative philosophy. It places complete emphasis upon the outcome, not the character or intent, of individual actions. Teleology is derived from a Greek term that means "outcome" or "result," and some of the most influential philosophers in the Western tradition—including Jeremy Bentham and J. S. Mill—have held that the moral worth of personal conduct can be determined solely by the consequences of that behavior. That is, an act or decision is "right" if it results in benefits for people, and it is "wrong" if it leads to damages or harm; the objective, obviously, is to create the greatest degree of benefit while incurring the least amount of damage or harm.

The benefits can vary. Material benefits are not the only ones that count, though they are certainly a good starting place for the calculations; but friendships, knowledge, health, and the other satisfactions we all find in life should be included as well. Think in terms of satisfactions, not pleasures; focusing on pleasures can lead to a very hedonistic and self-centered approach. The aggregate satisfactions or benefits for everyone within society have to be considered.

The benefits are not all positive. There are negative costs and adverse outcomes associated with each action, and they have to be included to establish a balance. The negative costs and adverse outcomes include pain, sickness, death, ignorance, isolation, and unhappiness. The aggregate harms or costs have to be considered, and then a balance of the net consequences can be computed.

This teleological ethical system—focusing on net consequences, not on personal characteristics or individual intentions—is termed Utilitarianism, a moral philosophy originated by Jeremy Bentham (1748–1832), a British thinker. The name of the philosophy is derived from the word *utility,* which had an 18th-century meaning that referred to the degree of usefulness of a household object or a domestic animal. That is, a horse could be said to have a utility for plowing beyond the cost of its upkeep. Utility has this same meaning, and this same derivation, in economic theory; it measures our degree of preference for a given good or service relative to price. In Utilitarian theory, it measures our perception of the net benefits and harms associated with a given act.

Utilitarianism is obviously close to the economic concept of cost–benefit analysis, particularly as the benefits are not to be confused with expediency and have to be calculated for the long-term consequences as carefully as for the short-term outcomes. Utilities, both benefits and costs, have to be computed equally for everyone. My satisfactions, and my costs, cannot be considered to be more important in some way than your satisfactions and your costs. The decision rule that is then followed is to produce the greatest net benefits for society; an act is "right" if, and only if, it produces greater net benefits for society than any other act possible under the circumstances. There are, of course, problems in measuring net benefits—the combination of positive and negative outcomes associated with the act—but mathematical precision is not required; we can approximate the outcomes and include them in our calculations.

Utilitarianism differs from the economic concept of cost–benefit analysis in that the distribution of the costs and benefits has to be included as well. That is, these are net benefits to society, and each individual within the society has to be considered equally and treated equally in the distribution. "The greatest good for the greatest number" takes precedence in Utilitarian theory over "the greatest good for a smaller, more elite number" in cost–benefit analysis. Of course, in full economic theory—as discussed in Chapter 2—the allocation of costs and the distribution of benefits are controlled by impersonal market forces.

To save time and to avoid the need to compute the full consequences of every decision and action, most Utilitarians recommend the adoption of simplifying rules. These rules, such as "always tell the truth" or "never renege on a contract," can be logically shown to lead to beneficial outcomes in all foreseeable cases, but the basis for the rules remains the balance of positive and negative consequences for the full society that comes from every act or decision.

What is wrong with Utilitarianism? Not very much, except for the possibility of exploitation. In the vast majority of cases, where no one is going to be hurt very badly, and particularly where it is possible to use financial equivalents for both the costs and the benefits, it is a familiar and useful form of analysis. But, there is always the possibility of justifying benefits for the great majority of the population by imposing sacrifices or penalties on a small minority. Utilitarianism fails because in reality it is two principles: greatest good and greatest number. At some point in our decision processes on important matters, these two principles come into conflict, and then we have no single means of determining what is the "right" or "best" or "proper" act. The principle of Utilitarian Benefits fails as a determinant of moral actions because it is impossible to balance the benefits awarded to the majority against the harms imposed upon a minority.

The Principle of Universal Duties

The ethical principle of Universal Duties can be summarized in two statements. Both, as you will soon see, are felt to have exactly the same meaning. You can't apply one to a moral problem without also applying the other, but the two formulations are thought to help in understanding the single principle. The first statement is, "Take no action that you would not be willing to see that others, faced with the same or an equivalent situation, should also be free or even forced to take." The second statement is, "Treat each person as an end in himself or herself, worthy of dignity and respect, never as a means to your own ends."

This is a deontological approach to managerial ethics. In essence, it is the reverse of teleological theory. "Deontology" is derived from another Greek term; it refers to the duties or obligations of an individual. This ethical principle states that the moral worth of an action cannot be dependent upon the outcome because those outcomes are so indefinite and uncertain at the time a decision to act is made. Instead, the moral worth of an action has to depend upon the intentions of the person making the decision or performing the act. If I wish the best for others, then my moral actions are praiseworthy, even though I happen to be an ineffectual and clumsy individual who always seems to be breaking something or hurting someone. It is assumed that we are not all clumsy and ineffectual people and, therefore, that good intentions will normally result in beneficial outcomes.

Personal intentions can be translated into personal duties or obligations because, if we truly wish the best for others, then we will always act in ways to ensure those beneficial results, and those ways become duties that are incumbent upon us rather than choices that are open to us. It is our duty to tell the truth. It is our duty to adhere to contracts. It is our duty not to take property that belongs to others. Truthfulness, legality, and honesty can be logically derived from the basic principles of all ethical systems. In deontological theory they are the duties that we owe to others, while in teleological theory they are the actions that bring the greatest benefit to others.

Our personal duties are universal, applicable to everyone, and, consequently, much of deontological theory is also termed Universalism, just as large portions of teleological theory are called Utilitarianism. The first duty of Universalism is to treat others as ends and not as means. Other people should be seen as valuable ends in and by themselves, worthy of dignity and respect, and not as impersonal means to achieve other people's ends. No actions can be considered to be "right" in accordance with personal duty if they disregard the ultimate moral worth of any other human being.

Immanuel Kant (1724–1804) proposed a simple test for personal duty and goodwill, to eliminate self-interest and self-deception and to ensure regard for the moral worth of others. The test is to ask yourself whether you would be willing to have everyone in the world, faced with similar circumstances, forced to act in exactly the same way. This is the Categorical Imperative; categorical, of course, means absolute or unqualified, and the precept is that an act or decision can be judged to be "right" and "just" and "fair" only if everyone must, without qualification, perform the same act or reach the same decision, given similar circumstances.

Kant starts with the simple proposition that it is unfair for me to do something that others don't do or can't do or won't do. This is not because the total effect upon society might be harmful if everyone took the same action, such as refusing to pay taxes. That would be a utilitarian doctrine based upon outcomes rather than a universal precept based upon duties. Instead, all of us owe others the duty of acting logically and consistently. I have a "will," or a view of the way I want the world to be, and my views must be consistent or I would have a "contradiction in wills," which would not be fair to others given my duty to act logically and consistently. That is, I should pay taxes not because if everyone else did not pay taxes the government would collapse and there would be chaos. Instead, I should pay taxes because I want a world of law and order and, therefore, I must also want to provide the financial support for that law and order. Law and order and taxes are right for me if, and only if, they are right for everyone else—that is, if they are "universalizable." Kant can be understood as attempting to tie moral actions to rational decisions, with rationality defined as being based upon consistent and universal maxims. Moral standards, according to Kant, are characterized by logical consistency.

The two formulations by Kant—(1) to act only in ways that I would wish all others to act, faced with the same set of circumstances, and (2) always to treat other people with dignity and respect—can be viewed as a single injunction. The first version says that what is morally right for me must be morally right for all others. Everyone is of equal value. If this is so, then no person's rights or benefits should be subordinated to anyone else's rights or benefits. If that is so, then we must treat all people as free and equal in the pursuit of their interests, which means that they must be ends, worthy of dignity and respect, rather than means to our own ends.

Universal Duties, particularly when supported by the Categorical Imperative test, is a familiar and useful guide to moral behavior. The common law is a form of Universalism: Everyone, faced with a just debt, should pay that debt and no one, needing money, should rob banks. Company policies that have a legal or ethical content are usually Universalist: All personnel managers, in considering promotions and pay increases, should include length of service as well as individual ability; and no product manager, in setting prices, should contact competitors or agree to trade constraints.

What is wrong with the principle of Universal Duties? It is a useful method of moral reasoning, but there are no priorities and there are no degrees. I might will that law and order be absolute, with no opposition to the government outside of the formal electoral process, while you might prefer greater personal freedoms. I might will that everyone pay taxes at 7 percent of their annual income, while you might believe that a graduated income tax would be more equitable. The principle of Universal Duties is another ethical system that seems to depend upon the situation of the individual for interpretation. Even the more basic formulation of the Categorical Imperative to treat each other as moral objects, worthy of dignity and respect, provides very limited help. It is difficult to treat others as ends and not as means all the time, particularly when so many people do serve willingly as means to our personal ends: Storekeepers are means of procuring our dinners; customers are means of earning our livelihoods; employees are means of staffing our factories. Both formulations of the Categorical Imperative have to be filled in with either Utilitarian Benefits (I should want some rule to be a universal law if the consequences of its adoption would be beneficial to others) or with Personal Virtues (I should want some rule to be universalized if I can be open, honest, truthful, and proud of its adoption). But those additives have to come from outside the formal Universal Duty concepts.

The Principle of Distributive Justice

The principle of Distributive Justice can be summarized in one simple statement: Never take any action that would harm the least among us, those with least income, education, wealth, competence, influence, or power. We don't have to help those people in the lower ranks of our society to any great extent; we just should never harm them.

None of the three classical theories—Personal Virtues, Utilitarian Benefits, and Universal Duties—can be used to judge all moral actions under all circumstances, and consequently two modern ethical systems have been developed based upon the primacy of a single concept rather than the advocacy of a single rule. The first of these, the principle of Distributive Justice, has been proposed by John Rawls, a member of the Harvard faculty. It is explicitly based upon the primacy of a single concept: justice. Justice is felt to be the first value of social institutions, just as truth is the first value of belief systems. Rawls explained that our beliefs, no matter how useful and complete, have to be rejected or revised if they are found to be untrue. In the same fashion our norms, no matter how efficient or accepted, must be reformed or abolished if they are found to be unjust.

Professor Rawls proposes that society is an association of individuals who cooperate to advance the good of all. At the same time, society and the institutions within it are marked by conflict as well as by collaboration. The collaboration comes about since individuals recognize that joint actions generate much greater benefits than solitary efforts. The conflict is inherent because people are concerned by the just distribution of those benefits. Each person prefers a greater to a lesser share and proposes a system of distribution to ensure that greater share. These distributive systems can have very different bases: to each person equally, or to each according to his or her need, to his or her effort, to his or her contribution, or to his or her competence. Most modem economic systems make use of all five principles: Public education is, theoretically, distributed equally, while welfare payments are on the basis of need, sales commissions on the basis of effort, public honors on the basis of contribution, and managerial salaries on the basis of competence.

Professor Rawls believes that all of these assorted distributive systems are unjust. He suggests that the primacy of justice in the basic structure of our society requires greater equality. Free and rational persons, he suggests, would recognize the obvious benefits of cooperation and, concerned about the just distribution of those benefits, would accept social and economic inequalities only if they could be shown to result in compensating benefits for everyone. "Everyone," particularly, should include the least advantaged members of our society: poor, unskilled, and with native intelligence but little education or training. According to Rawls, I would not object to your having more of the social and economic benefits of cooperation than I do, but I would not work hard, beyond the minimum level of effort required to maintain my present standard of living, just so that you could have more. I would want to share in that "more," or—at the very least— I would want to be assured that I would not lose the little I already had.

It is not hard to find evidence of this attitude within our society, so the theory of Distributive Justice does appear to have considerable empirical support. Professor Rawls, however, starts not with our society, but with society in a "natural state." This is the Veil of Ignorance existence at the beginning of time when people were still ignorant of the exact nature of the differences among them, when no one knew who was the most talented, the most energetic, the most competent or—for that matter—the most grasping. What reciprocal arrangement, he asks, would people under those conditions make for the just distribution of the benefits produced by their cooperation? This is the familiar idea of the Social Contract, and the basic question is, What principles would free and rational persons, concerned with furthering their own interests yet wishing to maintain the cooperative efforts of all, adopt as defining the fundamental terms of their association?

They would not select absolute equality in the distribution of benefits, Professor Rawls argues, because they would recognize that some of them would put forth greater efforts, have greater skills, develop greater competencies, and so on. They would not agree to absolute inequality based upon effort, skill, or competence because they would not know who among them had those qualities and who lacked them, and consequently who among them would receive the greater and the lesser shares. Instead, they would develop a concept of conditional inequality, where differences in benefits had to be justified, and they would propose a rule that those differences in benefits could be justified only if they could be shown to result in compensating benefits for everyone. "Everyone," once again, would have to include the least advantaged members of society. That is, the distribution of income would be unequal, but the inequalities would have to work for the benefit of all, and they could be shown to work for the benefit of all if it was obvious that they helped in some measure the least advantaged among us. If those people were helped in some small measure, or at least stayed the same, then it would seem clear that everyone else benefited to some greater extent, and then everyone would cooperate to produce even larger benefits.

Distributive Justice can be expanded from an economic system for the distribution of benefits to an ethical system for the evaluation of behavior in that acts can be considered to be "right" and "just" and "fair" if they lead to greater cooperation by all members of our society. What are the problems with this concept of distributive justice? It is entirely dependent upon an acceptance of the proposition that social cooperation provides the basis for all economic and social benefits. Individual effort is downplayed, if not ignored. We all recognize that certain organized activities can never take place unless some one individual is willing to take the risks and responsibilities of starting and directing those activities. That individual effort is ignored in Distributive Justice: It forms the basis, however, for the sixth and last ethical principle to be discussed.

The Principle of Contributive Liberty

The principle of Contributive Liberty can be also be summarized in one simple statement. Never take any action that would interfere with the rights of everyone—not just the poor, the uneducated and the weak—to develop their skills to the fullest. We don't have to help people. We just can never interfere with their attempting to help themselves.

The theory of Contributive Liberty (the phrase is my own, developed to contrast with Distributive Justice) is an ethical system proposed by Robert Nozick, also currently a member of the Harvard faculty. This system is another based upon the primacy of a single value, rather than a single rule, but that value is liberty rather than justice. Liberty is thought to be the first requirement of society. An institution or law that violates individual liberty, even though it may result in greater happiness and increased benefits for others, has to be rejected as being unjust for all.

Professor Nozick agrees that society is an association of individuals, and that cooperation between those individuals is necessary for economic gain, but he would argue that the cooperation comes about as a result of the exchange of goods and services. The holdings of each person, in income, wealth, and the other bases of self-respect, are derived from other people in exchange for some good or service, or are received from other people in the form of a gift. An existing pattern of holdings may have come about through application of any of the principles of distribution. These would be (1) to each equally, or to each according to (2) need, (3) effort, (4) contribution, or (5) competence. The patterns of holdings can be changed by transfers and those transfers by exchange or gift can be considered to be "just" as long as they are voluntary. Nonvoluntary exchanges or gifts, based upon the use of social force or other coercive means, would clearly be unjust.

Contributive Liberty can be expanded from essentially a market system for the exchange of holdings to an ethical system for the evaluation of behavior as long as individuals are allowed to make informed choices among alternative courses of action leading toward their own welfare. Those choices could be considered to be "right" and "just" and "fair" as long as the same opportunities for informed choices were extended to others. Justice, then, depends upon equal opportunities for choice and exchange, not upon equal allocations of wealth and income. What is wrong with this concept of liberty? It is based upon a very narrow definition of liberty that is limited to the negative right not to suffer interference from others; there may also be a positive right to receive some of the benefits enjoyed by others. That is, the right to life is certainly the right not to be killed by your neighbors, but it may also include the right to continue living through access to some minimal level of food, shelter, clothing, and medical assistance. And it is assumed that the food, shelter, clothing, and medical assistance are produced through personal initiative, not through social cooperation.

Conclusions on the Principles of Normative Philosophy

There are six major ethical systems, as summarized in Figure 4.2. They do not outwardly conflict with each other. An action such as lying that is considered "wrong" in one ethical system will generally be considered "wrong" in all others, but these ethical systems cannot be reconciled into a single logically consistent whole. Eventually conflict will arise over the primacy of the alternative norms and beliefs. Each ethical system expresses a portion of the truth. Each system has adherents and opponents. And each, it is important to admit, is incomplete or inadequate as a means of judging the true moral content of managerial decisions and actions.

The major implication for managers of this listing is that there is no single system of belief, with rationally derived standards of moral behavior or methods of moral reasoning, that can guide executives fully in reaching "proper" ethical decisions when confronting difficult moral problems. A moral problem, to repeat the earlier definition and sharpen the present discussion, is one that will harm others in ways that are beyond their own control. A decision to introduce a new brand of chocolate cake mix has no moral dimensions since others within the society are perfectly free to buy or to ignore the product. But a decision

FIGURE 4.2 Summary of Beliefs and Problems in the Five Major Ethical Systems

	Nature of the Ethical Systems of Belief	Problems in the Ethical Systems of Belief
Eternal Law	Moral standards are given in an Eternal Law, which is revealed in writings or apparent in nature and then interpreted by religious leaders or humanist philosophers. The belief is that everyone should act in accordance with the interpretation of the Law.	There are multiple interpretations of the Law, but no method to choose among them beyond human rationality, and human rationality needs an absolute principle or value as the basis for choice.
Personal Virtue	Moral standards are applied to the character of the person taking an action or making a decision. The principle is that everyone should act in a way in which they can be open, honest, truthful, and proud.	Some people can feel proud and be willing to be open, honest, and truthful about actions that many other people believe to be absolutely "wrong."
Utilitarian Benefits	Moral standards are applied to the outcome of an action or decision. The principle is that everyone should act to generate the greatest benefits for the largest number of people.	Immoral acts can be justified if they provide substantial benefits for the majority, even at an unbearable cost or harm to the minority; an additional principle or value is needed to balance the benefit–cost equation.
Universal Duties	Moral standards are applied to the intent of an action or decision; the principle is that everyone should act to ensure that similar decisions would be reached by others, given similar circumstances.	Immoral acts can be justified by persons who are prone to self-deception or self-importance, and there is no scale to judge between "wills." Additional principle or value is needed to refine the Categorical Imperative concept.
Distributive Justice	Moral standards are based upon the primacy of a single value, which is justice. Everyone should act to ensure a more equitable distribution of benefits, for this promotes individual self-respect, which is essential for social cooperation.	The primacy of the value of justice is dependent upon acceptance of the proposition that an equitable distribution of benefits ensures social cooperation.
Contributive Liberty	Moral standards are based upon the primacy of a single value, which is liberty. Everyone should act to ensure greater freedom of choice, for this promotes market exchange, which is essential for social productivity.	The primacy of the value of liberty is dependent upon acceptance of the proposition that a market system of exchange ensures social productivity.

to close the plant producing the cake mix, or to use a high-cholesterol shortening in the production of that mix, or to ask for government help in shutting off imports competitive to that mix, would have a moral content. Those actions do have an impact upon others. A product manager, faced, let us say, in an unlikely but perhaps not totally unrealistic problem of imported cake mixes from a foreign country that has very low wage rates and very high government subsidies, has to respond, and each response has moral implications. Lowering production means cutting employment, reducing the cost means compromising the quality, and requesting government help means endorsing restrictions.

There is no single system of belief to guide managers in reaching "proper" ethical decisions to difficult moral problems, but this does not mean that all of us are on our own, to do as we like in our decisions and actions that affect others. We do have obligations to other people. We cannot ignore those obligations. The difficulty comes in identifying our obligations and then in evaluating our alternatives, with no single set of moral standards to guide us.

What should we do? Instead of using just one ethical system, which we must admit is imperfect, we have to use all six systems and think through the consequences of our actions on multiple dimensions. Is this decision one of which we can be open, honest, truthful, and proud, or do we have to hide it and hope that no one notices? Is this action kind and compassionate, and does it lead to a greater sense of community, of brotherhood/sisterhood? Does this decision or action result in greater benefits than damages for society as a whole, not just for our organization as part of that society? Is this decision self-serving, or would we be willing to have everyone else take the same action when faced with the same or similar circumstances? We understand the need for social cooperation; will our decision increase or decrease the willingness of others to contribute? We recognize the importance of personal freedom; will our decision increase or decrease the liberty of others to act?

Moral reasoning of this nature, utilizing all six ethical systems, is not simple and easy, but it is satisfying. It does work. It works particularly well when combined with the economic outcomes and legal requirements forms of analysis. That combination, and its organizational consequences, will be the topic of Chapter 5, "Why Should a Business Manager Be Moral?"

Case 4-1

Susan Shapiro and Workplace Dangers

Susan Shapiro had an undergraduate degree in chemistry from Smith College, a master's degree in chemical engineering from M.I.T., three years' service as a sergeant in the Israeli army, and an MBA from the University of Michigan. The following is a nearly verbatim account of her experiences during the first month of employment with a large chemical company in New York.

> We spent about three weeks in New York City, being told about the structure of the company and the uses of the products, and then they took us down to Baton Rouge to look at a chemical plant. You realize that most of the MBAs who go to work for a chemical company have very little knowledge of chemistry. There were 28 of us who started in the training program that year, and the others generally had undergraduate degrees in engineering or economics. I don't know what you learn by looking at a chemical plant, but they flew us down South, put us up at a Holiday Inn, and took us on a tour of their plant the next day.
>
> As part of the tour, we were taken into a drying shed where an intermediate chemical product was being washed with benzine and then dried. The cake was dumped in a

rotating screen and sprayed with benzine, which was then partially recovered by a vacuum box under the screen. However, the vacuum box technology is out of date now, and never did work very well. Much of the solvent evaporated within the shed, and the atmosphere was heavy with the fumes despite the "open air" type of construction.

Benzine is a known carcinogen; there is a direct, statistically valid correlation between benzine and leukemia and birth defects. The federal standard is 10 parts per million, and a lab director would get upset if you let the concentration get near 100 parts for more than a few minutes, but in the drying shed it was over 1,000. The air was humid with the vapor, and the eyes of the men who were working in the area were watering. I was glad to get out, and we were only in the drying shed about three minutes.

I told the foreman who was showing us around—he was a big, burly man with probably 30 years' experience—that the conditions in the shed were dangerous to the health of the men working there, but he told me, "Lady, don't worry about it. That is a sign-on-job (a job to which newly hired employees are assigned until they build up their seniority so that they can transfer to more desirable work). We've all done it, and it hasn't hurt any of us."

That night, back at the motel, I went up to the director of personnel who was in charge of the training program and told him about the situation. He was more willing to listen than the foreman, but he said essentially the same thing. "Susan, you can't change the company in the first month. Wait awhile; understand the problems, but don't be a trouble-maker right at the start."

The next morning everybody else flew back to New York City. I stayed in Baton Rouge and went to see the plant manager. I got to his office by 8:00, and explained to his secretary why I wanted to see him. He was already there, at work, and he came out to say that he was "up against it that morning" and had no time to meet with me. I said, "Fine, I'll wait."

I did wait, until after lunchtime. Then he came up to me and said he didn't want to keep tripping over me every time he went in and came out of his office, and if I would just go away for awhile, he would promise to see me between 4:30 and 5:00.

It was 5:15 when he invited me to "come in and explain what has you so hot and bothered." I told him. He said that he certainly knew what I was talking about, and that every year he put a capital request into the budget to fix the problem, but that it always came back rejected—"probably by some MBA staff type" were his words—because the project could not now show an adequate return on investment, and because the present process was technically "open air" and, therefore, not contrary to OSHA regulations.

I started to explain that OSHA never seemed to know what it was doing—which is true, in my opinion—but he stopped me. He said he was leaving to pick up his family because his daughter was playing in a Little League baseball game at 6:30, and then they would have supper at McDonald's. He said I could go along, if I didn't mind sitting next to his five-year-old son "who held the world's record for the number of consecutive times he has spilled his milk in a restaurant." He was a very decent man, working for a very indecent company.

I told him I would go back to New York, and see what I could do. He did wish me "good luck," but he also asked me not to get him personally involved because he thought that "insisting upon funding for a project that won't meet targeted rates of return is a surefire way to be shown the door marked exit in large black letters." "The senior people up there are going to tell you that it's legal," he continued, "and you know, unfortunately, they're going to be right." (Verbal statement of Susan Shapiro, a disguised name, to the case writer)

Class Assignment

What would you do in this situation? You can either continue the campaign to change the benzine drying process or not. If you decide to continue, prepare a presentation that you would make to the "senior executives up there who are going to tell you that it's legal, and unfortunately they're right." If you decide to stop, be prepared to explain that decision to a close friend who wants to help you but also believes strongly in environmental protection and workplace safety. Remember, your career in the company may be at stake. It is suggested strongly that you use the analytical method that is the basis of this text, and that you examine the economic benefits, the legal requirements, and the ethical duties:

- *Economic benefits.* Always take the action that generates the greatest profits for the company because this will generate the greatest benefits for the society, provided that all markets are fully competitive, all customers are fully informed, and all external and internal costs are fully included.

- *Legal requirements.* Always take the action that most fully complies with the law, for the law in a democratic society represents the minimal moral standards of all of the people within that society, provided it can be shown that the self-interests of the various groups have been truly combined in the formulation process. The simple test of this prescription is "Would everyone accept this law under the conditions of the Social Contract or the Veil of Ignorance where no one knew what their self-interests actually were and consequently how they would personally be affected?"

- *Ethical duties.* Always take the action (1) that you would be willing to see widely reported in national newspapers, (2) that you believe will build a sense of community among everyone associated with the action, (3) that you expect will generate the greatest net good for the full society, (4) that you believe all others should be free or even forced to take in roughly similar situations, (5) that does not harm the "least among us," and (6) that does not interfere with anyone's right to develop their skills to the fullest.

Case 4-2

Wal-Mart and Expansion into Smaller Towns

Wal-Mart in 1994 was the world's largest retailer, operating a chain of modern discount stores throughout the United States and beginning to expand abroad. It had started as a single shop selling work clothes and household items in Bentonville, Arkansas, in 1969, but grew rapidly to a total of 2,136 stores handling a wide variety of consumer goods at the date of the case. The annual return to the shareholders since the 1980 listing on the New York Stock Exchange has averaged 32 percent; $10,000 invested at that time was worth $487,000 in 1994. The founder, Sam Walton, was known for his "folksy" approach to employees, customers, and stockholders alike. He drove a pickup truck to work through all the years of his company's growth and was the wealthiest person in the United States at the time of his death in 1993.

The success of the Wal-Mart chain has been extensively studied, and its outstanding financial performance is said to be based upon six strategic concepts that combine to produce large sales volumes and low operating costs at each of the stores:

- *Wide selection.* The typical Wal-Mart carries 35,000 items, about 35 percent more than the number handled by other discount chains such as K-Mart or national retailers such as Sears.
- *Low pricing.* The typical Wal-Mart has a price structure that is 5 to 8 percent lower than other discount chains and 15 to 20 percent below the national retailers.
- *Niche placement.* The typical Wal-Mart store is located in a rural community, with very low taxes, wages, and land costs, but then draws upon a large customer base in a 30-mile radius.
- *Accurate data.* Wal-Mart was the first large retail organization to build an online, real-time information system for prompt sales analysis and precise inventory control.
- *Direct shipment.* Wal-Mart shares their sales and inventory data by store with suppliers, who arrange for direct restocking without intermediate warehousing.
- *Central purchasing.* Wal-Mart purchases all items for all stores through a central buying unit that offers long-term, large-scale contracts in return for very low prices.

The large selections and low prices bring customers from relatively long distances, and consequently Wal-Mart generally develops a strip mall with a large grocery store as the other "anchor" tenant, and adds fast-food restaurants and specialty shops selling noncompeting items in between the two main chains, to concentrate shoppers at a "one-stop" location and collect rents from the other merchants. The strip mall is generally built as an interconnected line of single-story concrete block buildings with bare steel truss roofs, filled with 250,000 to 360,000 square feet of packed display shelves, and surrounded by 12 to 15 acres of asphalted parking lots and illuminated advertising signs. The resultant mall is huge. It is cheap. It may be unattractive but it is efficient. And it is often resisted by local people for all four of those reasons.

The resistance is concentrated, of course, among the local merchants in the downtown areas of the local communities who are concerned about their loss of business to the new complex if it is built. The local merchants are often joined by property owners and vacation visitors who are more worried about the shoddy appearance of the mall and its impact upon their traditional way of life. Together, these groups make the following points in their arguments:

- The downtown section will be "ruined" as the small, locally owned stores will be forced to close; they simply cannot compete against the economies of scale of Wal-Mart.
- The landscape also will be "ruined"; the large-scale architecture and huge parking lot of the new malls simply don't "look right" in an attractive rural setting.
- The vacation appeal may not be ruined, but certainly will be harmed; people don't want to drive hundreds of miles to find the same urban sprawl they left behind.
- The tax base will be altered; downtown businesses typically pay a large percentage of the town taxes. Once those businesses close, the burden shifts to the home owners.
- The job base will also be altered; downtown businesses and vacation resorts provide most of the local employment. Changes here could be disastrous.

The traditional response of Wal-Mart has been that they provide lower prices and better selections for local consumers, who are consequently much better off, and that the taxes they pay and the jobs they offer more than make up for whatever taxes and jobs are lost when local businesses close. Wal-Mart does not dispute that local businesses will close; their avowed aim is to dominate local retailing within every area in which they operate. In the few instances where that has not happened, Wal-Mart has simply closed the store and abandoned the mall. Numerous economic studies have confirmed the probable retail dominance; a new Wal-Mart strip mall will generally result in the closing of 35 to 40 local businesses within two to three years, which are usually boarded up rather than replaced. Those same economic studies show that the Wal-Mart strip mall does not quite make up for employment and tax losses, falling about 20 to 25 percent behind in both categories, also within the first two to three years.

A number of citizen groups in Petoskey, Michigan, have been particularly adamant in opposing a recently announced plan by Wal-Mart to build a large (360,000 square foot of retail space) mall on 67 acres of farm land the company owns adjacent to Route 131, the southern entrance into town. Petoskey is an old and picturesque village situated directly on the shore of Lake Michigan, about 30 miles south of the Straits of Mackinac at the top of the lower peninsula.

Petoskey was originally the site of a trading post and mission school for Indians. Development was slow until the arrival of the railroad in 1870. During the next 25 years Petoskey grew rapidly as a resort area, due to the inherent attractiveness of the region, easily reached by lake steamers or passenger trains from Grand Rapids, Kalamazoo, and Chicago. By 1985 there were 24 hotels and boarding houses, together with a thriving business district, all built with distinctive red brick architecture. The Methodist Church, which had run the mission school, converted their property to an educational camp for families, and added numerous cottages, lecture halls, concert facilities, and a down-town park along the waterfront. Gas lights installed at this time still operated in 1994. Restaurants and shops were intermingled, and customers tended to stroll the downtown area in the evening in an evocation of earlier days in small town America.

Some factories for food processing—the climate and soil close to the shore have long been known for producing superior fruits and vegetables—and furniture manufacturing using hardwood lumber from the nearby forests were started in the southern part of the town in the early 1900s, but those had mostly closed by the latter half of the century. A very small K-Mart had been built in one of the abandoned factories, but Wal-Mart had refused to consider that as an alternative due to the lack of parking, the inadequate space for product storage, and the inherent inefficiency caused by older, multiple-storied buildings.

Petoskey in 1995 was a prosperous, attractive town with a year-round population of 3,500 people that served as the trading center for Emmet County, which had a permanent population of 23,700 more. There were also 15,200 summer residents who owned property within the county, primarily along the shore, close to Petoskey. The area was almost totally dependent upon tourism during both the summer and winter; numerous golf courses and ski areas had been built close to the lake during the 1960s and 1970, and these facilities attracted a constant stream of short-term visitors.

Technically it was illegal for Wal-Mart to build upon the farmland that they owned, which had been zoned for farm, residential, or "light" commercial use. No one had ever anticipated that a large mall might be built on that site, though it was one of the few that was flat enough for commercial construction within the region. The original intent had been that the farmers might want to set up roadside stands to sell vegetables; that was the reason for the lenient zoning restrictions, to make it easier for the local farmers to survive. Courts, however, tended to interpret "light" commercial use broadly, and Wal-Mart was known for aggressive legal tactics, using large numbers of corporate attorneys in continuous hearings, suits, and appeals to simply override opposition. Small towns did not have the resources to oppose that effort. Vermont had successfully opposed Wal-Mart's entry into scenic or historic areas, but there zoning restrictions were both set and upheld by the state, not by the community.

Surveys of the Petoskey and Emmet County population bases have brought mixed results. A market research study conducted by an agency for Wal-Mart found that 47 percent of permanent residents in Petoskey and 62 percent of permanent residents in Emmet County approved of the concept of a new discount store for the obvious reasons: wider selections and lower prices. Ninety-three percent of summer residents throughout the area opposed the plan. Opposition leaders took photographs of an existing Wal-Mart strip mall in southern Michigan and of the boarded up central shopping district in that same town five years after the mall opened, displayed 24-in. × 36-in. enlargement of those photos in the lakeside park of Petoskey under the printed question "Do you want this urban sprawl in our town?" and gathered 22,000 signatures opposing the project over just a three-week period.

Class Assignment

You are the Michigan district manager for Wal-Mart. Petoskey is one of the few remaining "untapped" areas in the state; the nearest Wal-Mart stores are 45 to 60 miles away, at Gaylord to the east and Mackinac City to the north. At both locations store closings and the decay of the central business district did follow the introduction of the discount chain; neither, however, is a tourist destination so that the impact upon tourism can't really be measured and then applied to Petoskey. You have just received the appeal, signed by 22,000 people, saying "Please don't destroy our town; we love it just the way it is." What do you do, and why?

Do realize that it will not be easy to find an alternative site near the town. This is an area of steep hills and low mountains; there is little flat land close to the lake, and much of that has been taken for the numerous golf courses and summer homes. There are a number of suitable sites, large enough for the planned mall and flat enough for the needed construction, inland about 12 miles, but that is the area of lowest population density. Most people in Petoskey village and Emmet County, permanent residents and summer visitors alike, live close to the shoreline. Driving inland those 12 miles might create a problem for the permanent residents during the winter for this is an area of heavy snowfall.

Also realize that you will have to explain your decision, either to the corporate executives at Wal-Mart headquarters in Arkansas (if you do not build) or to the residents of Petoskey (if you do build). It is suggested strongly that you use the analytical method that is the basis of this text, and that you examine the economic benefits, the legal requirements and the ethical duties of the proposed expansion:

- *Economic benefits.* Always take the action that generates the greatest profits for the company because this will generate the greatest benefits for the society, provided that all markets are fully competitive, all customers are fully informed, and all external and internal costs are fully included.

- *Legal requirements.* Always take the action that most fully complies with the law, for the law in a democratic society represents the minimal moral standards of all of the people within that society, provided it can be shown that the self-interests of the various groups have been truly combined in the formulation process. The simple test of this prescription is "Would everyone accept this law under the conditions of the Social Contract or the Veil of Ignorance where no one knew what their self-interests actually were and consequently how they would personally be affected?"
- *Ethical duties.* Always take the action (1) that you would be willing to see widely reported in national newspapers, (2) that you believe will build a sense of community among everyone associated with the action, (3) that you expect will generate the greatest net good for the full society, (4) that you believe all others should be free or even forced to take in roughly similar situations, (5) that does not harm the "least among us," and (6) that does not interfere with anyone's right to develop their skills to the fullest.

Case 4-3

What Do You Owe to Yourself?

There are two major themes expressed within the first four chapters of this book. The first of these major themes is that everyone has a different set of subjective moral standards, or intuitive gauges of what is "right" or "wrong," "fair" or "unfair," "just" or "unjust." These standards and/or gauges are different because they are based upon the religious and cultural traditions and the economic and social situations of the individuals involved and are derived from the goals, norms, beliefs, and values of those individuals. This was earlier depicted in a graphic that is repeated in Figure 4.3.

The second of the two major themes emphasized within the first four chapters of this book is that—given that everyone has a different view of the moral standards which they use to judge their own behavior and the behavior of other people—we must clearly identify the benefits to some and the harms to others, the rights exercised by some and the rights denied to others, of managerial decisions and actions, and then use economic

FIGURE 4.3   **Individual Determinants of Moral Standards**

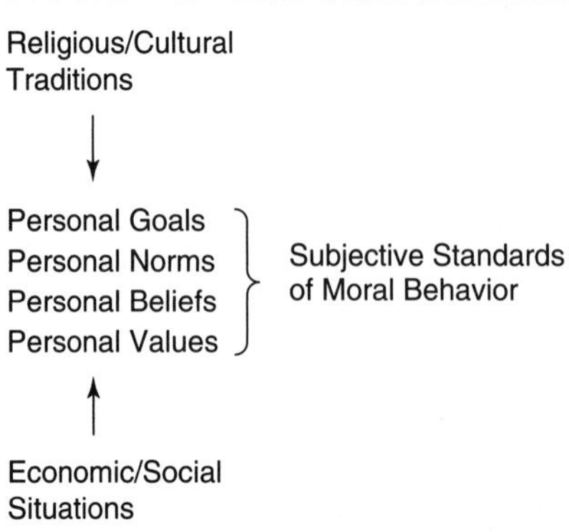

Religious/Cultural
Traditions

↓

Personal Goals ⎫
Personal Norms ⎪   Subjective Standards
Personal Beliefs ⎬   of Moral Behavior
Personal Values ⎭

↑

Economic/Social
Situations

FIGURE 4.4   **Analytical Process for the Resolution of Moral Problems**

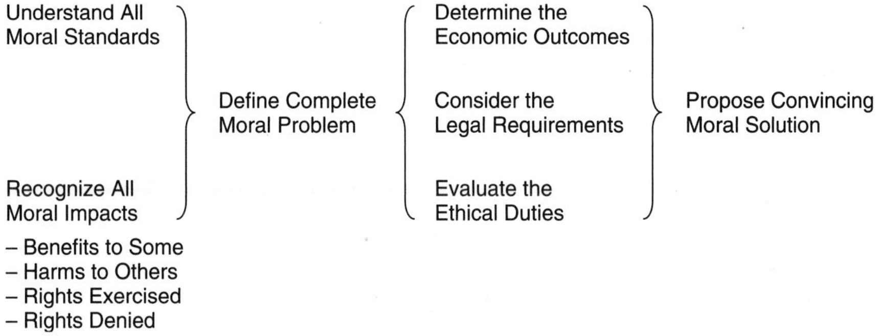

Understand All
Moral Standards

Define Complete
Moral Problem

Recognize All
Moral Impacts
– Benefits to Some
– Harms to Others
– Rights Exercised
– Rights Denied

Determine the
Economic Outcomes

Consider the
Legal Requirements

Evaluate the
Ethical Duties

Propose Convincing
Moral Solution

outcomes, legal requirements, and ethical principles to propose a *convincing* moral solution. This also was earlier depicted in a graphic that is repeated in Figure 4.4 above.

There is, however, one thing that has been left out of this analysis and those exhibits. Essentially you have looked at what you owe to others—workers, customers, and
owners—within your company, and at what you owe to others—local residents, national
citizens, and global inhabitants—within your society. But you haven't looked at what
you owe to yourself.

What do you owe to yourself? More money? More authority? More leisure? Maybe
your duties to yourself are more complex than just thinking about those three "goods,"
using that word in the classic sense meaning properties that almost everyone in the
world would like to have a little more of, for here you quickly run into the equally classic question "how much is enough?"

Maybe what you really owe to yourself is success in life. But then you have to define
what you mean by "success." The purpose of this short and unusual "case" is to ask you
to start to think about what you want from your life, what you believe would constitute
a successful life for you, one well worth living, one that might include more than just
money, authority, and leisure. There are five basic arguments I would like to make in
pursuing this exercise:

1. Most people do want more out of life than just additional money, authority, and leisure. There is a wide range of personal goals, with variable baselines (how much is
   enough) for each.
2. Selecting among those personal goals and establishing subjective baselines for each
   essentially define who that person is, what he or she stands for, and what constitutes
   his or her "character."
3. A person who knows what he or she stands for, and is known by others for his or her
   character, will be much more effective at resolving the inevitable conflicts between
   company, society and self. Why? People will know where that person is coming
   from.
4. A person who is more effective at resolving the inevitable conflicts between company, society, and self will be more successful at achieving his or her goals and,
   consequently, more successful in his or her life. In short, these factors are interrelated, as shown in Figure 4.5.

FIGURE 4.5 Your Definition of Success in Your Life

What do you owe
to yourself?

What are your
goals & values
and thus your
definition of
success in life?

What do you owe
to your employer?

What do you owe
to your society?

5. The Greek philosophers to whom you have been introduced in this last chapter—Socrates, Plato, and Aristotle—said that you should search not for success (happiness) in life, but for excellence in life. Maybe that is worth considering in management as well as in life.

Class Assignment

This is a very different case and assignment. It is also the last case following the last chapter in the section of this text that deals with the means by which you decide what you believe to be "right" and "just" and "fair" for everyone, or—to use the Greek terminology—what you believe to be "excellent" for your organization, your society, and your self. The next chapter in this book concerns the pragmatic effects of such moral, or "excellent," decisions and actions upon others within your organization and your society (do the diverse members actually cooperate more for the benefit of all if they believe they individually have been treated in ways that are "right" and "just" and "fair"?), and the last chapter in the book describes the practical means of spreading such excellent moral attitudes and—hopefully—such deliberately cooperative actions throughout the firm and the society.

The following questions ask you to consider what you value in life, what your believe would lead you to consider that your life has been successful. Clearly it would be inappropriate to discuss these very personal matters in a very public classroom. I assume, therefore, if your instructor decides to use this different—and difficult—case in class, that he or she will either set up a Web site where you can respond anonymously, or pass out printed forms where you can record your answers, also anonymously. The intent, once again, is not to discuss *in detail* the personal goals of specific members within the class. The intent instead is to show *in total* the wide variety of personal goals and values that exist among those different members of the class and to begin thinking about how those differences might be resolved. In short, the intent is to talk about what excellence in management might mean.

Start by thinking about your own goals, norms, beliefs, and values. What do you want to achieve in life? What is important to you? Select your personal goals in money, lifestyle, position, performance, reputation, family, and church from the following listing. Add your social values on independence, interdependence, protection of the poor, equality among individuals, improvement of the environment, and peace between nations. In my view this determination of your goals, norms, beliefs, and values, and your definition of success in your life, is worth considering for at least one class session while you are in college or at graduate school.

Determine your goals and values by ranking each category from 6 (highest in your priority) to 1 (lowest in your ranking). You may have as many 3s and 4s as you want, but limit yourself to one 6, which is then your most important goal or value, and to two 5s, which are your next most important goals and values. Pick at least one 1, which is your least important goal or value, and two 2s, which are also far down on your list of priorities. Put your choices on a home page set up by your instructor, or on an unsigned, and thus anonymous, form provided by your instructor.

Remember, 6 is the highest in importance in your opinion, 1 is the lowest, and you are limited to one 6 and two 5s, and to one 1 and two 2s:

1. Increases in my wealth, and the power, possessions, and lifestyle that go with money, are important to me: 1   2   3   4   5   6

2. Promotions in my company, and the authority and privileges that go with advancement, are important to me: 1   2   3   4   5   6

3. Performance in my job, and the security and respect that go with achievement, are important to me: 1   2   3   4   5   6

4. Reputation within my community, and the political offices and social activities that go with prominence, are important to me: 1   2   3   4   5   6

5. Attention to my family, and the affection and companionship that go with family life, are important to me: 1   2   3   4   5   6

6. Devotion to my church, and the sense of community and sharing that are part of most religions, are important to me: 1   2   3   4   5   6

7. Independence in my personal life, and the ability to achieve my own goals and follow my own rules, are important to me: 1   2   3   4   5   6

8. Interdependence with my fellow human beings, and the opportunity to set social goals and adopt mutual rules, are important to me: 1   2   3   4   5   6

9. Protection of the poor, and the need to help others within our society who have been less fortunate than I, are important to me: 1   2   3   4   5   6

10. Equality among races, genders, and ethnic groups, and the need to offer courtesy, respect, and opportunity for all, are important to me: 1   2   3   4   5   6

11. Improvement of the environment, and the need to show greater restraint in the exploitation of the earth's resources, are important to me: 1   2   3   4   5   6

12. Peace between nations, and the need to end oppression of any of the earth's peoples, are important to me: 1   2   3   4   5   6

Chapter 5

Why Should a Business Manager Be Moral?

We have looked at economic outcomes (Chapter 2), legal requirements (Chapter 3), and ethical duties (Chapter 4) as means of resolving the moral problems of management, and have found that none are completely satisfactory. None of those analytical methods can give us an answer that we can say with absolute certainty is "right" and "just" and "fair" when attempting to find the proper balance between the financial outputs and the social impacts of a business firm. And none of those analytical methods can give us a means of truly convincing the other people who have been affected by those outputs and impacts that our decision was indeed the "most right," the "most just," and the "most fair" in attempting to reach that balance.

But why is this important? Why should a manager attempt to be moral in his or her decisions and actions? And, particularly, why should a manager attempt to convince other people that he or she has reached the "most right," "most just," and "most fair" decision among all of the available alternatives? Perhaps we should all simply resolve not to lie, cheat, or steal, and then begin to look after the interests of the firm that has hired us to the very best of our abilities. Then we could forget about any need to be moral beyond those elementary "don't lie, cheat, or steal" rules, and particularly, we could forget about any need to convince others of the logical nature of our morality. A totally amoral person—one who did not stop to think about the "rightness" and "justness" and "fairness" of his or her decisions, but instead concentrated upon profits for his or her employer and benefits for his or her self—might be expected to be far more successful in purely financial terms for both entities over any reasonable period of time. Why should we all not do exactly that?

The answer on one level is that if we want others to worry about whether their treatment of us is "right" and "just" and "fair," then we have to worry about our treatment of them. Reciprocity is the most logical reason for morality. But the world is filled with people who are not logical in the sense of recognizing reciprocity and the need to be consistent. The world is filled with people who might well say, "We'll take our chances on your treatment of us later on, after we try to get what we want now, and if we do indeed get what we want now, then we won't have to worry about your treatment of us later on." How do we react to those people? Do we simply cede to them the first place in financial benefits and managerial positions, and hope that eventually they will learn that "what goes around comes around"? That is not a very satisfactory solution for most of the rest of us, who under that rationale would be forced to wait and hope for an eventual solution.

Beyond reciprocity, however, the reason for our moral actions toward others is—or perhaps ought to be—our concern for the quality of our lives. If we are concerned about the sort of profession we have entered, the sort of organization we have joined, the sort of society we are constructing, and the sort of person we are becoming, then we have to start thinking about our duties and responsibilities to others. What do we really owe to our professions? What do we really owe to our employers? What do we really owe to our society? And what do we really owe to our selves? And how do we reach a balance among all of those duties and responsibilities?

These are questions that people have worried about for centuries. In 399 BC, Socrates was put on trial in Athens for having "corrupted the youth of the city." He argued in his defense that all he had done was to ask the young people who attended his classes to consider the goals and standards of their lives. There was nothing wrong with this, he claimed, and ended with the closing statement that "the unexamined life is not worth living."[1] You can certainly interpret that expression following your own understanding, but perhaps he is saying that everyone should examine their duties and obligations to their professions, their organizations, their communities, and themselves. If so, it is necessary to get down to basics.

The most basic question in ethics is, "Do you have an obligation to leave the world a little better than you found it, or can you simply take what you want now, and let other people worry about making up for any shortfall later on?" Many people do recognize a personal obligation to other people to some extent, but have never thought strongly about its nature and terms, and have never sorted out that general duty into their specific responsibilities to their professions, their organizations, their communities, and their selves. And it has to be recognized that there are some other people who choose to ignore this injunction to "leave the world a little better than they found it." The question once again is whether we cede to those people the first place in financial rewards and managerial positions, and only hope that eventually they will become concerned with the quality of their lives and the nature and terms of their obligations to others. Perhaps we need something more than reciprocity of treatment and quality of life as the reason to be moral.

Trust, Commitment, and Cooperative Effort

Beyond reciprocity of treatment and quality of life, the third argument in favor of moral action in management is that of cooperative effort. Organizations are composed of individuals and groups who have to cooperate to be successful. In business firms we call those individuals and groups stakeholders.

The term *stakeholder* was composed to contrast with the more familiar *stockholder*. A stockholder is a person who owns a company. A stakeholder is a person who is associated with a company and, in a famous phrase, "can affect or is affected by the

---

[1] Plato (427–347 BC), "Apology," in *The Dialogues* [of Socrates], trans. B. Jowett (New York: Random House, 1987).

achievement of the organization's objectives."[2] The stakeholders in a business firm include the factory and office workers, functional and technical managers, senior executives, scientists and engineers, suppliers, distributors, customers, creditors, owners, and local residents. All, clearly, have an interest, a "stake," in the future of the firm. All, equally clearly, must contribute their efforts through cooperation and innovation if that future is to be successful and secure.

But why should these various individuals and groups contribute their best efforts, and be cooperative and innovative, for an organization that appears not to care about them? You are a worker on an assembly line in a factory. I am the manager of that factory. I recently downsized some of your friends who also worked on that assembly line. I have gradually made changes that increased the speed of that same assembly line. I continually argue that your hourly wages are too high, and your healthcare benefits too large. But now let us say that you have an idea for a simple change in the design of the product that you are manufacturing that would greatly facilitate the assembly and reduce the cost. After all, you work on that assembly day after day and hour after hour. You know far more about possible improvements in the manufacturing processes for that particular product than I ever will. Do you tell me about your idea?

The argument of this chapter is that under current conditions you probably will not tell me about your idea to greatly increase efficiency and reduce cost in my factory. Why? I would assume that you would not tell me because you would not trust me. You would think that I would take credit for the idea, ask for and receive a large bonus from the owners for having invented it, and fire a few more of your friends because your idea saved so much time and effort that they were no longer needed. I might even fire you so that I would not have to worry about your telling others that the idea for which I have received so much credit and reward was in reality your own.

What should I do in order to get you to tell me about your new idea? Perhaps I can do nothing now, but perhaps earlier I should have established an attitude that everyone within the company could expect to be treated in ways that could rationally be explained to be "right" and "just" and "fair." Perhaps I should have been moral.

Maybe the basic answer to the "Why be moral?" question is the need for a manager to build trust, commitment, and effort among all of the individuals and groups associated with his or her organization. Maybe trust is the essential first step, and perhaps we can't get commitment and effort without that trust. And maybe trust is built upon our making and explaining our decisions and actions in a way that most people—we can probably never convince all—can agree to be "right" and "just" and "fair." This the basic argument of this chapter, that trust of this nature requires, as shown in Figure 5.1, a recognition of moral responsibility, an application of moral reasoning, and a possession of moral character or courage:

- *Moral responsibility is the recognition of moral problems.* Perhaps this is the most essential managerial function of all: before we can start to think seriously about a moral problem, we first have to comprehend that people are actually being hurt or harmed, or are having their rights denied, by our company's decisions or actions. Many managers don't want to know if this is happening. If they don't know, the reasoning goes, they can't be held responsible. Perhaps, however, the only true social

[2] R. E. Freeman, *Strategic Management: A Stakeholder Approach* (Boston: Pitman, 1984), p. 46.

FIGURE 5.1 **Building Trust, Commitment, and Effort within Organizations**

Corporate management in extended organizations

{

Recognition of moral responsibility
—What is "duty"?

Application of moral reasoning
—What is "right"?

Possession of moral character
—What is "integrity"?

}

Trust
Commitment
Effort

responsibility managers can be said to have is to know what is happening to the members, the stakeholders, of their organizations.

- *Moral reasoning is the process of examining and then resolving these recognized moral problems in a way that will be convincing to others.* We can't just say, "Well, this will certainly benefit us so I know you'll understand" or, "I feel bad that this is happening to you, but we want to move forward." We as managers have to logically explain our decisions and actions, and rationally consider the economic outcomes, the legal requirements, and the ethical duties of the situation. Otherwise, we cannot build the trust, commitment, and effort among all the individuals and groups associated with the firm that will enable us to move forward.

- *Moral character is the possession of courage to first recognize a moral problem and then propose a "just" solution.* Many managers are not willing to face up to moral problems. They are not willing to say, "This is what is happening to some of the individuals and groups associated with our firm. These are the alternatives. And this is what I recommend and why I recommend it." They fear that their action will not be popular in some parts of their firm. That is why courage is a part of character and why integrity—the willingness to act on principle—is essential to build trust among all of the stakeholders in extended organizations.

Extended Organizations

What is an "extended organization"? The term is used in Figure 5.1 on the development of trust, commitment, and effort and is depicted in Figure 5.2 on the full meaning of that concept. Companies have become not only much larger, but also more dependent upon a wider range of other firms and institutions, beyond the formal boundaries and hierarchical controls of the firm. Material and component suppliers, for example, are clearly outside the formal boundaries and direct controls of a producing firm, yet they can easily influence the quality and cost of that company's goods and services. Many suppliers now participate in the original design of those goods and services, almost on a partnership basis, and most are now relied upon for just-in-time inventory systems, where failure to deliver could shut down the product lines of their customers.

Wholesale and retail distributors, as another example, are also outside the formal boundaries and hierarchical controls of a company, yet here they can influence the price

FIGURE 5.2 **An Extended View of Business Organizations (from LaRue Hosmer,** *Moral Leadership in Business,* **Richard D. Irwin, 1994, p. 193)**

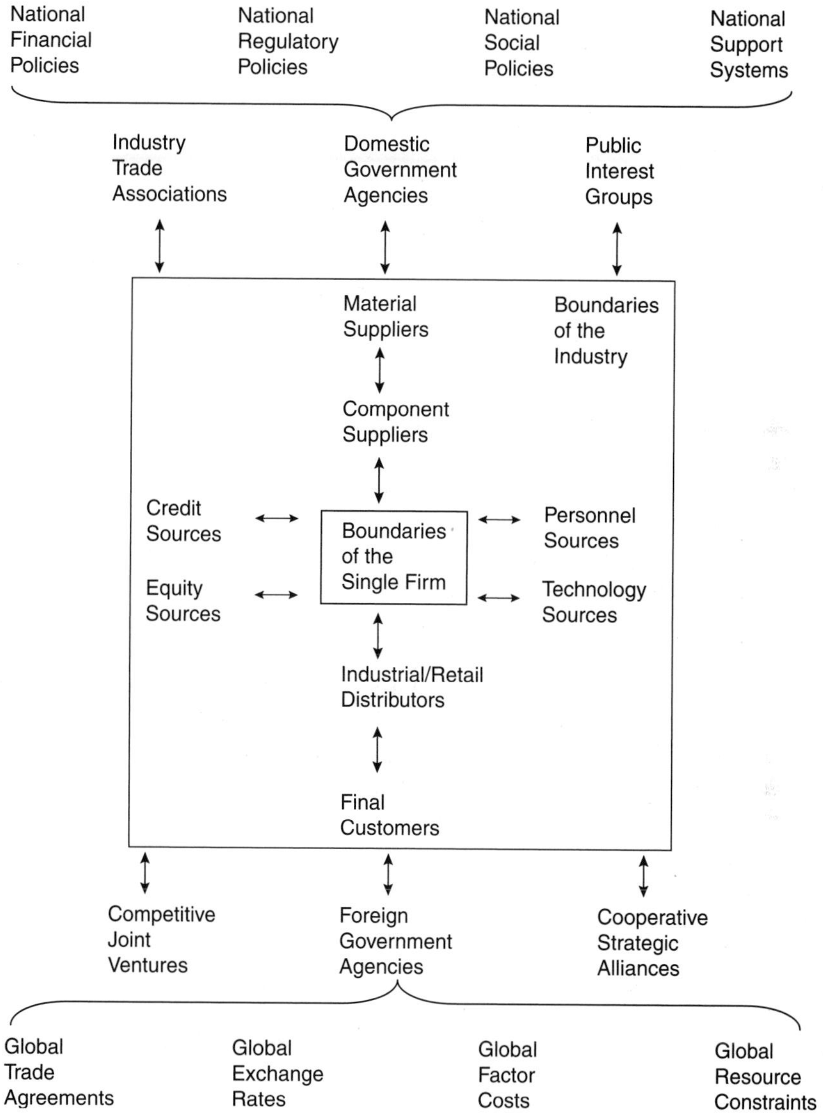

National Financial Policies	National Regulatory Policies	National Social Policies	National Support Systems

Industry Trade Associations   Domestic Government Agencies   Public Interest Groups

Material Suppliers   Boundaries of the Industry

Component Suppliers

Credit Sources ⟷ Boundaries of the Single Firm ⟷ Personnel Sources

Equity Sources ⟷ (Boundaries of the Single Firm) ⟷ Technology Sources

Industrial/Retail Distributors

Final Customers

Competitive Joint Ventures   Foreign Government Agencies   Cooperative Strategic Alliances

Global Trade Agreements	Global Exchange Rates	Global Factor Costs	Global Resource Constraints

of the product, the level of service, and the degree of satisfaction received by the final customers. Many distributors are now relied upon not only for the prompt transmission of information about current sales trends, but also for the accurate anticipation of future customer needs. Both are obviously essential for the long-term success of the producing firm.

Commercial banks, investment companies, research laboratories, and educational institutions are further examples of organizations that are outside the command-and-control hierarchy of a producing firm, yet can influence the long-term success of that company. They provide personnel, technology, equity, and debt. Their cooperation is essential, given the changed conditions of management. Companies with uneducated employees, obsolete methods, or inadequate funds cannot compete in a global environment.

Last, industry trade associations, public interest groups, and domestic and foreign political agencies are further examples of organizations that are outside the formal command-and-control hierarchy of the firm yet can affect the performance of each company. These associations, groups, and agencies help in determining (1) the national financial policies that set tax rules and interest rates, (2) the national regulatory policies that influence product/process designs and environmental requirements, (3) the national social policies that establish educational achievement levels and health care costs, and (4) the national infrastructure systems, which include the communication networks and the transportation methods.

If you doubt that companies are now dependent upon the governmental policies and national systems listed above, think for a minute about the domestic automobile manufacturers, who must meet mileage, safety, and emission standards in their cars and provide educational training and health care benefits for their workers. It was recently claimed that health care benefits added $1,100 to the cost of each American car, a charge not included in the cost of automobiles produced in Europe or Japan where the health care system is financed by public, not private, revenues. Companies are starting to compete based upon their country's educational and health care systems, in addition to their own product designs, manufacturing costs, and advertising messages.

Cooperation, Innovation, and Unification

Let us say that you accept for now that companies have become much larger, more extended, and less susceptible to the hierarchical command-and-control of the formal management structure. What does that mean for management, and particularly what does that mean for the need to be moral, to recognize and resolve the mixtures of benefits and harms, and the balances of rights and wrongs, that occur in the decisions and actions of the firm? The argument of this chapter is that moral management is necessary to build cooperative effort among the separate stakeholders in large, extended organizations in order to achieve the cooperation, innovation, and unification that are needed for success. There are three basic steps in this progression between moral management and organizational success. Each may be called a "thesis" of the chapter:

- *Trust builds committed effort.* The first major thesis is that (1) treating people in ways that can be considered to be "right" and "just" and "fair" creates trust, (2) trust builds commitment, (3) commitment ensures effort, and (4) effort is essential for success. Certainly there will be disagreements among the stakeholder groups on exactly what distribution of benefits and allocation of harms, on precisely what recognition and denial of rights, can be considered to be "right" and "just" and "fair" in any given situation. Certainly some stakeholder groups will prefer one decision or action, while other stakeholder groups will prefer others. But the first thesis of this chapter is that as long as all of the groups together can agree that the decision process itself has been "right" and "just" and "fair"—that is, that the decision process has considered the interests and rights of each of the groups according to known and consistent principles—then there should be an increase in trust and commitment among all of the stakeholder groups, and that increase in trust and commitment should, in turn, lead to an increase in effort.

- *Committed effort is essential for success.* The second major thesis of this chapter is that the effort that results from stakeholder trust and commitment goes far beyond that which is based only upon financial incentives or commercial contracts. Stakeholder trust and commitment result in a willingness to contribute "something extra," a readiness to act with both energy and enthusiasm for the benefit of the firm. A story by Edward Carlson, then president of United Airlines, illustrates very succinctly this willingness to contribute something extra. Mr. Carlson is quoted as saying, "The president of a company has a constituency much like that of a politician. The employees may not actually go to the polls, but each one of them does elect to do his or her job in a better or worse fashion every day."[3] Employees at all levels electing to their jobs in better rather than worse fashion is exactly what is meant in this text by contributing something extra. That committed attitude among all of the stakeholders—not just the employees, but suppliers, distributors, agencies, associations, and partners—is essential for the success of organizations today.

- *Success is becoming increasingly difficult to achieve.* The third major thesis of this chapter is that this committed attitude, this willingness to contribute something extra, this readiness to act with energy and enthusiasm for the benefit of the full organization on the part of all of the stakeholders, is more important now than in the past due to the changed conditions of global competition. Companies have become more aggressive. Technologies have become more advanced. Products have become more complex. Markets have become more diverse. Processes have become more oriented toward quality and cost. Customers in both the industrial and consumer segments have become more insistent upon value and choice. Changes in competitors, technologies, products, markets, processes, and customers have become more frequent. And the thoughtfulness, speed, and cost of the firm's reactions to those changes—or even better in their anticipations of them—have become more critical.

Unify and Guide

In summary, it is the argument of this chapter that it is no longer possible to manage organizations that must respond intelligently, quickly, and efficiently to technological, product, market, process, or customer changes on a command-and-control basis. Innovation is required, but corporate managers cannot command innovation. Cooperation is essential, but corporate managers cannot control cooperation. Something more is needed, and that "something more" is the trust, commitment, and effort that comes from moral management.

Let us assume that you accept for now the proposal that the old command-and-control form of management is no longer viable. Let us further assume that you also agree that the stakeholder groups—the people who are affected by and, in turn, can affect

---

[3] Thomas Peters and Robert Waterman, *In Search of Excellence: Lessons from America's Best Run Companies* (New York: Harper & Row, 1982), p. 289.

the performance of the organization—are now too diverse in their various activities for easy assimilation, and that they now extend too far beyond the hierarchical boundaries for easy direction. The question, then, is what takes the place of the outmoded command-and-control model? What generates a sense of trust, commitment, and directed effort?

Directed effort is obviously important. Undirected effort results only in chaos and confusion. But directed effort has to be the result of trust and commitment as well as of direction and planning. This leads us to the fourth major thesis of this chapter. Moral reasoning—the process that leads to a determination of what is "right" and "just" and "fair" in the treatment of others—is not peripheral to corporate management. It is central to corporate management.

Moral reasoning is not something to be considered, if at all, only after the important strategic, structural, technical, functional, and operational decisions have been made. Moral reasoning is not something to be published as a code of conduct that will be handed to each employee on his or her first day at work and then promptly forgotten. Moral reasoning has to become an integral part of the managerial process. It has to be combined with the other managerial decisions and actions at all levels of the firm to ensure trust, commitment, and directed effort.

The need for trust, commitment, and directed effort leads us to a form of management that might be called "unify and guide" rather than "command-and-control." Unification is the key. Unification means bringing all of the stakeholders of the firm—those within the company, those within the industry, and those within the society—together into an innovative and cooperative whole. Unification requires recognizing the impacts of company actions—both benefits and harms—upon the stakeholders of the firm, and then distributing those impacts through a process that is thought to be "right" and "just" and fair." Unification, based upon trust, commitment, and effort, is the moral responsibility of management. But this has to be combined with the practical responsibility of guidance.

A New Method of Management

Perhaps what is needed is a changed method of management, one that will extend the concepts of trust, commitment, and effort, and the results of cooperation, innovation, and unification, throughout the firm. The changed philosophy would balance the economic benefits, legal requirements, and ethical duties of the management, and be expressed in the values, goals, and missions of the company. This approach is portrayed graphically in Figure 5.3.

What is involved in this new method of management? It is based upon a changed philosophy that attempts to balance economic outcomes, legal requirements, and ethical duties. The argument of this text is that none of these approaches are complete and final in and/or by themselves, but that taken together, in balance, they lead to managerial decisions and actions that are "more right," "more just," and "more fair" than any approach used by itself. We as managers cannot claim that any one of our decisions or actions is absolutely "right" and totally "just" and completely "fair," but it is possible to logically explain the moral basis of our decisions and actions to others.

FIGURE 5.3 **Proposed Relationships between Managerial Decisions and Actions and Organizational Cooperation, Innovation, and Unification**

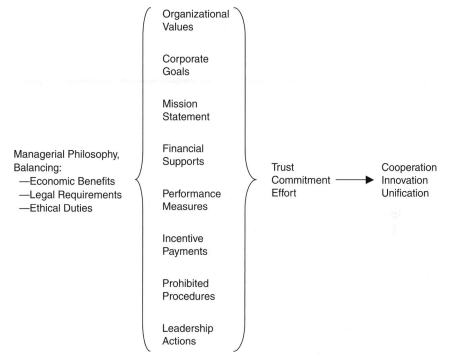

The further argument of this text is that a sequence of these decisions and actions that can be logically explained as "more right," "more just," and "more fair" than the considered alternatives should, over time, lead to trust, commitment, and effort among all of the participants—the stakeholders—in the organization. That trust, commitment, and effort among all of those participants or stakeholders should, again over time, lead to cooperation, innovation, and unification. That cooperation, innovation, and unification should, once more over time, lead to success for both business firms and service organizations operating under competitive global conditions. Why should a manager be moral? In my view being moral now is essential for being successful in the future.

Success in the future, however, will require more than just a moral approach to management now. This new philosophy of management—this new balance of economic outcomes, legal requirements and ethical duties—will have to be infused throughout the extended firm, reaching all suppliers, distributors, creditors, customers, and local residents, through the means portrayed in Figure 5.3. Those means will be described in much greater detail in Chapter 6, "How Can a Business Firm Be Moral?" For now, let me describe very briefly the first three steps in that process of infusion: the need to establish organizational values, corporate goals, and a mission statement combining those values and goals in clearly understandable and fully believable terms.

The mission statement states the reason for the company to exist. If you accept the fact that trust, commitment, and effort are essential to the success of the firm, for they lead to cooperation, innovation, and unification, then that reason for existence has to reflect values and goals that are meaningful for each and relevant to all of the various stakeholder groups:

- *Corporate values.* To avoid easy generalizations, think of corporate values as the duties the senior executives of the firm should—in your view—owe to the various individuals and groups associated with the firm who can, in one way or another, affect the future performance and position of the firm. These individuals and groups would include owners of all types (institutional and individual), employees at all levels, customers in all segments, suppliers, distributors, creditors, local residents, national citizens, and global inhabitants. What—again in your view—is important to each of these groups? What—once more in your view—should the senior executives of the company recognize as being important to each and to all of those groups? In short, how can the company begin to think about unification based upon similarities rather than separation based upon differences?

- *Organizational goals.* To avoid easy generalizations think of company goals as the end-points the senior executives of the firm should—in your view—set for the various dimensions of performance that are possible. What—again in your view— should the senior executives want to accomplish along such dimensions as financial performance, technological achievement, industry position, market share, customer satisfaction, manufacturing efficiency, employee loyalty, environmental protection, public reputation, and social contribution? What—once more in your view—should the various groups associated with the firm want to accomplish on each of these dimensions? Remember that scientists and engineers doubtless would like techno-logical achievement, while the owners and creditors might prefer financial perfor-mance. The two may not be as dissimilar as they at first appear; if the organization is well guided, there will be an obvious connection between them.

- *Mission statement.* Think of the mission statement as the means of combining the duties that the firm holds toward others with the goals that it has set for itself. What role, as a result of this combination, should the firm attempt to play within the market, the industry, the economy, and the society? It is frequently difficult to express mana-gerial values and organizational goals in explicit numerical terms. Consequently, it is suggested that you compromise with a mission statement that speaks only generally about the duties you want to observe and the end points you want to achieve, but much more specifically about the means you want to use and the standards you want to follow. The intent is to define the future of the firm, the scope of its activities, and the character of its people so clearly that everyone will understand, "This is where we're going to go, this is what we're going to do, and this is how we're going to do it." Think in terms of a document that will create a challenge for everyone associ-ated with the firm. Think also in terms of a document you would be proud to hand to employees, to show to customers, to send to suppliers and distributors, and to include in the annual report for owners.

Following this chapter are three cases on companies that most people will agree have done nothing "wrong." Instead, the senior executives at each company appear to have attempted to balance the economic outcomes, legal requirements, and ethical duties of their decisions and actions in a way that many people would find to be "right."

Do you agree that the company should have taken this action? If you agree, do you believe that this action should help to build trust, commitment, and effort among the employees, suppliers, distributors, and customers of the firm? If you agree on that point also, then start to think how to infuse this new philosophy of management throughout the extended company. Put together a list of the corporate values and the organizational goals that you think would accurately reflect the thinking of the senior executives, and prepare a mission statement that you think would create both a point of challenge and a source of pride to everyone associated with the organization.

Case 5-1

Johnson & Johnson and the Worldwide Recall of Tylenol

Johnson & Johnson is a long-established manufacturer of health care products and pharmaceutical drugs. The company is best known by consumers for products such Band-Aids and Tylenol tablets, but it is better known by physicians for minimally invasive surgical instruments and highly sophisticated diagnostic systems. It is a firm that has grown consistently over time, with a stock price that went from $12 per share in 1989 to $107 per share in 1999.

The company has a very unusual mission statement, or affirmation of the purpose of the firm, which focuses on corporate duties rather than financial profits. This statement has been widely distributed among active employees and is not considered to be "window dressing" or a hypocritical desire to appear socially concerned while everyone really focuses on the "bottom line." This was proven a number of years ago when a person in Chicago, for reasons that have never been discovered, put tablets containing cyanide in unsold bottles of Tylenol on store shelves throughout that city and the suburbs. Six people died. It could not quickly be proven that this had occurred purposely at the retail stores in Chicago and not accidentally at the manufacturing plant in New Jersey. Consequently, Johnson & Johnson removed, in a matter of days, every package of Tylenol from every store in America and abroad, at a cost of over $100 million, to protect their customers. Those packages were later replaced, free of charge to all retailers and to any customers who had returned unused portions of purchased packages, with new drugs in "tamperproof" containers. The senior executives at the time explained that this prompt and complete response was required by the credo or mission of the firm:

> We believe that our first responsibility is for the doctors, nurses, and patients, to mothers and all others who use our products and services.
>
> • In meeting their needs everything we do must be of high quality.
> • We must constantly strive to reduce our costs in order to maintain reasonable prices.
> • Customer orders must be serviced promptly and accurately.
> • Our suppliers and distributors must have an opportunity to make a fair profit.
>
> We are responsible to our employees, the men and women who work with us throughout the world.

- Everyone must be considered as an individual. We must respect their dignity and recognize their worth.
- They must have a sense of security in their jobs. Compensation must be fair and adequate and working conditions clean, orderly and safe.
- Employees must feel free to make suggestions and complaints.
- There must be equal treatment for employment, development and advancement for those qualified.
- We must provide competent management and their actions must be just and ethical.

We are responsible to the communities in which we live and work, and to the world community as well.

- We must be good citizens—support good works and charities and bear our fair share of taxes.
- We must encourage civic improvements and better health and education.
- We must maintain in good order the property we are privileged to use, protecting the environment and natural resources.

Our final responsibility is to our stockholders. Business must make a sound profit.

- We must experiment with new ideas. Research must be carried on, innovative programs developed, and mistakes paid for.
- New equipment must be purchased, new facilities provided, and new products launched.
- Reserves must be created to provide for adverse times.
- When we operate according to these principles, the stockholders should realize a fair return.

Class Assignment

The prompt and complete action by Johnson & Johnson was exceedingly well received by consumer advocates within the United States, but there was considerable grumbling among financial analysts and fund managers. The general feeling among many of the professionals on Wall Street was that $100 million was too large an amount to spend for all stores in all parts of the world. "They should have just taken the product off the shelves in Chicago where the deaths actually occurred, at maybe a cost of $2 million" was a common comment. What is your opinion? Should they have recalled just the Tylenol in the Chicago area, and waited to see what would happen, or were they correct in removing the product from all stores everywhere?

1. If you agree that the senior executives at Johnson & Johnson took an action that was "right" and "just" and "fair" in their worldwide recall of Tylenol, do you believe that this will have a positive impact upon the trust, commitment, and effort of the employees, suppliers, distributors, and customers of the firm? Will those people—those stakeholders—be proud of their firm? Will they think of it as "their" firm?
2. There is no need to consider the values and goals of Johnson & Johnson, and then to put together a mission statement for that company, because one already exists. Read it over once again, as if you were a brand-new employee of the company. The text said that a mission statement should be "both a point of challenge and a source

of pride" to everyone associated with the organization. Do you believe that this statement offers that challenge and pride? Are there changes/improvements that you would like to make?

3. If you disagree (1) that the senior executives at Johnson & Johnson took the proper action in their worldwide recall of Tylenol, (2) that this action should lead to further trust, commitment, and effort among the employees, suppliers, distributors, and customers of the firm, or (3) that the mission statement creates "a point of challenge and a source of pride" on the part of individuals and groups associated with the firm, be prepared to energetically argue your point of view.

Case 5-2

Procter & Gamble and the Focus on Stakeholders

Procter & Gamble is a very large consumer products company. It makes and markets laundry detergents, cleaning supplies, soaps and cosmetics, razors and blades, toothbrushes and toothpaste, infant diapers, paper towels, toilet paper, pet food, and a few snacks and beverages. Brands include Tide, Cascade, Dash, Cheer, Bounce, Mr. Clean, Swifter, Pantene, Olay, Head & Shoulders, Secret, Sure, Gillette, Pampers, Luvs, Always, Tampax, Charmin, Bounty, Iams, Pringles, and Folgers. The company is headquartered in Cincinnati, Ohio, and operates globally. Corporate sales in 2005 totaled $51.4 billion.

Procter & Gamble is also a very profitable consumer products company. For years it has recorded steady increases in revenues, profits, and stock prices. Sales revenues in 1995 were $12.17/share; in 2005 they had grown to $22.95/share. Annual profits in 1995 were $0.93/share; in 2005 they had grown to $2.53/share. Stock prices at the end of 1995 averaged $19.95/share; at the end of 2005 they averaged $59.00/share. Despite this excellent financial performance, Procter & Gamble does not focus on creating profits for *shareholders;* instead, they concentrate on establishing relationships with *stakeholders.*

Stakeholders, as described in the text, are people who are associated in some way with the company, and—in the famous phrase—can affect or are affected by the achievement of the company's objectives. These people include factory and office workers, functional and technical managers, senior executives, scientists and engineers, suppliers, distributors, customers, creditors, owners, and local residents. All, clearly, have an interest, a "stake," in the future of the firm. And all, equally clearly, must contribute their best efforts for the firm to continue to be successful.

The chairman and CEO of Procter & Gamble, A. G. Lafley, believes that this broader focus, on stakeholders rather than shareholders, is needed because of the broader range of demands, requirements, and responsibilities that are encountered in a global economy. He spoke of this broader range in an interview with a reporter from the *Wall Street Journal:*

> A. G. Lafley, Procter & Gamble's chief executive, doesn't talk much about shareholders. Instead, he talks about stakeholders.
>
> Who are those stakeholders? Well, add together the company's employees; the retailers and distributors and wholesalers the company sells to; its suppliers; the employees of those

retailers, wholesalers, distributors and suppliers,; the 2 1/2 billion people who consume P&G products; the communities all these people live in; and—oh yes—the people who happen to own Procter & Gamble common stock, and pretty soon the real question becomes:

Who on earth isn't a Procter & Gamble stakeholder?

Mr. Lafley makes no apologies for this expansive definition of his responsibilities. And he isn't particularly bothered when I suggest that it makes the CEO job sound like a global political role. "I've concluded I'm in it [the global political role] anyway, and I might as well deal with it."

A conversation with Mr. Lafley is a lesson in how dramatically CEOs like Mr. Lafley think it [once again, the global political role] has changed.

It's not that shareholders don't matter. In fact, shareholders are more demanding than ever. Mr. Lafley recalls that in the 1980s and early 1990s, his predecessors John Smale and Ed Artzt would meet with analysts and investors "only once a year in Cincinnati, give a formal, tightly prepared presentation, and then take very few questions." In contrast, Mr. Lafley has frequent contacts with investors and analysts.

But the outside demands don't stop with the investors. Consumers, he says, are also more demanding. "We used to think we were just taking care of the consumer buying Tide," he says. But "this consumer is also a citizen, is also a member of the community." He or she may care about how P&G treats the animals it uses in tests, for instance, or the company's policies regarding global warming. . . .

The problem with all this, as some critics see it, is that it distracts the CEO from his main job. "The shareholders hired the guy to be CEO and not Procter & Gamble's representative to the world," gripes Steven Milloy.

Mr. Milloy helps run a new group called the Free Enterprise Action Fund, a modest-sized mutual fund whose mission is to force CEOs to get back to basics and stop bowing to the agendas of activist groups.

On Friday, Mr. Milloy plans to be at the annual meeting of Goldman Sachs Group Inc., to complain about CEO Hank Paulson's conflict of interest in chairing the board of the Nature Conservancy, an environmental activist group. A few weeks later, he'll be on hand for General Electric Co.'s annual meeting, pushing a shareholder resolution that calls on the conglomerate to show the science behind its decision to embrace anti-global-warming measures.

"The role of these companies is to increase society's wealth by generating shareholder wealth," he [Mr. Milloy] says.

Mr. Lafley agrees that P&G's first job is to make money. Under his leadership, the company has done a good job of that. "If we aren't successful," he says, "we don't have a right to do the other stuff."

He says his definition of his job has evolved over time. "I came into this job in June of 2000, and my head was down for at least a year, year and a half, because the company was not performing well," he says. "Then when my head came up, all hell was breaking loose. We had Enron, WorldCom, Adelphia, Tyco."

That let him into a much broader "dialogue among stakeholders," he says. As he sees it, this is not an exercise of choice; it's a requirement of the job.

"Like it or not, we are in a global economy and a global political world," he says. . . .

"The responsibility is huge." (*The Wall Street Journal*, March 29, 2006, p. A2)[4]

Class Assignment

Where do you stand on the question of the proper focus of a business firm: stakeholders or shareholders? Should the senior executives of a large and prosperous consumer products firm be concerned about the rights and well-being of the wide range of the individuals and groups associated in some way with their company, or should they worry far more about increasing value and generating profits for the owners of the firm? You can obviously pick either side of the argument, but what reasons would you give to support your stand?

Let us set up a nonclassroom stage for this debate. Assume that it is about three years in the future, and that you have worked for a given company for about two years, ever since you graduated from your college or MBA program. Assume that you are returning from a business meeting in San Francisco, assume you find when you get to the airport that the plane is very full in the regular or tourist section, though a few seats remain in first class, and lastly assume that the clerk at the check-in counter notes that you are well dressed and very presentable in appearance—you came to the airport directly from your business meeting—and he or she says that they are going to move you into the first class cabin at no additional charge. This actually does happen upon occasion; you are pleased—as are most other such fortunate travelers—and do not object. When you get onto the plane, and find your assigned place, you recognize the individual who will be sitting next to you on the trip back to your home city: he or she is a senior vice president of your own company, leading the division for which you work. You introduce yourself, explain how you happen to be occupying a first class seat, and then open a book or magazine and start to read—or, even better, open your computer and start to work—as an indication that you are not going to disturb your seat row companion during the flight.

About 30 minutes into the flight, after coffee has been served and the seat belt sign turned off, your companion hands you his or her copy of the *Wall Street Journal,* points to the article quoted extensively above, and says "Read it and tell me what you think." You read it at breakfast, at the hotel, that morning, so you are generally familiar with the content, but you go over once again to make certain you understand that content. Now you have to respond to the senior vice president. You can't just agree with that person, you can't just be a "yes man" (or yes woman) because you don't know what he or she thinks. You've got to give your own opinion, but, obviously that opinion has got to be thoughtful; you are going to have to give the rationale that supports your opinion.

A major theme of this text is that it is necessary for managers at all levels to be able to support their opinions, to be able to logically convince others on what they believe to be "right" in any given context. It is suggested that you structure your response to the senior vice president by saying, "I like (or dislike) what Mr. Lafley has to say, and here are the three (or four or five) reasons I agree (or disagree) with him." It is certain that you will be evaluated by the senior vice president of your division. If you want to try for a home run, or chance the risk of a strikeout, you could add, "I think that it would work (or not work) in our company because . . ."

It is suggested *strongly* that you write out an outline of your response for this make-believe exercise before your class. You will find that opportunities to be favorably noticed by senior executives come along very seldom during your career; practice here so that you will be ready when—and if—this happens to you in real life.

Case 5-3

Nucor Corporation and the Treatment of Employees

Nucor Corporation is a new and different type of steel company. Traditional steel companies smelt iron ore, coal, and limestone in blast furnaces to produce cast iron, which is then refined while still in molten form through the use of Bessemer converters to generate steel ingots, which in turn are rolled into steel sheets, plates, bars, and beams for eventual sale to industrial customers. Nucor avoids the blast furnace and Bessemer converter processes; instead, this company melts scrap steel in electric arc furnaces, and then directly rolls the output into the needed sheets, plates, bars, and beams. It is a business model that is termed "mini-mill" because the plants are much smaller, with far lower capital investments, and are dispersed throughout the country, with far lower transportation costs for the incoming raw materials and the outgoing finished products. It is also a business model that has been exceedingly successful in the globally competitive steel business.

Steel was one of the first of the basic industries to become competitive on a global scale. The raw materials—ore, coal, and limestone—are easily available. The needed technologies—blast furnaces and Bessemer converters—are widely known. The output products—sheets, plates, bars, and beans—are readily shipped. Originally, most developing countries lacked the capital to build the expensive plants, but given that their labor costs and environment restrictions were far lower, the needed capital was soon provided by foreign investors. The resulting competition drove many of the traditional American and European steel producers into retrenchment or bankruptcy, or both.

Nucor, however, has performed very differently. Sales per share over the past five years, 2001 to 2006, have risen from $13.30 to $49.00. Cash flows per share over the same five-year period have gone from $1.29 to $6.90, and profits, from $0.36 to $5.50. The stock price, adjusted for stock splits, increased from $12.00 at the end of 2001 to $60.00 today. Nucor was able to take advantage of the sudden increase in the global demand for finished steel products that came from the rapid economic expansion of both China and India by shipping their products overseas, not by having to meet foreign competitors in U.S. markets.

Financial analysts cited the simpler production processes, the smaller investment needs, and the lower transportation costs (due to the dispersed plant locations) as the reasons for Nucor's continued success, but there was something else. That "something else" was discussed in an article recently published in *BusinessWeek:*

> It was about 2:00 p.m. on March 9th when three Nucor Corp. electricians [at different company mills, across the country] got the call from their colleagues at the Hickman (Ark.) plant. It was bad news: Hickman's electric grid had failed. For a mini-mill steelmaker like Nucor, which melts scrap steel in an electric arc furnace to make new steel, there's little that could be worse. The trio immediately dropped what they were doing and headed [for Hickman]. Malcolm McDonald, an electrician from the Decatur (Ala.) mill, was in Indiana visiting another facility. He drove down, arriving at 9 o'clock that night. Les Hart and Bryson Trumble, from Nucor's facility in Hertford County, N.C., boarded a plane that landed in Memphis at 11 p.m. Then they drove two hours to the troubled plant.

No supervisor had asked them to make the trip, and no one had to. They went on their own. Camping out in the electrical substation with the Hickman staff, the team worked 20-hour shifts to get the plant up and running again in three days instead of the antici-pated full week. There wasn't any direct financial incentive for them to blow their week-ends, no extra money in the next paycheck, but for the company their contribution was huge. Hickman went on to post a first quarter records for tons of steel shipped.

What's more amazing about this story is that at Nucor it's not considered particu-larly remarkable. "It could have easily been a Hickman operator going to help the Crawfordsville (Ind.) mill," says Executive Vice President John J. Ferriola, who oversees the Hickman plant and seven others. "It happens daily."

In an industry as Rust Belt as they come, Nucor has nurtured one of the most dynamic and engaged workforces around. The 11,300 nonunion employees at the Charlotte (N.C.) company don't see themselves as worker bees waiting for instructions from above. Nucor's flattened hierarchy and emphasis on pushing power to the front line lead its employees to adopt the mindset of owner-operators. It's a profitable formula: Nucor's 387% return to shareholders over the past five years handily beats almost all other companies in the Standard & Poor's 500 stock index, including New Economy icons Amazon.com, Starbucks, and eBay. And the company has become more profitable as it has grown. Margins, which were 7% in 2000, reached 10% last year. (*BusinessWeek,* May 1, 2006, p. 56f.) [5]

Nucor employees are known widely for their close-knit attitudes and cooperative behaviors. These come partially from the company's underdog identity at its begin-ning—the firm was derided then as an underfunded and unstable start-up by execu-tives at the industry giants that since have failed—but primarily from an insistence by Kenneth Iverson, the founder, that people will make exceptional efforts if you reward them richly, treat them with respect, and give them real power.

There is no question but that employees at Nucor can be rewarded richly. The pay rate for a frontline worker at that company is just $10.00 per hour, less than half the rate of experienced steelworkers at other companies, but there is a bonus, paid weekly, that is tied to the production of defect-free steel by an employee's entire shift. That bonus can triple the typical take-home checks. And there is an annual distribution based upon reported profit. Combined, these policies on basic pay, weekly bonus, and annual distribution result in production workers who frequently earn somewhat more than $100,000 per year.

But there are penalties that go with the rewards. If a given shift makes a bad batch of steel that is shipped to a customer and results in problems for and complaints from that customer, then the pay of all members of the shift is docked three times what the bonus would have been. Shift managers and department managers at each mill are also compensated on this reward-penalty policy. Their basic pay rates are about 75 percent of the industry average for their positions, but they receive annual distributions based upon the return on assets of their shift or their plant. In a good year, that annual distribution can equal their basic pay for the full year. The payment policy based upon shift or mill results is said to ensure a team approach to problems:

> This high stakes teamwork can be the hardest thing for a newly acquired plant [Nucor now buys many failed steel plants from large steel companies] to get used to. David Hutchings, a shift supervisor or "lead man" in the rolling mill at Nucor's first big

[5] Reprinted from May 1, 2006 issue of *BusinessWeek* by special permission, copyright © 2006 by The McGraw-Hill Companies, Inc.

acquisition, its Auburn (N.Y.) plant, describes the old way of thinking. The job of a rolling mill is to thin out the steel made in the hot mill furnace, preparing it to be cut into sheets. In the days before the Nucor acquisition, if the cutting backed up, Hutchins would just take a break. "We'd sit back, have a cup of coffee, and complain: 'Those guys stink.'" he says. "At Nucor, we're not 'you guys' and 'us guys'; all of us are 'us guys.' Wherever the bottleneck is, we go there and everyone works on it." (*BusinessWeek,* May 1, 2006, p. 56f.)

Executive pay is also geared towards team building. The annual distribution of plant managers at each production site, or of departmental managers at the headquarters office, depends upon the corporate return on equity, not on the performance of the plant or department.

> [The plant manager at] Nucor's Vulcraft plant in Grapeland (Tex.) remembers that he wasn't in the job two days before he received calls from every other manager in the Vulcraft division offering to help however they could. Vulcraft manufactures the steel joists and decks that hold up the ceilings of shopping centers and other buildings. "It wasn't just idle politeness. I took them up on it." And, they want him to, he notes. "My performance influenced their paychecks." (*BusinessWeek,* May 1, 2006, p. 56f.)

Even the pay of the chief executive officer at Nucor is tied tightly to performance, and limited to a set percentage of the pay of frontline steel makers. The pay of a typical CEO at an American company averages 400 times that of the typical workers within his or her firm; at Nucor it never goes above 14 times. Given that the average steel maker at Nucor makes over $100,000 in a good year, the chief executive officer at that company obviously does not suffer as long as company performance remains high: "In average to bad years, we earn less than our peers in other companies. That's supposed to teach us that we don't want to be average or bad. We want to be good" (*BusinessWeek,* May 1, 2006, p. 56f.).

The *BusinessWeek* article stressed the payment amounts and methods at Nucor, but there are other factors that help to create the distinctive attitudes and behaviors. The hierarchy at Nucor is compressed. There are only three levels between the chief executive officer and the frontline workers: vice president, plant manager, and shift leader. Responsibility at Nucor is delegated. Given the narrow hierarchy at the company, workers are expected to solve operating problems on their own, with just the approval of the shift leader. Stability at Nucor is emphasized. Newly hired members of the firm are told that they will have jobs as long as they remain cooperative and productive. Innovation at Nucor is stressed. Employees at all levels are expected to continually recommend improvements in the company's processes through their experiences at work, and in the company's products through their contacts with customers. And lastly, respect at Nucor is guaranteed; there is said to be only one cause for dismissal at Nucor, and that is treating a fellow employee with a lack of consideration and courtesy.

Class Assignment

The treatment of employees at Nucor is obviously very different from the treatment of employees at other "old line" industries such as steel, cars, car parts, textiles, clothing, and basic chemicals. List the treatment aspects that you would like if you were employed at Nucor, and then add the underlying policies on which those aspects are based, and the resulting attitude changes. For example:

Treatment Aspects	Underlying Policies	Attitudes Changes
High compensation ($100,000) for frontline workers	Low ($10/hr) hourly rate Substantial weekly bonus Large annual distribution	Worry about output quantity Worry about output quality Work cooperatively, as teams

Remember, not all of the treatment aspects and underlying policies that you might like at Nucor are compensation based, or even employee focused. Make certain that you include the full range.

Why don't other companies in other industries adopt these policies? There is nothing that is "rocket science" about them.

Would those other companies in other industries have been more successful if they had adopted these policies? At the time that this case is being written (fall 2006) Ford and General Motors are experiencing severe financial problems, with declining car sales and increasing annual deficits. Would that have happened if they had adopted these policies?

Lastly, it is easy to say that those other companies did not adopt these different policies because they did not know of them. Nucor came along later. But why did not those other companies originate these ideas? Once again, there is nothing "rocket science" about them.

Chapter 6

How Can a Business Organization Be Made Moral?

The first basic argument of the previous chapter was that people throughout the firm—employees, suppliers, distributors, customers, creditors, and owners—react positively when they believe they have been treated in ways that they consider to be "right" and "just" and "fair." This positive reaction consists of increased trust, greater commitment, and higher effort. I think that we can all agree that increased trust, greater commitment, and higher effort are keys to managerial success.

The second basic argument of the last chapter was that it is not enough for senior executives to balance economic outcomes, legal requirements, and ethical duties in ways that they believe to be "right" and "just" and "fair" and then stop. They have to go further and (1) be able to convincingly explain to others why their balance is "right" and "just" and "fair" and (2) thoroughly infuse that new philosophy of management or sense of integrity throughout the full firm in order to solidly establish the trust, commitment, and effort that is needed. Let us say, for example, that you are the president of the company I work for and you treat me very well, with a balanced consideration for my interests, but all the other managers treat me as if I don't exist, ignoring my well-being and neglecting my rights. Under those conditions, I think we can both agree that I am not going to evidence much of the trust, commitment, and effort that is so necessary for the success of our company in a highly competitive, rapidly changing global economy. The steps needed to infuse your philosophy of management throughout the firm, influencing the behavior of all of the other managers, are shown in Figure 6.1.

Rather than following this graphic with definitions, in very exact terms, of each of the steps in the process of infusing that new philosophy of management or sense of integrity throughout the firm, I should like to start with an example of the need for that infusion. The example is the wreck of the *Exxon Valdez*. This was a moral disaster that harmed in very substantial ways the Exxon Corporation and almost all of the individuals and groups associated with that firm: employees, owners, distributors, local residents, and state citizens. It was an accident that did not have to happen and one that could easily have been remedied far more quickly and completely than actually happened. It was, in short, a disastrous accident that occurred and a recovery process that was botched because no one cared, because no one trusted the management, evidenced any commitment or effort for the firm.

FIGURE 6.1   **Proposed Means of Infusing a New Philosophy of Management or Sense of Integrity throughout a Business Firm in Order to Achieve Greater Trust, Commitment, and Effort among All of the Stakeholders of That Firm**

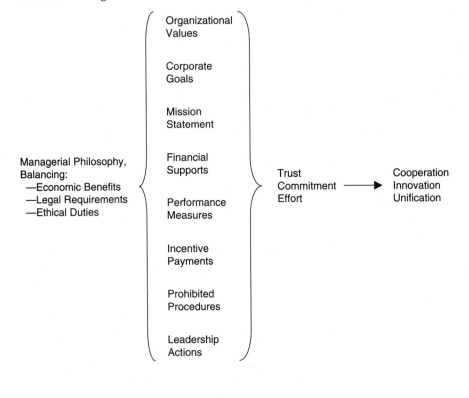

Example of a Moral Disaster

At 9:30 p.m. on Thursday, the 22nd of March, the oil tanker *Exxon Valdez* left the oil terminal at Valdez, Alaska, loaded with 1.26 million barrels of oil. The *Valdez* was the largest tanker owned by Exxon. It was nearly 1,000 feet long and weighed, fully loaded, 280,000 tons.

When the ship left port, it was under the command of Captain William Murphy, the harbor pilot. Harbor pilots are responsible for steering both incoming and outgoing tankers through the Valdez Narrows, a ½-mile-wide approach to the port of Valdez. After exiting the Narrows and achieving the sea lanes in Prince William Sound, Captain Murphy turned over command to Captain Joseph Hazelwood and left the ship. Captain Murphy testified later that he had smelled alcohol on the breath of Captain Hazelwood, but that he made no comment and took no action. He knew that it was common practice for both the officers and crew of oil tankers to drink while in port.

Captain Hazelwood, immediately after assuming command, radioed the Coast Guard and requested permission to alter course to avoid large chunks of ice that had broken loose from the Columbia Glacier and were floating in the outbound shipping lane. The permission was granted. Captain Hazelwood then turned over command of the vessel to Third Mate Gregory Cousins and went below to his cabin. Mr. Cousins was not licensed to pilot a ship in the sea channels approaching Valdez. Mr. Cousins and others later testified that it was common practice to turn over command of oil tankers to nonlicensed officers. Captain Hazelwood had set the automatic pilot to steer the ship southward into the inbound shipping lane, and he had instructed Mr. Cousins to maintain the course until after the ice chunks from the glacier were passed, and then to return northward to the outbound lane. No inbound traffic was expected, and permission for this course change had been granted by the Coast Guard, so no danger was anticipated. At 11:55 Mr. Cousins ordered a course change of 10 degrees right rudder to bring the tanker back to the proper lane within the channel. There was no response. At 12:04 the lookout, who was on the bridge rather than at the normal station on the bow of the tanker, sighted the lighted buoy marketing Bligh Reef, a rock outcropping only 30 to 40 feet beneath the surface. Mr. Cousins ordered emergency hard right rudder. Again there was no response. In the hearing that followed the accident, it was determined that either Captain Hazelwood had not informed Mr. Cousins that he had placed the ship on automatic pilot, or that Mr. Cousins and the helmsman had not remembered to disconnect the automatic pilot, which prevented manual steering of the vessel.

At 12:05 a.m. the Exxon Valdez ran aground on Bligh Reef. The hull was punctured in numerous places, and 260,000 barrels, approximately 11,000,000 gallons of crude oil, spilled from the badly ruptured tanks. It was the largest oil spill in the history of the North American petroleum industry.

At 12:28 a.m. one of the officers on the ship radioed to the Coast Guard that it was aground on Bligh Reef. "Are you leaking oil?" a Coast Guard operator asked. "I think so," was the reply.

At 3:28 a.m. members of the Coast Guard boarded the *Exxon Valdez* and reported that oil was gushing from the tanker. "We've got a serious problem," radioed the Coast Guard officer on board the tanker. "There's nobody here. . . . Where's Alyeska?"

"Alyeska" was the Alyeska Pipeline Service Company, which both managed the oil pipeline that brought crude oil 800 miles from the oil fields at Prudhoe Bay to Valdez and ran the oil terminal at Valdez. It was responsible, through a formal agreement with the state of Alaska, for the containment and recovery of all oil spills within the harbor and sea lanes. That agreement was expressed in a detailed written plan, 250 pages long, that listed the equipment and personnel that were to be kept available by Alyeska, and the actions that were to be taken by Alyeska, to react promptly to oil spills.

The stated goal of the written plan was to encircle any serious oil spill with floating containment booms within five hours of the first report of the occurrence, and to recover 50 percent of the spill within 48 hours. The stated goal was well known within the area, and accounted for the perplexity of the Coast Guard officer. When he reported, "There's nobody here," he was referring not to the captain and crew of the tanker, but to the oil spill recovery team and equipment from Alyeska.

The Coast Guard officer also noted the smell of alcohol on the breath of Captain Hazelwood, and reported to his base in very blunt terms that he suspected the captain was drunk. He was unable to establish the degree of intoxication, due to the lack of a testing kit, but he did request the assistance of the Alaska State Police to conduct the tests as soon as possible. Those tests were conducted the following morning, and did establish that the level of alcohol in Captain Hazelwood's bloodstream at the time was twice the legal limit.

At 6:00 a.m. on Friday, March 23 (six hours after the accident), officials from Exxon flew over the grounded tanker for the first time and reported a massive oil slick streaming away from the tanker. They contacted the Alyeska oil terminal, and ordered a quicker response and greater effort. The problem, the manager at that terminal reported, was that the single barge capable of handling the long containment booms had been out of service for two weeks and had been unloaded for repairs. Workers were preparing to reload the barge, he said, but the only employee who was capable of operating the crane needed for reloading had not yet reported for work. Later that morning the loading was completed and the barge was taken in tow by a harbor tug. At 2:39 p.m. the barge arrived at the wreck site, carrying all of the containment booms that were available at the terminal and a number of centrifugal pumps to help in removing the remaining oil from the *Valdez*.

At 7:36 a.m. on Saturday, March 24 (31½ hours after the accident), Exxon began pumping oil from the *Valdez* to a second tanker moored alongside, the *Baton Rouge*. At about the same time, seven Alyeska "skimmers," or barges with vacuum equipment designed to siphon oil off the surface of the water, arrived at the site. The skimmers, however, were designed to recover oil that had been bunched in a compact mass by containment booms. Those booms were still not in place due to a shortage of tugs and to some degree of confusion in the means of unloading the booms and placing them in the sea. By nightfall, only 1,200 barrels of oil had been recovered.

By 11:00 a.m. on Sunday, March 25 (59 hours after the accident), the *Exxon Valdez* was finally encircled by containment booms. It had taken 2½ days to get the booms in place, despite the original plan that called for full containment of any spill within five hours. Most of the oil was now outside the booms in a slick that covered 12 square miles, and the wave action had begun to convert the crude oil to an emulsified "mousse" mixture of oil and water that quadrupled the volume. This emulsified mixture now lay 5 to 9 inches thick upon the surface of the sea. The specific gravity of the emulsified mixture was very different from the specific gravity of either water or oil, and the skimmers were no longer effective except when working on fresh seepages close to the grounded tanker, within the booms.

At 6:00 a.m. on Monday, March 26 (78 hours after the accident), the Coast Guard admitted that the situation was out of control. The first two days had been calm, but Sunday night winds as high as 73 miles per hour had arisen, and driven the emulsified oil-and-water mixture 37 miles from the wreck site. It was swathing the islands and beaches throughout Prince William Sound with solid bands of black petroleum "gunk," the accepted term for the residue that is left after the more volatile elements in crude oil have evaporated. The skimmer barges and boom-tending boats had been forced to retreat to sheltered water. Flights into the Valdez airport, to bring additional supplies and people, had been halted. Most of the oil that had remained in the unruptured tanks of the *Exxon Valdez* had been pumped out, but it was now thought to be impossible to recover any further substantial amount of the spill. Eventually marks of this spill stretched 700 miles along the coast, spoiling fishery resources, wildlife refuges, and national parks in one of the most scenic regions of the country, and killing sea birds, fish, and mammals in one of the prime marine habitats of the world.

Nearly two months after the biggest oil spill in American history, Alaskan officials say not a single mile of beach has been completely cleaned and that the death tolls of birds, fish and mammals continue to mount.

Large patches of oil, untended in rough and remote seas, are still washing up on pristine Alaska beaches more than 500 miles from the reef in Prince William Sound where the *Exxon Valdez* went aground March 24.

The oil from the spill of 11 million gallons hit 730 miles of coastline, Alaskan state officials said today. Of that, only four miles have been declared cleaned. Less than one mile is totally free of oil, the officials said.

The ecological toll of the spill thus far includes more than 11,000 birds of 300 different species, 700 Pacific seal otters, and 200 bald eagles, according to a tally by the State Department of Environmental Conservation.

Biologists say that the actual number of dead wildlife could be three to five times higher than those found because many of the animals have been washed out to sea or taken by predators.

On some beaches in Prince William Sound the oil is more than three feet thick, lodged in the rocks and providing a reservoir of fresh contamination at every high tide. (*The New York Times,* May 19, 1989, p. 1) [1]

The causes of the accident, while obviously related to the intoxication of the captain and the subsequent command of the ship by an unlicensed third mate, were thought to be more complex than that simple explanation. Two additional factors were mentioned in the early hearings of the Federal Transportation Safety Board that investigated the oil spill.

- *Tired crew members.* The crew members on the tanker were said to have been exhausted from working long hours, and not fully alert. The *Exxon Valdez* normally carried a crew of 20 persons. This crew size was considered to be typical for crude oil tankers, but it was substantially smaller than that required by Coast Guard regulations and union requirements on merchant cargo ships. The oil companies had argued that the new technologies automated the operations of the tankers and eliminated the need for a larger crew. The modern equipment, however, had to be manned and maintained, and consequently the automation did not keep the officers and crew from working extensive amounts of overtime and frequently going long stretches with little or no sleep. Crew members on the *Exxon Valdez* testified that they had worked an average of 140 hours of overtime per month per person for the six months prior to the accident. One hundred and forty hours of overtime per month and 20 days at sea per month plus the regular 8-hour watches works out to be 15 hours per day.

   Many of the crew members were exhausted, a routine feeling on Exxon ships, they testified. (*The New York Times,* May 22, 1989, p. 10)[2]

- *Ignored sailing rules.* There were definite violations of sailing rules. Captain Hazelwood advised the Coast Guard that he was taking the ship on a southwesterly course, into the inbound shipping channel, to avoid floating ice chunks. That was considered to be perfectly proper, and normal under the circumstances, though permission was never granted for this maneuver except when the inbound lanes were completely free

---

[1] Copyright © 1989 by The New York Times Co. Reprinted with permission.

[2] Copyright © 1989 by The New York Times Co. Reprinted with permission.

of other shipping. Captain Hazelwood, however, did not advise the Coast Guard that he then altered course ever further to the south, out of the inbound shipping lanes and into waters close to Bligh Reef, or that he had engaged the autopilot. Permission for the further course change would almost certainly have been refused had the Coast Guard been informed, and Coast Guard rules are very definite that autopilots should never be used except in the open sea. Both improper actions certainly contributed to the final grounding of the ship.

> "Your children could have driven a tanker up through that channel." (Statement of Paul Yost, commandant of the U. S. Coast Guard, quoted in *The Wall Street Journal,* March 31, 1989, p. 1)[3]

Within Alaska, public reactions to the accident and to the lackadaisical practices that apparently led to the accident centered on the potential damage to the fishing resources and, consequently, on the harm to the livelihood of a substantial portion of the state's population. The Alaska coast from Prince William Sound northward is known as the richest salmon and crab fishing grounds in the world. Exxon assured the fishing boat operators that they would be compensated for any losses they suffered as a result of the oil spill, and explained that the company had insurance that would protect it against claims for negligence up to $4,500 million.

Outside of Alaska, public reactions to the accident and to the lackadaisical practices revealed in the hearings focused on the fouling of the environment and the destruction of the wildlife:

> Already thousands of birds have died, and biologists fear that a significant portion of the Sound's 12,000 sea otters—which lose buoyancy when just 10 percent of their body is covered in oil—may be in jeopardy.
>
> Those who know these bejeweled waters—rich in fish, fowl and fauna like few other places on earth—believe the damage will be monumental and long lasting. (*The Wall Street Journal,* March 31, 1989, p.1)
>
> Right now I'm still finding dead sea otters on the beach (61 days after the accident). Bald eagles feed on them, so I'm finding dead eagles. . . . Here I am, a scientist with a Ph.D., and as I watch these oiled birds trying to take off I start to cry. (Statement of a biologist at the Kenai Fjords National Park, quoted in *The New York Times,* May 19, 1989, p. 1f.)[4]

Public reactions to the accident also were not mollified when the chairman of Exxon, Mr. Lawrence Rawl, decided not to go to Alaska and supervise the cleanup operations directly. Instead, he remained in New York City and made no direct comment upon the oil spill or cleanup operations for seven days. Other officials with Exxon also refused to comment. The first statement by the president of Exxon U.S.A., the holding company for Exxon Shipping, which owned the grounded tanker, was made on May 9:

> We do not know what caused this accident. . . . Exxon's response was prompt and consistent with the previously approved contingency plan. (Mr. Bill Stevens, quoted in the *Detroit Free Press,* May 9, 1989, p. 7A)

---

[3] *The Wall Street Journal*, Central Edition [only staff-produced materials may be used] by N/A. Copyright 2005 by Dow Jones & Company, Inc. Reproduced with permission of Dow Jones & Company, Inc. in the format Textbook via Copyright Clearance Center.

[4] Copyright © 1989 by The New York Times Co. Reprinted with permission.

In fairness to Exxon, it should be explained that company officials felt that public reactions to the oil spill were extreme and did not take into account several mitigating factors. First, they thought that the public did not really understand that the company could not be held responsible for the intoxication of Captain Hazelwood. Second, they thought that the public did not fully realize that the company had been prevented from using chemical dispersants on the oil.

Chemical dispersants, it should be understood, do not destroy the oil. Instead, the effect of the dispersant is to lower the surface tension of the oil to the point where it will break up and disperse in the water in the form of tiny droplets. The problem is that these tiny droplets are in a size range that is easily ingested by marine organisms on the lower end of the marine food chain, and therefore gradually impact marine creatures on the higher end of that chain. The extent of that impact has never been studied under all climatic conditions. It is known that dispersants make an oil spill much less visible; there is no certainty that they make it any less toxic.

Despite the lack of certainty about the effect of the dispersants, company officials thought that chemicals should have been used as soon as it was apparent that the containment and recovery efforts had failed, and before the beaches were fouled and the wildlife killed. Mr. Rawl, the chairman of Exxon, in an interview with *Fortune* magazine, said environmentalists acting with the state of Alaska had prevented the company from applying the dispersants promptly:

> One of the things I feel strongly about—this catching hell for two days' delay—is that I don't think that we got a fair shake. The basic problem we ran into was that we had environmentalists advising the Alaskan Department of Environmental Conservation that the dispersants could be toxic. (Lawrence Rawl, quoted in *The New York Times,* May 22, 1989, p. 10)[5]

Mr. Lee Kelso, director of the Alaskan Department of Environmental Conservation, disagreed strongly that his department was responsible for any delay in the use of the chemical dispersants:

> Exxon was free to use dispersants on the vast majority of the oil slick, and did not do so. (Lee Kelso, quoted in the *The Wall Street Journal,* April 3, 1989, p. 1)[6]

Mr. Lee Raymond, president of the Exxon Corporation, said that he blamed "ultimately the Coast Guard" (*The Wall Street Journal,* April 3, 1989, p. 12) for the delay in the use of dispersants, explaining that it had required a test before granting permission.

Coast Guard officials denied that they had required testing, saying that it was only common sense to gauge the effectiveness of the treatment under the wind, wave, and water temperature conditions that existed at the time.

Government reactions to the oil spill centered not on the causes of the accident, and not on the consequences of the oil spill or the dispute about testing, but on the slowness and ineffectual nature of the cleanup. The federal attitude seemed to be that accidents

---

[5] Copyright © 1989 by The New York Times Co. Reprinted with permission.

[6] *The Wall Street Journal,* Central Edition [only staff-produced materials may be used] by N/A. Copyright 2005 by Dow Jones & Company, Inc. Reproduced with permission of Dow Jones & Company, Inc. in the format Textbook via Copyright Clearance Center.

do occur, that seamen have been known to consume excessive amounts of alcohol in the past, and that under conditions of stress people may forget about test conditions and requirements. But in the view of the government in Washington, there was no excuse for the inability first of Alyeska and then of Exxon to deal promptly and effectively with the spill itself.

The contingency plan that had been developed by Alyeska and approved by the state of Alaska envisaged containment within five hours and recovery of a minimum of 50 percent of the oil by skimmers within 48 hours. Containment, as stated previously took 59 hours, and estimates of the amount of oil actually recovered ranged from 0.4 to 2.5 percent. A number of reasons for the ineffectiveness of the response by Alyeska and Exxon were given in hearings held by the National Transportation Safety Board.

It should be explained, before discussing the results of these hearings before the National Transportation Safety Board, that the Alyeska Pipelines Service Company is not a subsidiary of the Exxon Corporation. It is a consortium owned by the seven oil companies that have drilling rights on the North Slope of Alaska and ship crude oil from Prudhoe Bay to Valdez. Representatives of all seven companies serve on the board of directors. Exxon is the second largest owner, and is said to participate actively in the management of the company.

The first reason given for the slowness of response was a shortage of equipment. The oil spill contingency plan required Alyeska to maintain two barges, loaded with containment booms and ready for use. At the time of the spill, only one barge was available. The other had been scrapped as old and obsolete, but its replacement was still in Seattle. There was a requirement in the contingency plan that Alyeska notify the state Department of Environmental Conservation if any equipment was out of service for any period of time. Alyeska now concedes that it failed to provide this notification.

The barge that was available had been damaged by a storm in January. It was still considered to be seaworthy, but the containment booms had been unloaded to facilitate repair. Repairs had been delayed, according to testimony by Alyeska officials, because the company had been unable to locate a licensed marine welder. Environmentalists at the hearing displayed the Valdez telephone book that listed four companies that claimed to provide licensed marine welding services.

Seven thousand one hundred feet of containment booms were stored at the oil terminal. The contingency plan did not specify an exact lineal footage that was to be kept in stock, but it can be understood that 7,100 feet would be enough to contain a spill around a 1,000 foot tanker only if the booms could be placed quickly, before the oil spread out upon the surface of the water. Three thousand feet would be required just to encircle the hull.

Ten skimmers, which are large suction units that can be mounted on barges and used in essence to vacuum oil from the surface of the sea, were available as promised in the contingency plan. However, replacement parts were not kept in stock, and equipment breakdowns were common as the machines were not designed to work on the emulsified mixture of oil and water that was formed rapidly through wave actions on the noncontained spill.

Other equipment that was needed either was missing or could not be found quickly. Heavy ship fenders, essential for the second tanker to come alongside the *Exxon Valdez* and pump out its remaining oil, couldn't be located for hours because they were buried under 14 feet of snow. Half of the required six-inch hose, needed for the pumping, never was found and replacement had to be flown in from Seattle. The emergency lighting system, to illuminate the boom-laying and oil-pumping work at night, was finally discovered off base, being readied for use in the Valdez winter carnival.

As a final example of the shortage of equipment, it was determined after the accident that there never had been enough chemical dispersant stored in Valdez to treat the oil spill, even had there been no disagreement or misunderstanding about permission to use this material.

> Records made available this week show there was prior approval to use dispersants in the area of the spill and that only 69 barrels of dispersants were on hand in Valdez for a job that called for nearly 10,000 barrels.
>
> Six days after the spill, Exxon still had only a fraction of the amount needed to fight the disaster, according to records and the company's testimony this week. (*The New York Times*, May 22, 1989, p. 10)[7]

In addition to the shortage of equipment, there was also a shortage of personnel. The oil spill contingency plan required Alyeska to have a crew of 15 persons on duty at all times. These were not oil spill experts. These were hourly paid workers responsible for the normal operations of the terminal, but according to the plan they should have included all of the skills and trades necessary to respond to emergencies, whether oil spills at sea, oil leaks on land, or oil fires at the terminal.

At the time of the spill, only 11 workers were on duty. Unfortunately, none of those people knew how to operate the crane, which was needed to load the barge with the long and heavy containment booms. A crane operator was finally located, but he was also the only one who knew how to drive the fork lift, and he spent the morning after the accident, when speed in response was essential, running back and forth between the fork lift and the loading crane.

Last, there was a lack of training. Alyeska had dismissed its oil spill response team in 1981. This was a group of 12 persons originally set up to contain and then clean up spills throughout Valdez Harbor and Prince William Sound. The duties of the spill response team were assigned to regular employees at the plant. At the time of dismissal, Alyeska had claimed that this arrangement would be superior as they would have "120 people trained in oil spill response rather than 12."

> Some of the cited 120 scoff at this. One senior employee says he has had "zero oil spill training, none." He recalls being summoned to two spills over the years. "I didn't know what the hell I was supposed to do, and when I found the guy I was supposed to report to, he did not know what the hell we were supposed to do either. We just stood there watching." (*The Wall Street Journal,* July 16, 1989, p. 1)[8]

Some of the operating managers within the oil industry have been greatly concerned by this tendency to replace specialized teams with personnel from the general workforce:

[7] Copyright © 1989 by The New York Times Co. Reprinted with permission.

[8] *The Wall Street Journal,* Central Edition [only staff-produced materials may be used] by N/A. Copyright 2005 by Dow Jones & Company, Inc. Reproduced with permission of Dow Jones & Company, Inc. in the format Textbook via Copyright Clearance Center.

You either have a team of people who are dedicated to a specific task, and trained to perform that task under any and all conditions, or you have nothing. The Valdez terminal didn't have that trained team, and it showed.

We run into this same problem continually with fire drills. Previously, every refinery had a fire department, with fire engines, a fire chief and a fire crew. Now, they just have the engines and, if they are lucky, they still have a chief who knows what he is doing and can teach the others. We are not lucky, and we don't still have a chief. It is company policy to run a drill once every six months. The bell rings, and all of the 9:00 to 5:00 desk jockeys jump on the truck, and away they go. When they get there, they don't know how to turn on the hydrant, they don't know how to work the pump, they don't know how to lay the hose and fight the fire, and they don't know what is safe and what isn't. We have not had a fire since the department was disbanded, but when we do it is going to get very bad, very fast.

I can understand exactly what happened at Valdez. They had not had a major spill in 18 years, but when they did it got very bad, very fast. (Statement of oil industry executive made in confidence to the case writer)

The shortage of equipment, the shortage of personnel, and the lack of training were caused, it now appears, by deliberate policy decisions reached by the senior management of Exxon Corporation, who pushed strongly for cost reductions at Alyeska during the mid-1980s. These policy decisions were not taken arbitrarily. They were in response to a change in the basic economic conditions of the oil industry.

Oil prices fell from $32/barrel in 1981, at the height of the power of the OPEC (Organization of Petroleum Exporting Countries) to $12/barrel in 1987, and then rose slightly to stabilize in the range of $15 to $20/barrel. The large oil companies are vertically integrated, with divisions for the exploration, production, and refining of crude oil, and for the distribution and marketing of oil products. The lower price for crude oil brought exploration nearly to a halt and severely reduced the profits that come from production.

The large, vertically integrated oil companies reacted slowly to the changed economic conditions, but the reaction—when it came—was dramatic and harsh. Costs were reduced. Employees were discharged. The changes at Exxon were particularly dramatic because the company for years had prided itself on a generous, almost paternal attitude towards its employees. In January 1986 Mr. Clifton Garvin, chairman of Exxon Corporation since 1975, commented to *Fortune* magazine about personnel policies at the time of his company's selection as one of the 10 "most admired" firms in the United States.

Six months later, Exxon Corporation was in the midst of an extensive restructuring effort that would eventually change the company from one of the "most admired" to one of the most disliked. The company planned a 2 percent budget cut. They gave workers 60 days to decide whether or not to resign with their partially funded pensions. It added that if it did not get enough volunteers, it would resort to involuntary terminations, with no pensions. Analysts estimated that the 26 percent budget cut, almost totally aimed at mid-level managers and hourly paid workers, would reduce employment approximately one-third.

The generous, almost paternal attitude of the company toward Exxon employees had disappeared. Nearly one-third of all the company's workers, almost all of those over 50 years of age, were told they had to retire early or be fired:

With oil companies cutting production in the face of falling crude oil prices and a hard-noised head chopper named Lawrence Rawl in the president's chair, at least part of Exxon's worldwide workforce of 145,000 seemed destined for the block. In late April, the world's largest oil company offered 40,500 employees the option to retire early or quit with compensation. (*Fortune,* May 16, 1986, p. 11)

The new chairman of Exxon, Mr. Lawrence Rawl, who replaced Mr. Clifton Garvin in the spring of 1986, apparently believed that he had been selected by the board of directors to reduce costs and increase earnings, despite the probable impact upon employee morale.

The cutbacks in staff extended throughout Exxon to the Exxon Shipping Company—the 20-person crews on that company's oil tankers reportedly were to have been reduced to 15 persons had the accident not intervened—and to the Alyeska Pipeline Company:

When oil prices began falling in 1981, the owners of Alyeska ordered it to save even more on costs. In late 1982, Alyeska managers prepared what they thought was a lean budget and presented it to a meeting of the owners' committee in San Francisco. According to former Alyeska officials who were briefed on the meeting at the time, committee members cited a figure, roughly $220 million, and asked if the budget was under that; told that it wasn't, they rejected it out of hand.

"There was an overall attitude of petty cheapness that severely affects our ability to operate safely," recalls Mr. Woodle who came over from the Coast Guard to run the terminal's marine operations just in time to see their budget slashed by about a third. "I was shocked at the shabbiness of the operations." (*The Wall Street Journal,* July 6, 1989, p. 1)

Management of a Moral Company

The oil spill from the *Exxon Valdez* coated 750 miles of Alaska coastline. It severely impacted the livelihood of commercial fishermen, almost destroyed the food sources of native Indians, and resulted in the death of 40 percent of bald eagles in Alaska, killed 80 percent of sea otters in Prince William Sound, and eliminated 200,000 birds along the coast. It nearly ruined the reputation of the Exxon Corporation and resulted in a $2.4 billion fine by the federal government and a $2.8 billion penalty in a civil trial. Senior executives truly wish that the careless accident and delayed cleanup had never happened. The causes and consequences of that careless accident and delayed cleanup are summarized in Figure 6.2.

How could it have been avoided? The argument of this chapter is that it would have required a series of changes, starting with a different philosophy of management and then continuing with different corporate values, organizational goals, and mission statement, as shown graphically once again in Figure 6.3. The balance of this chapter will discuss the stages in that figure, with a short explanation of the recommended changes in each stage, and then a brief comment about the performance that would be expected from Exxon employees following those changes.

Philosophy of Management

If the total focus of corporate management is placed on financial benefits for the stockholders, with little or no attention paid to the well-being and/or rights of the other

FIGURE 6.2 **Actions That Led to the Wreck of the *Exxon Valdez* and the Slow Cleanup of the Resulting Oil Spill**

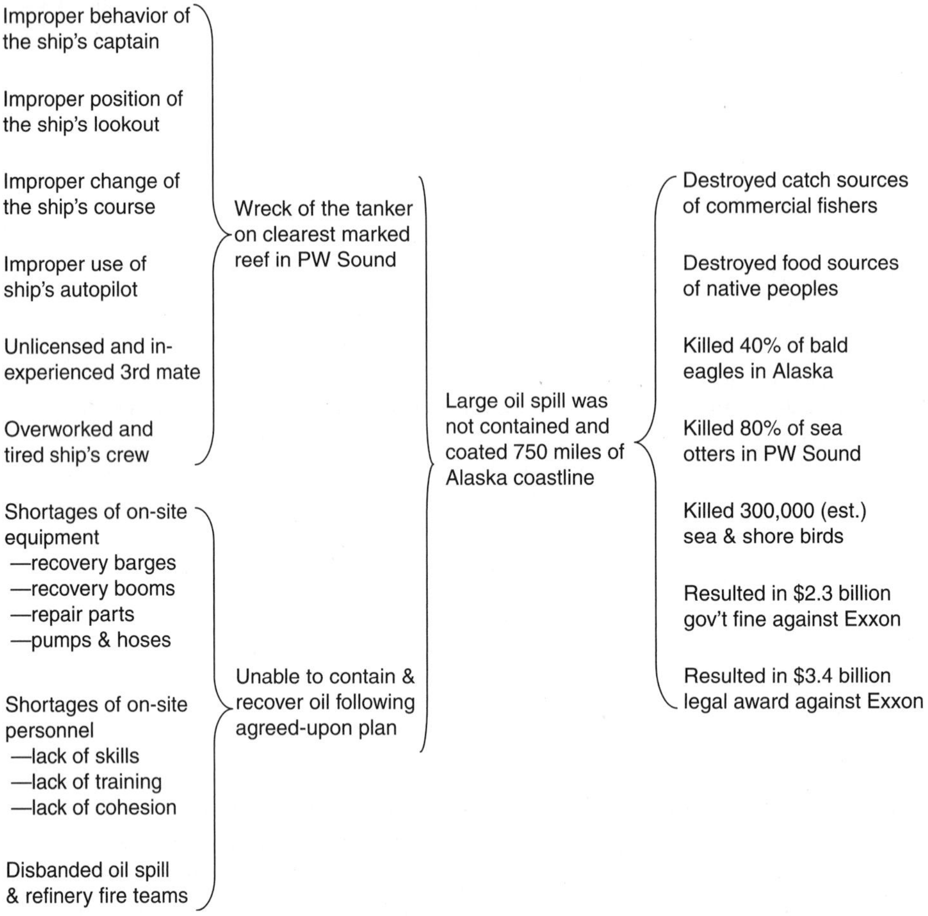

Improper behavior of the ship's captain

Improper position of the ship's lookout

Improper change of the ship's course

Improper use of ship's autopilot

Unlicensed and in-experienced 3rd mate

Overworked and tired ship's crew

Wreck of the tanker on clearest marked reef in PW Sound

Shortages of on-site equipment
—recovery barges
—recovery booms
—repair parts
—pumps & hoses

Shortages of on-site personnel
—lack of skills
—lack of training
—lack of cohesion

Disbanded oil spill & refinery fire teams

Unable to contain & recover oil following agreed-upon plan

Large oil spill was not contained and coated 750 miles of Alaska coastline

Destroyed catch sources of commercial fishers

Destroyed food sources of native peoples

Killed 40% of bald eagles in Alaska

Killed 80% of sea otters in PW Sound

Killed 300,000 (est.) sea & shore birds

Resulted in $2.3 billion gov't fine against Exxon

Resulted in $3.4 billion legal award against Exxon

stakeholders, the result—according to this text—will be a lack of trust, commitment, and effort among those other stakeholders.

This is clearly what happened at Exxon Corporation. At the time of the wreck, Exxon was being managed with sole attention to the financial well-being of the stockholders. Lawrence Rawl boasted that he was "bottom line" oriented, that he planned to fire employees and cut expenses to increase profits, with no concern for those to be fired in the company or to those to be harmed in the community. Under economic outcomes, the company did not recognize the external costs that were imposed upon the commercial fishers, the native Indians, and the active environmentalists. Under government requirements, the company did not obey the law, in the form of the spill response contract with the state of Alaska. Under ethical duties, the company was not open, honest, and truthful about their actions and did not select the greatest net benefit for society or act in a way they would be willing to have all others act. The result was a clear lack of committed effort by employees

FIGURE 6.3   Proposed Means of Infusing a New Philosophy of Management or Sense of Integrity throughout a Business Firm to Achieve Greater Trust, Commitment, and Effort among All of the Stakeholders of That Firm

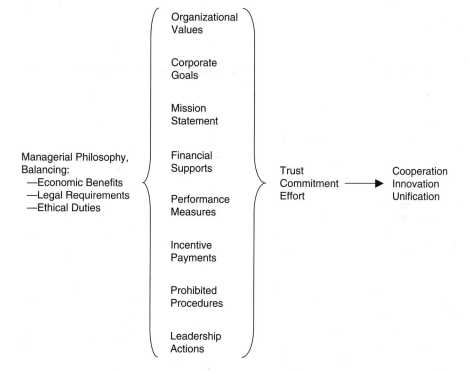

on the tanker: no one was willing to report the frequent drunken behavior by the captain or to object to the continual violations of sailing rules that jointly led to the tragic accident. The result was also a complete lack of committed effort by employees at the terminal: no one made an attempt to correct the shortage of equipment and the absence of training that led to the slow response. That lack of trust, commitment, and effort brought about, eventually, a huge cost to the company and a heavy charge to the society.

Corporate Values

To avoid easy generalizations, think of corporate values as the duties the senior executives of the firm should—in your view—owe to the various individuals and groups associated with the firm who can, in one way or another, affect the future performance and position of the firm. These individuals and groups include owners of all types (institutional and individual), employees at all levels, customers in all segments, suppliers, distributors, creditors, local residents, national citizens, and global inhabitants. Think about what issues are probably important to each of those individuals and groups. Then think about the extent to which the senior executives of the firm should recognize those factors that are important to each of those individuals and groups. In short, think about how the company should begin to plan for unification based upon similarities rather than separation based upon differences.

Clearly Exxon owed profitable operations to the owners, but they also owed them the duty of avoiding large fines and penalties. Perhaps they could not have owed continued employment to all of the workers, given the changed conditions of the oil industry, but they could have provided those workers with better conditions, such as less forced overtime on the oil tankers, and improved training, such as better instruction for the response teams. It would be hard to argue that they did not owe an unharmed environment to the local residents, and forthright information on the level of preparation to the state officials. None of these duties, beyond profits owed to the shareholders, apparently were recognized by the senior executives at Exxon.

Organizational Goals

To avoid easy generalizations, think of company goals as the end points the senior executives of the firm should—in your view—set for the various dimensions of performance that are possible. What—again in your view—should the senior executives want to accomplish along such dimensions as financial performance, technological achievement, industry position, market share, customer satisfaction, manufacturing efficiency, employee loyalty, environmental protection, public reputation, and social contribution? What—once more in your view—should the various groups associated with the firm want to accomplish on each of these dimensions? As with the corporate values there will be differences among these groups. Scientists and engineers doubtless would like to emphasize technological achievement, while the owners and creditors probably would prefer to focus on financial performance. The two may not be as dissimilar as they at first appear; if the organization is positioned correctly within the industry, there will be an obvious connection between the two. Again, think about how the company should begin to plan for unification based upon similarities rather than separation based upon differences.

Exxon placed total emphasis upon financial performance, and set very explicit goals along that dimension. The accident, and the total of $5.2 billion in fines and penalties, could have been avoided with greater emphasis upon technological achievement (better methods of tanker control and spill cleanup), employee morale (less drinking by tanker officers and more training for terminal employees), environmental protection, and public reputation. The basic question in proposing goals for a corporation is whether it is possible to plan for profits or whether it is necessary to plan for the activities that lead to profits. Exxon, it is very clear, planned for profits.

Mission Statement

The mission statement is the means of combining the duties that the firm owes to others with the goals that it has set for itself. What role, as a result of this combination, should the firm attempt to play within the market, the industry, the economy, and the society? It is frequently difficult to express corporate values and organizational goals in explicit numerical terms. Consequently, many firms compromise with a mission statement that speaks only generally about the duties they want to observe and the end points they want to achieve, but much more specifically about the means they want to use and the standards they want to follow. The intent is to define the future of the firm, the scope of its activities, and the character of its people so that everyone will clearly understand: "This is where we're going to go, this is what we're going to do, and this is how we're going to do it." Think in terms of a document that will create a challenge for everyone associated with the firm. Think also in terms of a document you would be proud to hand to employees, to show to customers, to send to suppliers and distributors, and to include in the annual report for owners.

Exxon, at the time of the wreck of the *Exxon Valdez,* did not have a mission statement. Instead, it had a code of conduct, which is reproduced below:

> Our company policy is one of strict observance of all laws applicable to its business:
>
>> A reputation for scrupulous dealing is itself a priceless company asset.
>> We do care how we get results.
>> We expect candor at all levels and compliance with accounting rules and controls.
>> It is the established policy of the company to conduct its business in compliance with all state and federal antitrust laws.
>> Individual employees are responsible for seeing that they comply with the law.
>> Employees must avoid even the appearance of violation.
>
> Competing or conducting business with the company is not permitted, except with the knowledge and consent of management.
>
>> Accepting and providing gifts, entertainment, and services must comply with specific requirements.
>> An employee may not use company personnel, information, or other assets for personal benefit.
>> Participating in certain outside activities requires the prior approval of management.

What would have happened had Exxon Corporation had a mission statement similar to the one adopted by Johnson & Johnson that was printed in Chapter 5? Here the order of priorities was very clear: customers, suppliers, distributors, employees, and local residents come first, with company owners at the very end. Just having a different mission statement that emphasized duties and goals in set rankings, rather than policies and prohibitions without priorities, probably would not have avoided the wreck or improved the cleanup. But it is the argument of this text that having such a mission statement bolstered by proper financial supports, performance measures, incentive payments, prohibited procedures, and leadership actions would have made a substantial difference.

Financial Supports

Within every firm, in very simple terms, someone has to sell the products (marketing), manufacture the goods (production), and supervise the cash flows (finance). In slightly more complex terms, someone also has to gather the data (information systems), develop the people (human resources), and apply the technologies (research and development). In somewhat further complex terms, someone has to select the strategy (strategic planning), define the tasks (activity planning), and design the structure (organizational planning). People at all of these levels, from the least to the most complex, need money, or, more properly, the authority to spend money, in order to follow the policies and achieve the goals set in the mission statement.

Financial supports provide that authority to spend money to accomplish results. This money comes in two forms: capital and cost. Capital represents the long-term investments needed for buildings, equipment, and inventory; those amounts are "capitalized," or recorded as an asset on the balance sheet. Cost represents the short-term expenditures required for employee salaries and outside services; these amounts are "expensed," or deducted from revenues on the income statement. The issue in financial supports is whether the capital is allocated and the costs are budgeted to maximize the profits for the company or to fulfill the duties and meet the goals listed in the mission statement.

It is very clear that Exxon had not made the long-term capital investments that were needed for equipment and inventory to contain and then recover the oil spill. Only one of the two barges specified in the contract with the state of Alaska to transport the containment booms to the site of a spill was available, and that had been damaged and not repaired. An adequate number of containment booms were not available. Spare parts for the skimmers were not in stock. Only 69 barrels of chemical dispersants were on hand; not the 10,000 barrels that were required. Obviously the emphasis here had been on profits, not duties and goals.

It is also very clear that Exxon had not budgeted the short-term cost amounts that were needed for personnel and training to be able to contain and then recover the oil spill. The specialized oil spill recovery teams had been disbanded. Only 11 general-purpose workers were on duty at the time of the wreck, not the 16 specified in the contract with the state of Alaska, and those employees had not been specifically trained to respond to oil spill emergencies. There was a lack of cohesion in the containment and recovery efforts caused, in the view of the marine managers of the Valdez terminal, by "an overall attitude of petty cheapness that severely affected our ability to operate safely" (*The Wall Street Journal,* cited previously). Obviously here also the emphasis had been on profits, not duties and goals.

Performance Measures

Performance measures are the means of evaluating the performance of the persons assigned to the various critical tasks designed to implement the strategy and achieve the mission of the firm within capital investment and expense budget constraints. Many of these performance measures are financial in nature, simple restatements of the capital allocations and revenue/expense budgets. Others are numerical, and related to such aspects of job performance as unit output, customer satisfaction, product performance, workplace safety, employee morale, and environmental preservation. Setting these performance targets for people assigned to critical tasks is felt to be an important aspect of corporate management; it is frequently said "If you can't measure 'em, you can't manage 'em." The issue in performance measures, as in financial supports, is whether the measures are set to maximize the profits of the company or to fulfill the duties and meet the goals of the mission statement.

None of the published accounts of the hearings and trials that followed the wreck of the Exxon Valdez spoke specifically of the performance measures that were in use by the Exxon Corporation. It can be assumed, however, given the restrictions on capital allocations and limitations on budgeted expenses, that all of them focused on profits. It would appear that none of the managers at Valdez were measured on the availability of response equipment and inventory or on the training of recovery employees.

Incentive Payments

Incentive payments are the means of rewarding the performance of the persons assigned to the various critical tasks designed to implement the strategy and achieve the mission of the firm. They are the method by which the people supervising the programs and managing the divisions are rewarded for meeting the performance targets that they have been assigned. These rewards can be financial (bonuses or commissions), positional (promotions and raises), or reputational (recognition and praise). They are usually tied very closely to the performance measures; if an individual meets the target that was set on—for example—divisional profit, customer satisfaction, or workplace safety, then the incentive payments reward that achievement. These rewards for meeting performance targets often have an impact upon the occurrence of moral problems, particularly if the size or the importance of the incentives for the manager can overcome that person's judgment as to what is best for the firm. Bonuses and commissions that form a very high percentage of a manager's total compensation package often lead to "cutting corners" and "taking risks."

Again, none of the published accounts of the hearings and trials that followed the wreck of the *Exxon Valdez* spoke specifically of the incentive payments. It can be assumed here also, however, that most if not all of them focused on rewarding the managers who met their profit and cost objectives. Had those managers received a bonus or a promotion or even just recognition and praise for having response equipment and inventory on hand or for having trained employees ready to react, the spill probably would not have been left uncontained for 59 hours rather than the 5 hours specified in the contract with the state of Alaska.

Prohibited Procedures

Prohibited procedures are a published listing of procedures and/or actions that simply will not be tolerated by the company. This listing of behavioral standards, often termed a code of conduct, generally differs in two important ways from the mission statement. The mission statement is usually very idealistic; the conduct code is frequently very realistic. The mission statement is very general; the code is very specific. Examples of prohibited acts that are often included in a code of conduct are "Employees of this company may accept no gifts, lunches, dinners, or other forms of entertainment with a value over $25.00," or "Employees of this firm must never falsify accounting records or expense accounts." There often is an emphasis on financial limits, not mission priorities, in these prohibited procedures.

The code of conduct of the Exxon Corporation was reproduced earlier in this chapter. Essentially it says that laws should never be broken, bribes should never be paid, and benefits should never be accepted. It does not, however, say that ships' officers should never be intoxicated, safety equipment should never be unavailable, or safety training should never be neglected.

Leadership Actions

It is often possible for the senior executive of an organization to take a dramatic action, or issue a memorable statement, that will indicate to members of the organization the relative weight to be given to profitable outcomes versus social impacts. It is easy, in many business organizations, to forget the values, goals, and priorities of the mission statement if those differ from an everyday focus on financial performance. It is hard, in most business organizations, to get people, even diligent employees, to carefully read memos or attentively listen at meetings about social performance. This is particularly true in large organizations in which there are hundreds of memos and numerous meetings. Senior executives, however, simply by the way they publicly choose to spend their time or voice their concerns, can clearly indicate their priorities.

Apparently no senior executive at Exxon had been at the Valdez terminal to publicly inspect spill response capability, or had attended environmental meetings to energetically endorse spill prevention technology, since Lawrence Rawl became chairman. Mr. Rawl did not go to Prince William Sound after the grounding of the tanker, which seems to indicate his position on the "financial performance versus social performance" question. Prior to the wreck there were many things senior executives could have done, had the company included environmental protection in the mission statement, to convey the importance of that protection. Inspection of sites, interviews with employees, and presentations of awards would all have been possible. These were not done at Exxon, and the result was not only severe damages to the society but huge charges against the company.

Conclusion

The last two of the three cases following this chapter describe companies (Enron is one) that focused totally on profits. Persons within those companies took actions that were profitable over the short term but brought harm to customers, employees, and/or local residents over the long term. Eventually those actions became publicized, which resulted in large declines in public reputation, customer loyalty, and employee support and eventually brought about substantial governmental fines, legal claims, and stockholder losses.

The first of these three cases, however, is very different. It asks you to develop a mission statement for *your* school of business administration. Try to put together a statement that combines the duties *you* believe your school owes to others with the goals *you* believe it should set for itself in order to define the role *you* believe it should attempt to play within your world, your country, your state, and your community. The following will be the last line of text in this book. I want to use it to emphasize that—in my view—the most basic reason for a moral approach to management is to inspire others to contribute to a cause worth serving, not to prevent them from acting in ways that are not worthy.

Case 6-1

A Mission Statement for *Your* School of Business Administration

Your school may or may not have a mission statement. The text in Chapter 6 defined the content and purpose of mission statements for business firms, where such statements have frequently been adopted, many with very beneficial effects. The following is an only slightly different description proposed for academic institutions; it contains the same elements but is adjusted to reflect the less easily defined nature of the duties and goals that need to be set for colleges and universities.

A mission statement for an academic institution should be the means of combining the duties that the college or university owes to others with the goals that it has set for itself. It essentially should be an effort to define the role, resulting from this combination of duties and goals, that the institution wants to play within the world, the nation, the state, and the community. What does an academic institution owe to students of all types (undergraduate, graduate, professional, or arts and sciences), to faculty in all disciplines, to administrative personnel, staff employees and maintenance workers at all levels, and to alumni, supporters, and residents in all regions? What does the institution want to achieve along each of the dimensions of performance that are possible in teaching, research, and service, to what extent, in what order of priority?

It is exceedingly difficult and frequently divisive to express academic duties and goals in exact terms; consequently, many colleges and universities never make the effort. They don't attempt to define the future of the institution, the scope of its activities and the nature of its efforts so that everyone will clearly understand: "This is where we're going to go, this is what we're going to do, and this is how we're going to do it." They don't lay out a challenge for those associated with the institution so that everyone—students, faculty, administrators, employees, workers, alumni, supporters, and residents alike—can fully participate and help. In short, they don't prepare a document that talks about purpose and contribution, one that they would be *proud* to hand to others, and then ask for their trust, commitment, and effort.

Instead of a visionary statement of the proposed "this is where we're going to go, this is what we're going to do, and this is how we're going to do it" nature, colleges and universities far more frequently resort to what they often term a "code of ethics," or a "code of conduct." This is usually a negative statement. It does not say, "This is our purpose and function; this is the contribution that together we can make within our world, our nation, our state, and our community; this is what we challenge you to do." Instead, it more generally declares, "We don't want trouble in our everyday routine; this is what we forbid you to do." These codes of conduct really constitute, in that vertical listing of policies and procedures that was shown in Figure 6.3 of the text, the "prohibited procedures" near the bottom, and they often apply only to students, not to the full range of students, faculty, administrators, etc.

Student Assignment

Firstly, look to see if your school, college, or university has a mission statement. If it does, read it and determine if it is a true mission statement as defined in Chapter 6, perhaps modified as explained above, expressing positive intentions, or more a code of conduct as described in the previous paragraph, filled with negative prohibitions. It is suggested strongly that you reread the mission statement of Johnson & Johnson, from Chapter 5, and the code of conduct of the Exxon Corporation, printed earlier in Chapter 6, so that the differences between these two document forms are completely clear to you. Then:

1. Does the mission statement of *your* school, college, or university challenge you, as one of the students, and challenge members of the faculty, administrators, employees, workers, etc., in their respective positions as well, to strive for excellence? Does it provide you and others with a reason to contribute your trust, commitment, and effort to a "cause worth serving"?

2. If you believe that the mission statement of your school, college, or university does *not* challenge you to strive for excellence, does *not* provide you with a reason to contribute your trust, commitment, and effort to a cause worth serving, or if that document simply doesn't exist, then start to think about what should be in that statement for *your* business school.

3. Focus at first on the duties: What does *your* business school owe to you and your fellow students, to faculty members, administrative staff, office and maintenance

workers, alumni supporters (if a private institution), or local/state citizens (if a public institution)? Put those in a sequence of importance, following your priorities. Why should others accept your priorities?

4. Now start to think about the goals: What should *your* business school attempt to achieve along the different dimensions of performance—teaching, research, and service—that are possible? Think of "service" as what *your* business school should do, if anything, to help people in its broader community. Where, in your view, should the focus be put, and why?

5. Now put those duties towards others and those goals for itself together into a mission statement that defines what *your* business school should want to do, where it should want to go, and how it should want to act. Try to be challenging. Attempt to be realistic. Make an effort to set up a "cause worth serving" of which you and everyone else can be proud.

6. Finally, set up some performance measures. How would you measure the performance of you and your fellow students at *your* business school? How would you measure the performance of the faculty members, the administrators, the office staff, and the hourly workers? How would you measure the satisfaction of alumni supporters and local/state citizens?

Case 6-2

Two Companies in Need of Redirection

Two short cases that depicted moral problems encountered by recent graduates of a program in business administration were included earlier in this text. These cases—"Sarah Goodwin" and "Susan Shapiro"—depicted very fundamental moral problems, for in each instance they placed the career of the individual in jeopardy if he or she refused to accept the situation. The recent graduates had to decide what they would or would not accept; that is, they had to decide where they would "draw the line."

Now you have been promoted. Put yourself in the place of the president of one of those companies. Just to help your memory, the moral problems involved (1) a large retail chain that was shipping defective food products to the ghetto for sale to the poor, and (2) a major chemical company that continued to operate a production process even though it was harmful to the health and well-being of the employees.

Assume that you are the president or a very senior vice president, clearly at a managerial level where you can make whatever decision you believe would best serve the interests of your company. You also have a reputation as a "doer," a man or woman who has managed company operations very successfully in the past, with continually rising sales and increasing profits, and consequently a person who tends to get his or her own way in dealing with both superiors and subordinates. In short, no one will openly oppose your suggestions. That does not mean, however, that people further down in the organization, at the functional or operating levels, will automatically accept and support your directions just because they are your directions. People tend to resist change, and you will probably have to recommend some fairly major changes in the mission, structure, and systems of the firm. How will you convince others that those major changes truly are needed?

Assume finally that you have just found that the situation described in the case not only exists in your firm, but is widespread within your firm. That is, if you decide to be the president of the chemical company, you now understand that almost all of your chemical plants have production processes that are economically attractive and technically legal but medically and environmentally harmful. You are shocked. You say to your spouse that night at dinner, "I had no idea this was going on, but it obviously is and I've got to do something to stop it."

Class Assignment

What are you going to do? Chapter 6 of this text suggested that you think in terms of a sequence moving from a new managerial philosophy through changes in organizational values, corporate goals, mission terms, financial supports, performance measures, incentive rewards, prohibited procedures, and leadership actions that should eventually lead to increases in the trust, commitment, and effort of all of the employees and/or other stakeholders. See Figure 6.4.

FIGURE 6.4   Proposed Means of Infusing a New Philosophy of Management a Sense of Integrity throughout a Business Firm to Achieve Greater Trust, Commitment, and Effort among All of the Stakeholders of That Firm

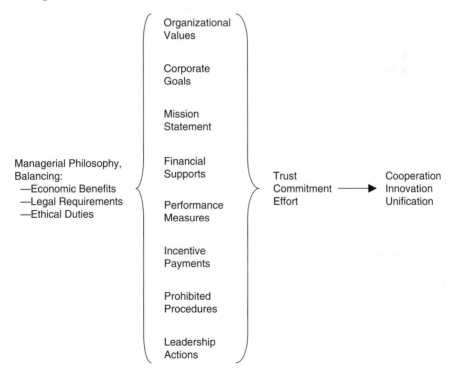

Case 6-3

Enron Corporation and the Need for Complete Revision[*]

Enron Corporation was formed in 1985 through the merger of two natural gas pipeline companies. The result was the largest gas distribution network in the United States, with 38,000 miles of pipeline stretching from the production sites in the southwestern and mountain states to the industrial users and residential customers in the northeastern and midwestern regions.

Originally the natural gas industry had been regulated by the federal government. Pipeline companies purchased gas at federally approved costs from the producers and then sold that gas at federally approved prices to the users. The demand was steady and the margins were set. It was hard for a pipeline company not to make money:

> In the beginning, the gas business operated just like any regulated public utility. Producers sold their natural gas at just and reasonable rates to interstate pipeline companies that, in turn, transported that gas for sale to local distribution companies at just and reasonable rates. . . . It was a steady, lucrative monopoly for the pipelines. Everyone knew, year in and year out, how much money they'd be taking in. (Swartz with Watkins, 2003, p. 25)[9]

All this steadiness and certainty changed soon after the merger. The natural gas industry was deregulated, and purchase costs at the wellhead and sales prices at the distribution point began to swing wildly, back and forth, with daily changes in supply and demand. Kenneth Lay, the newly appointed president of Enron, saw this as an opportunity, not as a problem:

> Enter Ken Lay who believed that the opportunity to let the market set the price of gas, instead of the government, promised enormous benefits to everyone. In the coming years, the fight to deregulate would become his mission. . . . Rules were made to be broken, and success went to the businessman who was ready to embrace change—someone who was a "visionary." (Swartz with Watkins, 2003, p. 25)[10]

Kenneth Lay's vision was to use complex financial instruments called derivatives and hedges to absorb the risks of the cost and price swings. Derivatives are essentially

---

[*] *Note:* This case was prepared with the assistance of Jeremy Jepson, a 2004 graduate of the Masters of Public Policy program at the University of Michigan. Additionally, this case is based on three recently published books: (1) Brian Cruver, *Anatomy of Greed: The Unshredded Truth from an Enron Insider* (New York: Carroll & Graf Publishers, 2003); (2) Loren Fox, *Enron: The Rise and Fall* (Hoboken, NJ: John Wiley & Sons, 2003); and (3) Mimi Swartz with Sherron Watkins, *Power Failure: The Inside Story of the Collapse of Enron* (New York: Doubleday, 2003).

[9] From *Power Failure: The Inside Story of the Collapse of Enron* by Mimi Swartz and Sherron Watkins, copyright © 2003 by Mimi Swartz. Used by permission of Doubleday, a division of Random House, Inc.

[10] From *Power Failure: The Inside Story of the Collapse of Enron* by Mimi Swartz and Sherron Watkins, copyright © 2003 by Mimi Swartz. Used by permission of Doubleday, a division of Random House, Inc.

contracts to either buy or sell a set amount of a given commodity—in this case, natural gas—at a set cost or price at a set time in the future. The risks of these future contracts could be reduced in part by having a huge database that contained all costs and prices for the past purchases and sales of natural gas, and records of all economic situations and weather conditions that might have affected the past supply and demand of that natural gas. Computer-based models could then be developed to forecast future supply and demand levels and the expected cost and price changes over time. The risks of these future or derivative contracts could be further reduced by the use of hedges. Hedges essentially are offsetting derivative contracts where the price of one commodity is expected to move in opposite directions to the price of another, given a certain event. For example, the price of natural gas could be expected to increase in the event of severe winter weather in the Northeast or Midwest; the price of lumber and other building materials could be expected to decline as that same harsh winter weather reduced construction activity throughout the region.

Both derivatives and hedges sound simple when described briefly; in reality they are statistically very complex, and require people who are technically trained to develop the derivative models and imaginatively minded to envisage the hedge relationships. Kenneth Lay believed that it was the people who would set Enron apart and enable his company to succeed in a very competitive environment:

> "My goal when I first come into this business was to try to get a superstar in every key position. You must have the very best talent, and then let them develop a good strategy." That was the gospel of Key Lay. A company staffed with the best and the brightest, who were allowed to develop to their fullest potential, could not be beat. (Swartz with Watkins, 2003, p. 35)[11]

Industry deregulation, quantitative finance, and entrepreneurial talent all came together at Enron during the 1990s, and the company grew very rapidly. College graduates with high grades but no experience were hired as analysts and put through a two-year training program. Those that succeeded were very well paid; those that failed were let go with very short notice. MBAs were hired only if they had three to five years of experience in investment banking or corporate consulting. The MBAs were not put through a training program; instead, they were expected to contribute right from the start. Again, those who succeeded were very well paid; those who did not were told to look for other opportunities. Enron became known for their aggressive, innovative, entrepreneurial culture:

> Throughout the 1990s, the company increasingly developed a name as a center for smart, ambitious, young professionals. The gleaming 50-story office tower in downtown Houston buzzed with activity from early in the morning until late at night. It was more than just an office. It was the place to be. For those interested in the latest trends in the energy business—or in business period—Enron was the place either to learn the ropes or to land when a person was ready to succeed. (Fox, 2003, p. 77)[12]

---

[11] From *Power Failure: The Inside Story of the Collapse of Enron* by Mimi Swartz and Sherron Watkins, copyright © 2003 by Mimi Swartz. Used by permission of Doubleday, a division of Random House, Inc.

[12] Reprinted with permission from John Wiley & Sons, Inc.

These aggressive, innovative, determined-to-succeed employees became very good at what they did, and what they did was to analyze huge amounts of data, develop derivative contracts based upon that analysis, and then market hedge trades to offset the risks. The earlier "winter weather affects the price of both natural gas and construction lumber" example may have made the process of creating and selling futures and options seem straightforward and routine; in reality it frequently was intricate and complex, as illustrated by the following anecdote:

> Enron also had the usual football and basketball pools, but the traders added so many complicated financial instruments on top of the standard bets—swaps, derivatives, costless collars, and other semi-comprehensible financial structures—that only the shrewdest people really knew what they were betting on (a game or a series of games) and how much they were actually in for ($10, $500, or much, much more). Many knew how to maneuver themselves into a winning position no matter what. As one trader described his bets on the January 1996 Super Bowl, "If Pittsburgh wins I make $1,500, but if Dallas wins I make $1,500." (Swartz with Watkins, 2003, p. 80)[13]

Enron, during the period 1996 to 2000, grew very rapidly. It had become a large, integrated energy company, trading futures contracts for both gas and electricity, with a number of newly formed divisions assigned to apply what was felt to be a proven business model to other commodities (drinking water, scrap metal, bandwidth capacity, etc.) throughout the world. It was staffed with innovative, intelligent, and self-confident employees at the senior executive, middle management, and commodity trading levels alike. Kenneth Lay, as CEO, attempted to hold these diverse products, distant locations, and aggressive workers together through stated values, assigned goals, performance reviews, and incentive payments:

1. *Stated values.* The core values of the company were described simply, but emphasized continually with posters on walls throughout the building and pamphlets handed out in every training program. There were four of these basic values:

- *Respect.* We treat others as we would like to be treated ourselves. We do not tolerate abusive or disrespectful treatment. Ruthlessness, callousness, and arrogance do not belong here.

- *Integrity.* We work with customers and prospects openly, honestly, and sincerely. When we say we will do something, we will do it; when we say we cannot or will not do something, then we won't do it.

- *Communication.* We have an obligation to communicate. Here, we take the time to talk with one another . . . and to listen. We believe the information is meant to move, and that information moves people.

- *Excellence.* We are satisfied with nothing less than the very best in everything we do. We will continue to raise the bar for everyone. The great fun here will be for all of us to discover just how good we can really be. (Cruver, 2003, pp. 42–43)

---

[13] From *Power Failure: The Inside Story of the Collapse of Enron* by Mimi Swartz and Sherron Watkins, copyright © 2003 by Mimi Swartz. Used by permission of Doubleday, a division of Random House, Inc.

2. *Assigned goals.* The goals of the company were also stated simply and emphasized frequently. There were two types: companywide and division-only. Companywide goals focused on the stated need for Enron to be the leader, originally in the natural gas industry, then in the energy industry, and finally in the global economy. Brian Cruver, who worked as a trader at Enron and is the author of one of the books upon which this case is based, described his reception as he entered the lobby of the building on his first day at work in 1999:

> I looked up and saw a banner the size of a mobile home. "From the World's Leading Energy Company To the World's Leading Company." The banner hadn't been there a week earlier [when he had interviewed for the job]. (Cruver, 2003, p. 3)[14]

   Divisional goals were designed to forward that leadership ambition. They concentrated on "meeting the numbers," which meant growing the business and attaining steady increases in revenues and returns. New product divisions were given time to get established, but once established they were expected to contribute to the overall sales, profits, and success of the firm.

3. *Performance reviews.* There were few excuses for failure. Success was simply expected, and it was ensured by a semi-annual weeding-out process that was formally termed the Peer Review Committee but that most employees simply referred to as "rank and yank." A committee consisting of senior executives asked "peers"—all workers within a given group or division—to fill out forms evaluating other members of the group or division on such qualities as innovation, effort, and imagination. Those forms were combined with accounting records that detailed the financial performance of the group or division, and then each member was ranked on a forced curve from 1 to 5. Ones were considered to be excellent; they were termed "water walkers," but there could be only 10 percent of them. There could be 15 percent of the 2s, 35 percent of the 3s, 25 percent of the 4s, and there had to be at least 15 percent of the 5s. The 5s were considered to be failures. They might be great performers, but that performance mattered only relatively to the other employees within the group or division, and the past performance of that group or division relative to other groups and divisions.

   People who got 5s were "redeployed," which meant that they were given a desk, a computer, a telephone, and two weeks to find another job in or out of Enron. The section of the building that contained those desks, computers, and telephones was called "the departure lounge"; going there "meant that you got fired, only in a really slow and painful way" (quotations are from Cruver, 2003, p. 63).

4. *Incentive payments.* Employees at Enron who received 1s and 2s in a steady series on their semi-annual evaluations could expect substantial rewards, with position promotions, salary increases, year-end bonuses and—best of all, in the view of the large numbers of financially oriented people who had been attracted to Enron—big stock options:

---

[14] From the book *Anatomy of Greed: The Unshredded Truth from an Enron Insider* by Brian Cruver. Copyright © 2002 by Brian Cruver. Appears by permission of the publisher, Carroll & Graf Publishers, a Division of Avalon Publishing Group, Inc.

The Enron millionaire factory was in full force through the '90s, and into the new millennium. Shiny new MBAs from the top schools, former consultants from McKinsey and Andersen, and military geniuses making the transition to private industry—they all came to Enron seeking a fortune. If they could survive the culture, the PRC, and the demands of meeting growth targets from quarter to quarter, then they believed that they had won something much more valuable than a lottery ticket. . . .

It wasn't the salary, though many executives took home a few million a year. It was the bonuses and the stock options. The bonus was the reward for meeting targets, from quarter to quarter. It was paid at the beginning of the new year based on the prior year's performance. The size of the bonus often dwarfed the employee's salary. There was literally no cap on the bonus. . . .

The stock options were a long-term incentive, although it didn't take Enron stock very long to leave the option price in the rearview mirror. A typical executive would accumulate options by the tens or hundreds of thousands. By the time the options were vested and could be cashed out, they would be worth millions. (Cruver, 2003, pp. 67–68)[15]

It was not just the money that brought people to Enron. It was also the opportunity to be a part of something that was totally new and different. The company put together a recruiting video in 1998 that talked about the wisdom of open markets and the need for individual innovation, and that wound up with an unrehearsed conversation between Kenneth Lay and Jeffrey Skilling:

"A lot of organizations like to stamp out the nonconformist, the nonconvention thinker," Lay said, "but a lot of times they're the people who really are the future because they're thinking about things differently, they're coming up with new ideas." "Yes," Skilling replied, "you know when you work for Enron you're going to see the newest things, the newest products, the newest services, the newest ways of thinking about things."

As they spoke, the video cut to scenes of bright young Enron employees hammering out their differences on whiteboards, and weathered men inspecting pipelines at dusty, remote locales. A smiling Asian woman draped a lei over a beaming Ken Lay, while her countrymen in business suits nodded and bowed gracefully. "If there's one thing I hope we can achieve," Lay said, "it's to create an environment where our employees can come in here and realize their potential."

Skilling waited just a beat before agreeing. "It's a wild ride," he said, and then both men laughed. They laughed the way people do when they've pulled off something they never thought they could." (Swartz with Watkins, 2003, p. 105)[16]

The challenging divisional goals and the rigid performance reviews meant that high reported profits were important for each group or division; the members were evaluated on whether they "met their numbers" relative to all other groups and divisions. The generous stock options meant that high reported profits were important for the company as a whole; the stock market responded quickly to increased earnings and thus hastened the day when senior executives, middle managers, and option traders alike could "take their money and run," retire with a substantial fortune.

[15] From the book *Anatomy of Greed: The Unshredded Truth from an Enron Insider* by Brian Cruver. Copyright © 2002 by Brian Cruver. Appears by permission of the publisher, Carroll & Graf Publishers, a Division of Avalon Publishing Group, Inc.

[16] From *Power Failure: The Inside Story of the Collapse of Enron* by Mimi Swartz and Sherron Watkins, copyright © 2003 by Mimi Swartz. Used by permission of Doubleday, a division of Random House, Inc.

This dual focus on reported profits at the divisional and organizational levels brought about accounting and banking methods that—everyone admitted—were on the edge of legality and that—no one confessed—would eventually lead to the bankruptcy of the firm. These accounting and banking methods were termed "mark to market" accounting and "special purpose entity" financing.

Mark-to-market accounting essentially is a way to recognize the profits associated with long-term futures contracts. Jeffrey Skilling, the president of Enron, had made his reputation early in the transformation of the company when, as a trader, he arranged a huge futures contract to sell natural gas to an electrical utility in New York State over a 20-year period at a high but set price, and then hedged all of the supply contracts so that substantial profits were assured.

Standard accounting treatment of those profits would force the company to wait for the completion of the first fiscal year following the signing of the contract, add up all of the revenues received from the sale of the gas associated with the contract, deduct all of the variable costs for the purchase of the gas and the operation of the pipeline system to deliver the gas, and finally subtract all of the overhead expenses that came from making the offer, negotiating the contract, and arranging the hedges. Standard treatment would require that this same process (accrual accounting) be followed for each subsequent year over the length of the contract. The problem was that the overhead expenses, almost all of which came in the first year of the contract, were very large and would exceed the revenues of that year. Enron would be forced to report a substantial loss for a contract that every other natural gas supplier and/or pipeline company in the country wished that they had had the skill, the resources, and the nerve to arrange.

There was an alternative accounting treatment, termed "mark to market." Enron, due to its huge trading volume, had been able to build up price and cost curves that showed the gradually increasing selling prices and purchase costs for natural gas that were expected over time. That is, the cost of gas to be purchased for delivery tomorrow on the "futures" market was expected to differ only slightly from the cost of gas to be purchased for delivery today on the "spot" market because there is very limited risk of change in the supply/demand ratios over that very short time period. The cost of gas to be purchased for delivery in five years, however, was expected to differ very markedly from the cost of gas to be purchased for delivery today because there is so much more that can go drastically wrong (or dramatically right) in those supply/demand ratios. Hundreds of thousands of futures trades recorded by Enron over lengthy periods of time generated hundreds of thousands of data points on price and cost charts, and those data points formed gradually increasing price and cost curves that could be claimed to represent <u>market</u> valuations of the increasing risks.

These price and cost curves could then be applied to the "book" for the original contract that listed all of the futures contracts and hedge swaps for the full 20-year period associated with the original sale, and then the profit could be estimated, based upon these <u>market</u> valuations. The term "market" has been underlined in both sentences because it is important to recognize that these valuations are not random estimates, but are based upon economic exchanges between assumedly intelligent and experienced traders, each allegedly acting in his/her own self-interests and/or in the self-interests of his/her firm. If the expected profits for the full contract were reported, then the "front-loading" of the overhead costs would not matter and, it was felt, a much more accurate picture of the financial performance of the firm could be recorded. It would be necessary, of course, to redo these market-based computations at the start of each subsequent fiscal year, using the then current—and doubtless somewhat different—price and cost curves, but this did not appear to create any particular difficulties given the availability of high-speed computer equipment.

At this time (mid-1990s) mark-to-market accounting had been formally approved by the Financial Accounting Standards Board (FASB), and was part of the published 30,000-page listing of those approved standards. It was not approved for and could not be used by manufacturing companies, which were forced to record sales revenues, variable costs, and the allocated portions of fixed expenses at the time of shipment of their physical products, but it was extensively used by financial institutions, consulting firms, and service providers. It could easily be argued that Enron was operating essentially as a combined financial institution, consulting firm, and service provider in the natural gas industry and thus was entitled to use mark-to-market accounting despite their delivery of a physical product. The use of this new accounting method was quickly approved by the company's auditor (Arthur Andersen), the company's legal advisor (Vinson and Elkins), and the company's board of directors.

> Enron's board went along with its risky accounting strategies. In one presentation to the board's audit committee, in February 1999, David Duncan—Andersen's lead partner on the Enron account—included a handwritten note that read: "Obviously, we are on board with all of these, but many push limits and have a high 'others could have a different view' risk profile." In the discussion that followed that meeting, Andersen didn't recommend changing any accounting practices, and board members didn't advocate a more prudent approach or even request a second opinion. Board members didn't characterize Enron's accounting structure as high-risk, but as "leading edge" or innovative—the sort of innovation they expected given the big fees they paid Andersen. (Fox, 2003, p. 158)[17]

"Special purpose entity" financing, the second of the accounting and banking edge-of-legality methods that eventually brought about the bankruptcy of the firm, essentially is a way to provide additional capital for a high-growth firm without that added capital appearing either as debt or equity on the liability side of the balance sheet. Large amounts of additional debt on the liability side of the balance sheet would reduce the creditworthiness of the firm and raise their interest cost. Large amounts of additional equity would reduce the rate of increase in earnings per share and lower their stock price.

Andy Fastow, the chief financial officer of Enron, thought that he had found a way to get the additional capital that Enron needed without affecting either the interest cost or the stock price of the firm. He called this new method "special purpose entity" financing, or SPE. All that was required was to form a subsidiary that was partially owned by a different firm or individual and nominally controlled by that different firm or individual; as such, according once again to the 30,000-page book of the FASB standards, the subsidiary could report their profit and loss figures separately from those for Enron, and their assets, liabilities, and equity did not have to appear on the Enron balance sheet. Assets could be transferred from Enron operations to a newly formed subsidiary, bonds could be sold by Enron bankers to fund those recently transferred assets, but

---

[17]Reprinted with permission from John Wiley & Sons, Inc.

then the money (which was considered payment for the Enron assets) could be used by Enron managers for general corporate purposes without either the assets or the bonds of the subsidiary having to be consolidated on the Enron balance sheet. These conditions fully met the requirements of the Financial Accounting Standards Board and the Securities and Exchange Commission, were quickly approved by Arthur Andersen, solidly endorsed by Vinson and Elkins, and enthusiastically affirmed by the Enron board of directors.

At the end of 1998, Enron had $7.8 billion in long-term debt on the balance sheet, and another $7.6 billion in debt that had been recorded off the balance sheet, in special purpose entities. Andy Fastow felt that he had been given clear authority to continue these processes of what he felt to be financial sophistication, not financial manipulation:

> To effectively juggle Enron's capital needs, Fastow transformed the finance department much the way Skilling had transformed Enron's sales department. He more than doubled the finance staff, loading it with experts in investment banking, commercial banking, and corporate finance. Rather than just raise debt or issue stock, Fastow's finance department became a manager of risk; it sold securitizations, parceled out the company's risk into other vehicles, took on investing partners, and marketed debt as a way to participate in the sure growth of everything that Enron touched. "Essentially, we would buy and sell risk positions," Fastow explained. (Fox, 2003, pp. 156–57)[18]

The mark-to-market accounting methods greatly improved the income statements of Enron, and the special purpose entity financing methods greatly improved the balance sheets. Now the company was ready to grow, and the booming stock market of the late 1990s was ready to reward in very substantial terms all public firms that could post consistent gains in earnings per share, and to severely penalize all those that failed. This was the New Economy. All limits were thought to be off. Recessions were felt to be a relic of the past. People throughout the financial community believed that a threshold had been passed, and that continuous growth in the order of 10–15 percent per year was not only possible, but that it was the duty of senior corporate executives to generate steady increases in shareholder value within that exalted range:

> The stock price became the indicator of corporate health; senior managers became, in a weird way, more focused on their shareholders than their customers. Quarterly earnings reports, once ignored by all but the most compulsive auditors and investors, suddenly became crucial to a company's public image. This was where [quarterly earning reports] a business could prove that its growth was on the proper, speedy trajectory. So, like everyone else, Enron began projecting, and then miraculously meeting, earnings targets four times a year, to glowing reviews from analysts and the business press. A company that missed its numbers got the same treatment in reverse. Wall Street analysts would hammer the company and the stock price plummeted. (Swartz with Watkins, 2003, p. 69)[19]

Kenneth Lay, fully supported by Jeff Skilling and Andy Fostow, determined that Enron should meet substantial growth targets—10 to 15 percent or more—each year.

[18] Reprinted with permission from John Wiley & Sons, Inc.

[19] From *Power Failure: The Inside Story of the Collapse of Enron* by Mimi Swartz and Sherron Watkins, copyright © 2003 by Mimi Swartz. Used by permission of Doubleday, a division of Random House, Inc.

They thought that this would be easy. Enron was now trading futures contracts in electric power as well as natural gas, and the total demand for electric power was huge, 20 times the size of the market for gas. The companies operating in that industry tended to be large and slow, accustomed to the regulatory approval process that was just ending. Enron, on the other hand, was large and fast, accustomed to the competitive price system that was just getting started within the natural gas and electrical generating industries. They had the mathematical models, computer capabilities, experienced traders, cultural attitudes, and funding methods needed for speed and growth. Skilling gave a talk in 1995 on his expectations for success under the new conditions in the combined energy (electricity and gas) industry and tried not to gloat:

> I don't know who is going to win. They [the winners] will have to be very fast-moving; this market is moving at just unbelievable speed. . . . They are going to have to be very creative; we don't know what the products and services are going to look like 5 to 10 years from now, so you will have people designing those. I think that competitive advantage won't be based on assets any longer. It won't be based on pipes and wires and generating plants; it will be based on intellectual capital. (Fox, 2003, pp. 75–76)[20]

What went wrong? Enron had expanded globally and was now operating in Europe, Asia, and Africa. Many of the public utilities in these areas were state-owned and refused to issue futures contracts for the sale of electric power. Enron had to build their own generating plants in order to push their way into the newly unregulated markets abroad. Teeside, in northern England, was an example of one of those new plants. It was built to be a showcase: a large-capacity, high-efficiency gas-fired co-generation (produce both steam and electricity) project that relied upon Enron's ability to pull together many diverse players into one totally integrated effort. The gas, at the time still classified as a waste product of crude production, would come from the North Sea oil fields and be processed by a major petroleum company in Scotland. The steam would be used by ICI Polymers, a division of one of the largest chemical firms in Europe, for industrial processing, and the electricity would be distributed through local utilities for retail sale to consumer and commercial customers alike. The plant design was very advanced: it took half the land of equivalent coal-fired plants, produced half the carbon dioxide emissions of those plants, and employed half the number of workers. The only problem was the lack of substantial competition for the use of the North Sea gas; Enron had signed long-term contracts based upon their anticipated price curves, but the competition never developed, and, consequently, Enron wound up paying above-market rates for the gas despite the existence of numerous hedges that relied upon nonexisting contradictory trends. The Teeside plant was unprofitable, but it was not shut down. Kenneth Lay was disappointed, but not abashed:

> For Enron [it was originally seen as] a triumph of the corporation's multitasking capabilities—a sort of hard asset version of the existing supply contracts in that Enron was able to pull together many facets of a complicated project. "We believe Enron is uniquely qualified to develop all aspects of a large integrated natural gas project such as the one at Teeside," said Lay. . . . "Rather than resisting change, we're trying to lead it and prosper from it." (Fox, 2003, p. 47)

---

[20] Reprinted with permission from John Wiley & Sons, Inc.

Dabhol, in southern India, was another example. The plant, once again of very modern design, had been built to generate electric power for sale to Maharashtra, India's poorest state, using liquefied natural gas transported by refrigerated ships from the oil-producing nations bordering the Red Sea. Enron owned 70 percent of this project. Bechtel, which had done the construction, owned 20 percent, and General Electric, which had supplied the equipment, owned 10 percent. Elections changed the ruling party in Maharashtra, and the new officials claimed that the contract price per megawatt hour that had been negotiated with the prior administrators was far too high. Allegations that this contested contract price had been approved only as a result of extensive bribery payments were openly made and popularly believed. Enron had essentially hedged the purchase price by having a subsidiary contract with the Indian national government that required that entity to buy the electric power if the state of Maharashtra reneged, but the bribery allegations made this a "third rail: you're dead if you touch it" political issue. The Dabhol plant was closed down and put up for sale at 20 percent above construction costs; there was no adjustment made for the presumably far lower price that would be received for an unused power plant in a politically hostile nation.

There were objections within the company to the refusal to recognize and reevaluate these failed power projects. All of them had been transferred to Enron Global Power, a publicly traded subsidiary in which Enron owned 52 percent of the stock and large pension funds and wealthy individual investors the balance. James Alexander had been appointed to be head of that subsidiary. He was responsible for renegotiating the contracts and then either starting or selling the plants. Asked to take over one more failed project, he complained to Kenneth Lay that the current market value should be substituted for the past construction cost for each plant, and that the losses should be recognized. This, he continued, was almost impossible given that the company's performance measures and incentive payments were based totally on projected profits and would penalize severely any recorded losses. Almost everyone in the company would lose, he explained, if the accounting records were corrected, but it was necessary to do so for financial accuracy. His recommendations were ignored:

> Lay listened to Alexander's recounting of the conflicts of interest and suspicious accounting practices for about fifteen minutes. Then he grew distant. He wouldn't meet Alexander's eyes, and he stopped responding. Finally he said, "I'll take it up with Rich [Richard Causey, chief accounting officer at Enron]." The meeting was over. (Swartz with Watkins, 2003, p. 70)[21]

Other problems came in the use of mark-to-market accounting to establish the value of long-term contracts for trading nonenergy commodities such as scrap metal, raw steel, wastepaper, packaging materials, etc. Futures markets for natural gas and electric power were well established, and the resultant price and cost curves projected far into the future were thought to be reliable. Futures markets for the nonenergy commodities were not as well established, particularly abroad, and, consequently, the price and cost curves based upon market forces were not as reliable and sometimes not even available. Personal estimates of the traders had to be used in the place of the market-based

[21] From *Power Failure: The Inside Story of the Collapse of Enron* by Mimi Swartz and Sherron Watkins, copyright © 2003 by Mimi Swartz. Used by permission of Doubleday, a division of Random House, Inc.

models. Each trader had a price curve for his or her commodity, constructed partially from market data-points but primarily from personal projections, and he or she would fight fiercely for the validity of that price curve. Why? Because his or her semi-annual evaluations, salary increases, bonus payments, stock options, and even continued employment under the rank-and-yank system all depended upon the recorded profit that came from the price curve. Brian Cruver, the MBA from the University of Texas who went to work for Enron just eight months before the collapse, noted this problem in his first few weeks upon the job:

> Enron, more than any other energy company, dealt in commodities and derivative structures that were far too unusual to have an established [futures market] price. It was an issue of liquidity. If the deal required a price on something that was rarely bought and sold, then the price had to be made up. . . . The trader's expertise on a commodity was difficult for someone from RAC [the Risk Assessment and Control Division at Enron] or Arthur Andersen to credibly question. . . .
>
> This was mark-to-market accounting, and Enron linked individual bonuses to this mark-to-market value. As a result, the strategy was less about booking profitable deals or controlling the risk of deals, and more about booking as many of the biggest [and most computationally complex] deals possible. (Cruver, 2003, p. 80) [22]

Allegedly it was possible, when trading derivatives, to separate risks from returns and to price both by open market exchanges in a complex series of hedges. But errors could be made and losses then would occur. Serious errors were made and severe losses had occurred in the energy-trading division of Enron in the third quarter of 1997. That division has been assigned a goal of a $100 million profit for that quarter, but instead they would have to report a loss of $90 million, for a combined shortfall of $190 million. That shortfall would affect the profit reported by the company at the conclusion of the quarter and the steady growth in quarterly profits that was felt to be essential in maintaining the confidence of the investment community and the price-to-earnings ratio of the company. Enron had never missed its earning targets. Jeffrey Skilling, the CEO, told the traders to quickly find a way to recoup the loss and regenerate the profit. There were weekly and then daily meetings. None of their proposals seemed certain to work. Skilling felt they were not being innovative enough. "You're looking for your lost car key under the streetlight because the light's better there" (Swartz with Watkins, 2003, p. 92). Look elsewhere was his unstated command. They did so and found a potential gold mine.

The energy-trading division had been buying companies and investing in plants that could convert natural gas to electrical energy at times of high demand and—consequently—high prices. These were the "peaking" plants. It would be possible, one of the members of the energy trading division suggested, to look upon these plants as purchases for eventual resale rather than investments for immediate use. If they could be classified as purchases for resale, then their values could be increased through mark-to-market accounting to cover this shortfall in profits and—given the large reservoir of value in those plants—future shortfalls as well through the use of optimistic price curves. Sherron Watkins, a coauthor of one of the books about the success and failure of Enron that have been used as the basis for this case, had, years earlier, worked as an auditor for Arthur Andersen. That company, she felt, could not and would not approve. But she had forgotten the pressures that were being placed on the auditing partners at Andersen:

> By the mid-1990s it was clear that Andersen needed Enron more than Enron needed Andersen, both for the prestige [of representing this large and well-known firm] and for the billings, which were closing in on $1 million per week. Consequently, as Enron pushed Andersen to approve ever more aggressive accounting techniques, Andersen had more trouble pushing back. . . . Given that, it was not surprising that Andersen's Enron team signed off on the plan to use mark-to-market accounting to help cover the $190 million loss. (Swartz with Watkins, 2003, p. 96)[23]

Sherron Watkins expressed her concerns informally to Kenneth Lay but received no encouragement to continue. The general attitude among the senior executives within Enron seemed to be that Arthur Andersen was acting properly, that they were being paid very substantial fees to be both innovative and aggressive in the interests of the firm, and that both of those qualities were needed to adapt Old Economy accounting rules to New Economy financial needs.

Last, the special purpose entities developed by Andy Fastow had been intended to hide debts; it was soon discovered that they made an equally suitable means to hide losses. The state-of-the-art generating plants abroad that had not worked out quite as planned could be put into a package and then sold to a group of outside investors who needed to supply only a minimal (3 percent) amount of equity, with the balance in debt guaranteed by a pledge of unissued shares of Enron stock. The peaking-power plants within the United States that had been overvalued through mark-to-market accounting could also be put into a similar package and also sold to a group of outside investors under the same 3 percent equity and 97 percent debt guaranteed by unissued shares of the company's stock.

The early financial packages, particularly those that contained the gas exploration and supply contracts from the Gas Bank, had worked out very well for outside investors. Pension funds, such as CalPERS (California Public Employees Retirement System), insurance companies, and investment banks had competed to invest because they received high cash flows and excellent capital returns. But as the SPE vehicles were increasingly used to hide losses, the cash flows dwindled and the capital returns disappeared. It became more and more difficult to place these packages. Andy Fastow again came up with a solution. He, his family, and—to some extent—his friends would supply the needed 3 percent in equity, borrow the balance backed by unissued shares of Enron stock, and attempt to rescue the failed project or projects. This was illegal because (1) it contravened the clear requirement that control of the entity had to be outside Enron, and (2) it ignored the conflict of interest that would occur between Andy Fastow as a senior executive at Enron and Andy Fastow as a private investor in the SPE. Benefits that went to Fastow and his family/friends clearly could not go to the stockholders of Enron. However, these

---

[23] From *Power Failure: The Inside Story of the Collapse of Enron* by Mimi Swartz and Sherron Watkins, copyright © 2003 by Mimi Swartz. Used by permission of Doubleday, a division of Random House, Inc.

transactions were again approved by Arthur Andersen, the auditing firm, with the provision that the conflict be at least partially revealed in the company's annual report. On page 48, in footnote 16, of the 2000 report the following statement appeared:

> In 2000 and 1999, Enron entered into transactions with limited partnerships (the Related Party) whose general partner's managing member is a senior officer of Enron. The limited partners of the Related Party are unrelated to Enron. Management believes that the terms of the transaction with the Related Party were reasonable compared to those which could have been negotiated with unrelated third parties. (Cited in Cruver, 2003, p. 60) [24]

Jeff McMahon, then treasurer of Enron, objected strongly to the conflicts of interest inherent in the special purpose entities financed by Andy Fastow, hierarchically his superior, and arranged to meet with Kenneth Lay. According to a handwritten note of that meeting, Jeff McMahon complained that "I find myself negotiating with Andy on Enron matters, and am pressured to do deals that I do not believe are in the best interests of the shareholders" (Fox, 2003, p. 202). According to McMahon, Skilling ended the meeting by saying that he understood the concerns that had been expressed and that he would look into the matter. No further action was taken.

Early in 2001 the Enron stock price, which had been on a steep upward climb for nearly 10 years, began to falter. Apparently the cause was a series of rumors about the decline in quality of the company's reported earnings and the absence of transparency in the company's accounting records. Then, in August 2001, Jeffrey Skilling resigned as chief executive officer, a post he had held for only six months. Kenneth Lay quickly replaced him and sent the following message to all employees, first saying that the departure was for "personal reasons," and then trying quell the natural concerns:

> I want to assure you that I have never felt better about the prospects for our company. . . . Our performance has never been stronger; our business model has never been more robust; our growth has never been more certain; and most importantly, we have never had a better nor deeper pool of talent throughout the company. We have the finest organization in American business today. Together we will make Enron the world's leading company. (Cruver, 2003, p. 91) [25]

Sherron Watkins replied with what was to become, when presented months later to a congressional committee investigating Enron, her famous one-page memo. Originally sent anonymously, she acknowledged authorship the next day and requested a meeting with Kenneth Lay. She was worried, she said, that Skilling's abrupt departure would raise suspicions about Enron accounting practices, and she believed that those practices could not withstand outside scrutiny:

> Has Enron become a risky place to work? For those of us who didn't get rich over the last few years, can we afford to stay?

[24] From the book *Anatomy of Greed: The Unshredded Truth from an Enron Insider* by Brian Cruver. Copyright © 2002 by Brian Cruver. Appears by permission of the publisher, Carroll & Graf Publishers, a Division of Avalon Publishing Group, Inc.

[25] From the book *Anatomy of Greed: The Unshredded Truth from an Enron Insider* by Brian Cruver. Copyright © 2002 by Brian Cruver. Appears by permission of the publisher, Carroll & Graf Publishers, a Division of Avalon Publishing Group, Inc.

Skilling's abrupt departure will raise suspicions of accounting improprieties and valuation issues. Enron has been very aggressive in its accounting—most notably [she named a series of the special purpose entities arranged by Jeff Fastow]. We do have valuation issues with our international assets and possibly some of our [energy-trading] mark-to-market positions. . . .

The spotlight will be on us, the market just can't accept that Skilling is leaving his dream job. I think that the valuation issues can be fixed and reported with other goodwill write-downs to occur in 2002. How do we fix the [special purpose entities]? They unwind in 2002 and 2003, we will have to put up Enron stock and that won't go unnoticed.

To the layman on the street, it will look like we recognized funds flow of $800 mm from merchant asset sales in 1999 by selling to a [special purpose entity] that we capitalized with a promise of Enron stock in later years. Is that really funds flow or is it cash from equity issuance?

I am incredibly nervous that we will implode in a wave of accounting scandals. My eight years of Enron work history will be worth nothing on my resume, the business world will consider the past successes as nothing but an elaborate accounting hoax. (Excerpts from Sherron Watkins's memo to Kenneth Lay, cited in Swartz with Watkins, 2003, pp. 361–62)[26]

Sherron Watkins followed up her original memo with a longer document providing greater detail about the accounting treatments of the special purpose entities and mark-to-market valuations that had concerned her. She then met with Kenneth Lay and verbally expressed her concerns. Kenneth Lay asked Vinson and Elkins, the Houston law firm that represented Enron, to investigate the allegations. Their response essentially was that the accounting treatments, while aggressive, were not illegal, that those treatments had originally been approved by Arthur Andersen, the company's auditor, and that, consequently, no further action was needed.

Jeffrey Skilling's departure, while considered curious by outside observers, particularly those connected to the investment banks and brokerage houses on Wall Street, appeared not to trigger the suspicions and start the investigations that Sherron Watkins had anticipated. Enron's stock price stabilized at about $30/share, down from over $100 at the start of 2001. Kenneth Lay and many of the other senior executives at Enron spent much of their time attempting to reassure investors and employees, though at the same time they were selling large amounts of their own holdings of Enron stock:

On September 26, Lay again told employees the company's stock seemed like a bargain and that the third quarter was "looking great"—only weeks before Enron would fall apart and its stock price plunge. "My personal belief is that Enron stock is an incredible bargain at current prices, and we will look back a couple of years from now and see the great opportunity that we currently have."

However, Lay made this series of comments touting Enron's stock not long after he and other senior executives had sold large amounts of their Enron shares. Between February 1999 and July 2001, Lay sold more than 1.8 million shares of Enron stock for total proceeds of $101.3 million. . . . In all, Enron officers and a few directors unloaded a

[26] From *Power Failure: The Inside Story of the Collapse of Enron* by Mimi Swartz and Sherron Watkins, copyright © 2003 by Mimi Swartz. Used by permission of Doubleday, a division of Random House, Inc.

whopping $1.1 billion in Enron stock from January 1999 through July 2001. (Fox, 2003, pp. 252–53)[27]

The final ending came with surprising quickness on October 16. Enron announced its earnings for the third quarter of 2001, which had ended September 30. Total recurring net income, it was said, had increased to $393 million, up from $292 million the year before:

> Our twenty-six percent increase in recurring earnings per diluted share shows the very strong results of our core wholesale and retail energy businesses and our natural gas pipelines. (Enron third-quarter earnings report for 2001, cited in Cruver, 2003, p. 116)[28]

Apparently the growth was continuing. Everything seemed to be well. But then came the first shocker. Nonrecurring charges of $1.01 billion were to be deducted from the stated earning figures, resulting in a loss for the quarter of $618 million. These nonrecurring charges, Kenneth Lay explained, were to write off a few failed investments and to restructure a few poorly operating divisions. But this was followed by a second shocker. There was to be a write-down of $1.2 billion in shareholders' equity, with the minimal explanation that this was associated with the "related party transactions" that had been briefly noted in a footnote to the 2000 annual report.

Enron had been forced to reveal the second related-party adjustment because approximately $3 billion in notes issued by other special purpose entities was coming due, and clarification of the status of the related-party claims was needed to permit sales of some of the pledged assets in order to be able to repay those notes. The company, apparently, had anticipated a subdued reaction to both the "nonrecurring charges" and the "equity write-down" announcements. Enron executives believed, it would seem, that there was still a reservoir of trust and respect for their company among members of the financial community and that both adjustments would just be seen as long-needed but relatively minor corrections. Instead, there was a flurry of disappointment and anger. The *Wall Street Journal,* the next morning, in a front-page story, revealed that Andy Fastow, the chief financial officer of Enron, was the "related party" and was "eligible for profit participations that could produce millions of dollars [of profit for himself] in transactions with Enron." Brian Cruver, the MBA from the University of Texas who had started work at Enron only 10 months earlier, described his reaction to this account:

> I sat at my desk and read through the article two more times. I stopped seeing the numbers and the partnerships and the Enron spin. I started to see a huge red stamp across the pages of the most respected business publication on earth. It read, "This company [Enron] cannot be trusted." (Cruver, 2003, p. 120)[29]

[27] Reprinted with permission from John Wiley & Sons, Inc.

[28] From the book *Anatomy of Greed: The Unshredded Truth from an Enron Insider* by Brian Cruver. Copyright © 2002 by Brian Cruver. Appears by permission of the publisher, Carroll & Graf Publishers, a Division of Avalon Publishing Group, Inc.

[29] From the book *Anatomy of Greed: The Unshredded Truth from an Enron Insider* by Brian Cruver. Copyright © 2002 by Brian Cruver. Appears by permission of the publisher, Carroll & Graf Publishers, a Division of Avalon Publishing Group, Inc.

Other articles followed in different newspapers and news magazines with exactly the same message. Congressional hearings were scheduled in an attempt to ascribe blame. Traders at other energy firms refused to deal with Enron, worried about their financial stability. Lenders at commercial and investment banks refused to negotiate with Enron for exactly the same reason. The stock price plummeted. The company was bankrupt. It just took a few more weeks for everyone—investors, creditors, managers, and members of the general public—to formally acknowledge that undoubted fact.

Class Assignment

Assume that you were a member of the staff of one of the senior vice presidents at Enron in 1997. This was the year when the first major accounting misrepresentation and/or financial manipulation occurred. That misrepresentation and/or manipulation was the use of mark-to-market accounting to adjust the recorded value of purchased companies in order to cover a $180 million shortfall in the expected earnings of the energy trading division, as was recounted earlier in this case. Assume that the senior vice president, for whom you worked, heard of this artificial transaction, called a meeting of his/her staff and said, "If this sort of thing continues, we're dead. It will take awhile, but we'll lose everything we've worked so hard for around here for so long. We've got to change the way we do business. What would any of you suggest?" Put together a package of suggestions for that senior vice president.

Index